BASIC PRINCIPLES

OF DATA PROCESSING

PRENTICE-HALL INTERNATIONAL, INC. *London*
PRENTICE-HALL OF AUSTRALIA, PTY. LTD., *Sydney*
PRENTICE-HALL OF CANADA, LTD., *Toronto*
PRENTICE-HALL OF INDIA PRIVATE LTD., *New Delhi*
PRENTICE-HALL OF JAPAN, INC., *Tokyo*

BASIC PRINCIPLES

OF DATA PROCESSING

JAMES A. SAXON

President
Saxon Research Corporation
San Diego, California

WESLEY W. STEYER

Chairman
Division of Business and Data Processing
San Joaquin Delta College
Stockton, California

PRENTICE-HALL, INC.
ENGLEWOOD CLIFFS, N.J.

©1967 by
PRENTICE-HALL, INC.
Englewood Cliffs, N.J.

Current printing (last digit):

10 9 8 7 6 5 4 3 2

Library of Congress Catalog Card Number: 67-16391
Printed in the United States of America

To Tottie and Audrey

ACKNOWLEDGEMENT

The authors wish to thank the many persons who have helped to make this book possible; the students who served as "guinea pigs" in its development, Susann M. Johnston, who did such an admirable job of typing the manuscript and most especially, Mr. Herman S. Englander, Mr. James Shannon and Mr. H. Rowe, who took great pains with detailed technical reviews and with constructive criticism which was most helpful throughout the entire project.

The authors would also like to thank the following companies for the use of their photographs:

IBM equipment courtesy of International Business Machines Corp., White Plains, N. Y.

NCR equipment courtesy of National Cash Register Co., Dayton, Ohio

UNIVAC equipment courtesy of Sperry Rand Corp., New York, N. Y.

CDC equipment courtesy of Control Data Corp., Minneapolis, Minn.

PREFACE

This book has been written as a first semester text in the instruction of basic data processing. The approach taken by the authors was to avoid exhaustive treatment of subject matter—a treatment which is felt to transcend the needs of the student at this level. Instead, the salient points of each topic are discussed in a fairly brief and easy-to-understand manner, each such topical area being followed by a short sequence of review questions to drive home the important features of the material being covered.

A knowledgeable instructor can build his daily lectures around the nucleus included in the text with a great deal of ease, thus giving him the leeway of free choice of topical inclusion or exclusion and still allowing the student to retain, in the text, the basic knowledge and terminology required for reference purposes.

The treatment of including review questions after each discrete unit of information instead of at the end of each chapter is also unique to this text. Considerable tryout of the technique on typical student groups indicated the advisability of such a technique. The series of questions at the end of chapters are seldom completed by students unless they are forced to do so by a firm requirement by the instructor. One of the reasons for this is that a student must search through the entire chapter to locate the answer to a problem or question, and students would rather avoid this painful process.

If, on the other hand, the questions are posed immediately after the topic has been covered, the student is more apt to turn back one or two pages to reabsorb the answer that he failed to completely absorb during his first perusal of the subject matter. This technique contains a certain amount of automatic reenforcement which has been found to be quite valuable in studies of topical retention.

The Table of Contents indicates a detailed Course Outline. This outline is suggestive in nature and is certainly not to be taken as the only sequence of instruction to be followed. The outline does agree with the content of the book, but an instructor may determine his own sequence of instruction if it differs from the suggested outline by merely assigning material to be studied in the sequence he desires.

The basic precept followed in the development of the text was to provide first semester students of data processing with material that is easy to read and that will not tend to confuse the novice with extraneous subject matter not pertinent to his present needs.

JAMES A. SAXON

San Diego, California

WESLEY W. STEYER

Stockton, California

CONTENTS

APPENDICES

1 INTRODUCTION

BACKGROUND

The Data-Processing Mystery

The term *data processing* is a relatively new one and is grossly misunderstood by many people. The mention of data processing with reference to a course of study in school or to a daily way of life in the working world can, and often does, prompt a response of curiosity as to the nature of this "mysterious" phenomenon. Data processing is a tremendously interesting subject, but it need not be mysterious. Many students of data processing have been surprised at the basic simplicity of data processing. Learned step by step, a student suddenly realizes that he has entered into this new world that was once strange and forbidding. Strange words and ideas become understandable, ordinary, and a regular part of the day-by-day vocabulary and conversation.

Data Processing Defined

What are data? What is processing? What is data processing? At the risk of oversimplification, data might be defined as *meaningful information*. The limitation to meaningful information is important for it implies that meaningful conclusions can be drawn from the information. Data then are items of information stated in terms of dollars and cents, quantities, degrees, feet and inches, tensile strength, color, ohms, grade points, blood pressure, etc. The list is practically endless.

1

Processing refers to handling or manipulation. It should be skillful handling and purposeful manipulation. So data processing is purposeful manipulation of meaningful information done in a skillful manner to accomplish results that are likewise meaningful.

Data processing is the reassembling of facts into more meaningful terms, the summarizing of a mass of information into a form from which judgment can be made and responsible action taken.

EXAMPLE:

Suppose each student in a data processing (or other) class were to fill out a form such as the following:

```
┌─────────────────────────────────────────────────────────┐
│  Name: _____         │
│                                                           │
│  Student Number: _____         │
│                                                           │
│  Sex:              M         or        F                  │
│                                                           │
│  Age: _____         │
│                                                           │
│  Class:   Fresh.   Soph.   Jr.   Sr.   Grad.              │
│                                                           │
│  Employed:         Yes       or       No                  │
│                                                           │
│  Marital Status:        Married        Single             │
└─────────────────────────────────────────────────────────┘
```

After the cards are filled out and gathered together, they represent merely a mass of unprocessed data. Each card may be of interest individually, but, in order to gain an over-all view of the composition of the class, the cards need to be grouped according to similar responses. The data need to be classified. If an analysis of the class according to sex is desired, the cards would be grouped by sorting them into two classifications, male and female. No meaningful results have been obtained, however, until the cards are counted. Once the totals are obtained, the new summary data do have meaning. The instructor now has a small bit of valid information about the class from which he may determine how the class should be taught.

Now look more carefully at the relatively simple form being used for illustration. How many different classifications can be made? The cards could be arranged by age groupings, class status, employment status, or marital status. In addition, the cards might be assembled into order by student code or into alphabetical order by student name. But these are not the only results which could be obtained. Subclassification might be made; i.e., those cards representing freshmen could be further sorted down by employment status and the results would reflect an interesting and possibly revealing situation. Even with the limited example being used, an almost unlimited number of groupings and subgroupings could be obtained. For instance, how many of the *male seniors* who are *not employed* are *married?*

Systems versus Machines

The reader may well wonder that the definition and illustration of data processing made no reference to sophisticated or even simple machines. This is as it should be, for data processing should be understood as a system and not as a machine or machines. What is meant by a system as opposed to machines? A system is a regular, orderly way of performing an operation. Data processing refers to the regular, orderly, systematic procedure for performing the data-processing function, that of assembling meaningful data into meaningful summary form. Machines can be used to do this. The machines are tremendously fast, very flexible, and extremely reliable.

The Processing Cycle

Every data-processing application follows a basic processing cycle. That is, each job or application will adhere to three basic steps, no matter how large or small the job may be. These three steps were present in the example given above. They are input, processing, and output. This cycle can be expressed in symbolic form as follows:

Irrespective of the method used to process data, this cycle will be followed. The example used earlier started with new data as input, which were processed or summarized into output. The entire operation was performed manually. The data were recorded manually, sorted manually, and counted and reported in summary form manually.

REVIEW QUESTIONS

1. Give a brief definition of the following terms:
   a. Data
   b. Processing
   c. Data processing

2. List the three major steps in a processing cycle.

METHODS OF PROCESSING DATA

As indicated above, data may be processed in a strictly manual manner. No machines are employed in the process. Of course, this method is called just that, manual data processing. In addition, there are three other methods of processing data. These are mechanical, electromechanical, and electronic.

Manual and Mechanical

The distinction between manual and mechanical data processing is not a clear one. A basically manual system may be mechanized in varying degrees. At an arbitrary point a system may then be referred to as mechanical. The typewriter, for instance, might be used to record input data and/or to report the output data. An adding machine or a counting device could be used to accumulate or tally the quantitative data. As machines are added and more complicated procedures developed, these would include other recording devices such as cash registers, credit-card imprinters, check writers, and other mechanical aids to the manual process.

The processing steps of the cycle might be made more efficient with the addition of mechanical devices to the basically manual method, such as desk calculators, posting, bookkeeping or accounting machines, a slide rule, or even an abacus.

The output or reporting step, in turn, could be facilitated with the use of printing devices, such as the typewriter or a similar device used in conjunction with a posting or bookkeeping machine. The use of duplicating equipment for multiple-copy production of output is a further example of mechanization.

The manual and mechanical methods will remain predominate methods of processing data and deserve their place in a study of data processing along with the more publicized electromechanical and electronic methods.

Automatic Features of Manual Systems

Although *automatic* generally implies a machine process, it need not be so. Automatic results might be obtained from a basically manual data processing system. The use of carbon paper is an example. By its use multiple copies of a document can be obtained from a single recording. This "write-it-once" principle, the idea of acquiring multiple recordings from a single recording and the consequent elimination of separate recordings, is referred to as *integrated data processing,* or IDP. Integrated data processing is represented again at the manual processing level by the use of window envelopes. The recording of the name and address on the letter serves also for the addressing of the envelope.

The integration of a data-processing procedure because it eliminates rerecording reduces the possibility of error. Whether we like it or not, the elimination of the human being in the processing cycle will reduce the error rate. Take another example of integrated data processing, that of the use of a credit card at the service station. The name, address, and account number are originally recorded on the credit card, but all subsequent recordings are merely copies of it. The chance for error is virtually eliminated. Imagine the error rate if every service station attendant were required to copy this information onto each credit ticket. Integrated data processing may be defined as the reduction or elimination of duplication in the processing of data.

Electromechanical

As indicated above, the line dividing manual from mechanical data-processing methods was found to be less than distinct and, in fact, had to be thought of as a matter of degree of mechanization. The electromechanical method is, however, distinctly different from either manual or mechanical. The previous methods never required data to be in any form except the familiar symbols on familiar paper documents. The electromechanical method requires a machine-readable document, the best example of which is a punched card. The human operator does not enter the raw data directly into the electromechanical machines. Instead, the operator enters the punched card from which the machines are capable of "reading" the data. The electromechanical method is also referred to as the punched-card method, the electric accounting-machine method (EAM), the unit-record method, and the tabulating method.

The electromechanical method has been in use for some time but still represents a concept unfamiliar to most people. For this reason additional chapters of this book will be devoted to an explanation of this method.

Electronic

Electronic data processing (EDP) is the glamorous facet of data processing. It is here that the unbelievable is commonplace. Electronic data processing is processing by computer. A computer is used for the same reason that any other machine is used—because it does certain jobs better than a human being. In particular, it handles more information and it handles it much faster. Phenomenal speeds are the earmark of EDP. These processing speeds are measured in millionths and even billionths of a second.

The distinguishing characteristic of electronic processing is the form the data takes. The electromechanical method required the data to be in a machine language, a code in the form of holes in cards. The electronic method requires that the data be translated into magnetic and electronic impulses in and on electronic devices. The data are then manipulated or processed by transporting them within the system on wires, printed circuits, microcircuits, magnetic cores, magnetic tapes, etc.

However, the basic simple data-processing cycle is still the central theme. Raw data go in, are processed in a prescribed manner, and the results are transmitted out in the form of output.

REVIEW QUESTIONS

3. List four methods of processing data.

4. Give a brief explanation of each of the four methods.

5. What do the letters EAM represent?

6. What do the letters EDP represent?

7. Define the term "integrated data processing." What two advantages can you name for this concept?

BASIC DATA-PROCESSING FUNCTIONS

The basic data-processing functions are merely expansions on the processing cycle of input, processing, output. These functions (or steps) are recording, classifying, sorting, calculating, reporting, and communicating. One or more, if not all, of these functions must be performed in the solution of a data-processing problem. Inasmuch as this is so, each of these functions will be discussed later as it applies to the various data-processing methods. The discussion below is for the purpose of defining each of the functions as an integral part of the system regardless of the method being employed to process the data.

Input

Recording is the basic input function. If data are to be processed, they must be set down. A record must be made of it. Perhaps it could be stated that the data must be "captured." There are several forms in which data can be recorded. The most commonplace is the written document using the traditional symbols to represent letters and numbers. Data may, however, be recorded as holes in cards, holes in strips of paper, electronic impulses on metallic or metallic-coated surfaces. These *coded* methods are used to satisfy the limitations of the machines and their inability to "read" symbols with the same facility as human beings.

Classifying is closely associated with recording. Classifying is the assigning of a group identification. Unless data units can be grouped into meaningful classifications, it is impossible to reconstruct the data into summary form and the whole idea of data processing breaks down. For instance, it is necessary to classify sales data according to customer or sales area, product group, date of sale, or any number of other groupings. Classifying very often involves a type of coding, either numeric, alphabetic, or alphameric, and these classification codes are assigned to describe or identify the data unit. A code number is assigned the customer, another number to each product line, and others to salesmen, etc. Much of the classification is done by recording preassigned codes at the time data are being recorded or when the data are rerecorded into machine language. Another familiar example of classification is the method of classifying a transaction according to its accounting characteristics. What account is to be debited, and what account is to be credited? A natural extension of this procedure would be to assign a code from a chart of accounts.

Although recording and classifying have been referred to as input functions, they may be more accurately thought of as functions preceding input without which input cannot be accomplished.

Processing

Sorting is a very important processing function. If data are identified and recorded, then an accumulation of such data can be arranged into homogeneous groupings. Sorting is the function which brings order out of disorder. Transactions might be sorted into sequence according to classification such as customer names. In so doing, the data would be in alphabetic order, and coincidentally all the data for each customer would be grouped together. Or some other classification might be chosen, such as date, and a new order would replace the old order with new significance for further processing. Except where there is only one occurrence for each classification, sorting is grouping. It can be accomplished in a variety of ways. Grouping may be accomplished by sorting into sequence as mentioned above, by extraction, where data of a particular group are selected out of the mass of data, or by combining or merging like groups into a single grouping.

The calculating function, although usually the most difficult for the human being to perform, is the easiest to comprehend. Calculating is computing, and both refer to the basic arithmetic processes of addition, subtraction, multiplication, and division. Fortunately machines compute very efficiently and very rapidly and thereby relieve man of a mental burden much as the engine and motor relieved his physical burden. Calculating or computing actually creates new data. The computation of hours worked times rate of pay creates a new item, gross pay. The accumulation or addition of a series of sales amounts for a particular salesman creates a new item, total sales for that salesman.

Output

The purpose of any data-processing procedure is to obtain the desired output. All of the other functions are performed so that meaningful results become available. The results obtained must then be put into understandable form. The reporting function is the presentation of the results of the input and processing functions. Reporting is the function of output.

The output of a data-processing procedure might be reported in a variety of ways. The most traditional and understandable is the printed report. Printed reports are endless in variety and form ranging from address labels, statements of account, and report cards to voluminous statistical, scientific, and analytical reports. On the other hand, output is not limited to reporting in printed form. Summarized data can be communicated in graphic form or line drawings such as charts and maps. Output can be reported as pictures such as are obtained when relaying pictures from space. Reporting does not have to be done on paper documents. Output can be reported on a screen or in audible form.

In addition, output may be reported in machine-level language such as those used to enter data into the system. One reason for doing this would be so that the data could easily reenter the system for subsequent machine processing. These machine languages are typically recorded on punched cards, punched paper tape, magnetic tape, and other magnetic type media.

Communication is the function which links all of the other functions together into a system. Communication is data transportation or data transmission. The transporting of data can be as simple as moving a paper document on which data are recorded from one location to another or carrying a deck of punched cards into which data have been recorded from one machine to another, to the transmitting of data in the form of electronic impulses from distances of a fraction of an inch to millions of miles.

REVIEW QUESTIONS

8. What two functions must be accomplished prior to the processing of data?

9. Name two functions of the processing cycle.

10. What is the basic output function?

HISTORY AND DEVELOPMENT

Since data processing has been defined as a process or system, it should become apparent that no single invention, discovery, or development is solely or even in a predominately major way responsible for the status of data-processing techniques today. Many factors have contributed to the development of data processing. It is also interesting to observe that in several instances ideas were ahead of the technological developments for the implementation of the ideas. Some men were ahead of their time. Many men made contributions both direct and indirect. History records the names of some of the contributors, but others go unnamed. In some cases need was the obvious mother of the invention, while in other instances ideas seemed to be born just because it was time.

Development of Symbols

The limitation of man's mind in its memory ability represents the first need to be fulfilled. Up to a point man was able to "store" information gathered from his observation, but soon he could not remember all of what he saw or experienced. The solution was to record, or make a record, of what he wanted to remember. Additional problems arose. How was he to represent abstract ideas? The drawing of pictures on cave walls or the carving of notches on trees was done on a one-for-one ratio until this became burdensome and impractical, and then it was necessary to invent symbols to represent quantities and qualities. Finally these symbols expressed on paper with a writing instrument such as a pen or pencil are illustrative of the basic recording technique for data processing. This method or similar methods continue as useful tools, even though their use extends back thousands of years.

Mechanical Printing

Improvements on the pen-and-paper technique are apparent. Printing with type was invented in China and later (independently) in Europe by Johann Gutenberg about the middle of the 15th century. Improvements on the printed technique were few and slow to appear. Recently, however, new methods have appeared. Photographic processes, offset printing, and typesetting by electronics are examples of modern methods applied to an ancient art with noteworthy revolutionary effect.

Because of its flexibility, the typewriter tends to better illustrate mechanization of the data-processing functions. The typewriter is used for recording and reporting, for input and output. The first practical, commercially feasible typewriter was invented in Milwaukee in 1867 by C. L. Sholer. It was manufactured by the firm of E. Remington. A working model of an electric typewriter was produced in 1920 by Smathers.

Development of Mathematics

Just as it is impossible to identify and credit all of those responsible for the development of symbols as a means of human expression, it is also impossible to know and credit those who contributed to our basic mathematical concepts. It is reasonable to assume that, as man found the need for and developed symbols to express quantitites, he also would need to manipulate these symbols in an expression of changes in quantities. Addition and subtraction concepts would naturally evolve. Evidence that man used his fingers as an aid to the development of one of his numbering systems is apparent in the base-10 system. The system utilizes 10 symbols, zero through nine (0–9), which is, of course, equal to the digits (fingers) on our hands. Later we shall discuss the digital computer.

It is possible to name several men who have made major contributions to the field of mathematics, which have in turn brought about profound changes in the history of man. A Scottish mathematician, John Napier (1530-1617), invented logarithms and developed the first logarithmic table. Napier is credited also with introducing the decimal point in writing numbers.

Blaise Pascal (1623–62), a French scientist and religious philosopher, included in his broad area of scientific contributions certain computational concepts. He laid the foundation for the modern theory of probabilities. Students of statistics will recall Pascal's triangle, a triangular table of odds.

Each contribution of men will have had its prerequisite in the contributions of others. Sir Isaac Newton (1642–1727), inspired by the works of Euclid and Descartes, developed his version of calculus in 1665. He was reluctant to publish his findings, however, and Gottfried Wilhelm von Leibniz (1646-1716), a German mathematician, developed and subsequently published his version of calculus in 1684. Newton published his findings in 1704.

At the age of three, Karl Friedrich Gauss, while watching his father (a foreman) add up the payroll, noted and called his father's attention to an error he had made in arithmetic. This contribution was not the last which Karl Gauss was to make to the world of mathematics. He made many important contributions to mathematical theory. Of particular interest, however, is his application of mathematical theory to electricity and magnetism. He also laid the framework for recent and current investigation of relativity and atomic energy.

Recent and contemporary contributors to the ever growing field of mathematics and the areas of mathematical applications include, of course, Albert Einstein (1879–1955), whose contributions as a theoretical physicist included the mathematical formulation of his general theory of relativity. A process of reasoning using a mathematical approach of symbolic logic is a development of George Boole, an English logician. Boolean algebra can be applied to such areas as abstract reasoning or computer design. John Von Neumann, whose mathematical genius sets him apart, has contributed "game theory" with application to decision making in business as well as international politics.

Development of Accounting

Mathematics in its present state is the result of an almost continual addition to the accumulation of knowledge in the field as evidenced by the many men who made their individual contributions. Only a few of those whom history has marked in bold-face type have been mentioned above. Conversely, the principles which have guided commercial activity over most of the world for five centuries have gone essentially unchanged. A treatise on bookkeeping called "Particularis de Computis et Scripturis" was published as part of a larger work in 1494, and the ideas developed in it are in common use today. The author was an Italian named Luca Paciolo. His works were varied and included original contributions to the fields of algebra, geometry, proportion, architecture, and mathematical games.

Paciolo's treatise on bookkeeping translates as "Details of Accounting and Recording" and includes the type of discussion that would be found in an accounting book today. He covered the use of journals and ledgers, posting and posting references, checks and balances, recording of original entries, and closing of the nominal accounts through the Profit and Loss Summary Account into the Capital Account. He stressed internal controls and the need for auditing.

Paciolo was the first to extract the best of the then existing practices and formally record them into a scholarly volume. A book, *Paciolo on Accounting,* by Brown and Johnson makes extremely interesting reading for students of accounting. And students of data processing should find the following paragraph taken from this book of particular interest:

> Directly or indirectly through the Dutch and the English, Paciolo laid the foundation for our present accounting literature and our knowledge of bookkeeping. The so-called modern aspects of the accounting process are reflected largely by streamlined and sophisticated techniques for data collection, its processing, and the preparation of reports. Although one frequently finds expensive electronic equipment performing the accounting process, the entire structure governing these processes is the

same as it was when Paciolo outlined it in 1494. Of course, it is possible that accountants will not always adhere to the double entry process, but they have been doing so for almost 500 years.[1]

Development of Computing Devices

Concurrent with the development of ideas and theories, there has been a search for ways of speeding up simple computations and relieving man of the drudgery of monotonous repetitive calculations.

A frame into which a series of rods are mounted, each rod being strung with a number of beads, has been used successfully as a calculating device for many centuries. This device is called an *abacus*, and it may have first appeared as long as 5,000 years ago in ancient Babylonia. It has appeared in varied forms in many civilizations. The Chinese were probably the first to use the bead approach, while the Babylonians used small disks in grooves cut in boards. The abacus is still in widespread use, especially in the Orient. The abacus is a digital device that is used for counting and thereby computing on the basis of digits as in a digital computer.

A much later device but one using simple manipulative skill, as does the abacus, is the slide rule. The slide rule is based on the principle of the logarithm and the logarithmic scale of John Napier and did not appear until 1850 as a modern calculating device. The slide rule is a measuring device, not a counting device such as the abacus. Because of its capabilities for solving arithmetic problems by means of measuring instead of counting, it is referred to as an analog device. Analog computers also utilize the principle of measuring instead of counting.

The use of gears and wheels to count is also not new. Many devices, not totally unlike the mileage indicator on your automobile, have been conceived and used. Evidence points to such devices being used by the Greeks even before the birth of Christ.

Blaise Pascal was the son of a tax collector and drew the assignment of adding up columns of figures for his father. At the age of 19 he had grown tired of the job and invented an arithmetic machine to relieve him of the drudgery. It could be used for adding and subtracting and consisted of gears and wheels housed in a box.

Other machines were invented including ones by Leibniz, Thomas, Parmalee, and a more familiar name, Burroughs. Each of these had as its purpose the performance of a simple arithmetic operation. The Burroughs machine was the direct forerunner of the adding machines of today.

---

[1]R. Gene Brown, Ph.D., CPA, and Kenneth S. Johnson, Ph.D., *Paciolo on Accounting*, McGraw-Hill Book Company, Inc., New York, 1963.

A more ambitious effort was undertaken by Charles Babbage (1791-1871), an English mathematician. In his Difference Engine and especially his Analytical Engine, Babbage was attempting to build 20th-century computers with 19th-century technology.

The underlying idea of the Difference Engine was that level differences between the values computed by a formula are always constant so that the values themselves may be reached by simple addition. Babbage built a small working model in 1822 and with the aid of a government subsidy built a much larger model that was completed in 1859 and used to calculate life tables by insurance companies.

The Analytical Engine was conceived by Babbage in 1833, and his plans contained all the basic principles of modern-day computers. In this effort he failed because of the myriad of technical difficulties encountered when parts could not be engineered to required specifications and tolerances. However, the concepts which were incorporated into drawings and blueprints made by Babbage reappeared almost 100 years later and are incorporated into our present-day computers. These concepts include punched-card input and output, typewriter output, data storage, and arithmetic unit.

Today computing devices are more likely to bear the names of companies and have model numbers or have fetching names such as Stretch or Larc. Computers many times more powerful, efficient, and fast than those built or proposed in the early development stages are commonplace in today's business and scientific world. Improved technology made new and reliable component parts available and facilitated the implementation of ideas. The honor of being the first electronic computer goes to Mark I. Professor Howard G. Aiken, a Harvard University physicist, was primarily responsible for its development. Mark I was completed in 1944, seven years after work started.

About 1946 at the Moore School of Electrical Engineering at the University of Pennsylvania, another pioneer computer was making its appearance. It was named ENIAC and was developed by J. Presper Eckert and John W. Mauchly. ENIAC is the abbreviation for Electronic Numerical Integrator and Calculator. Its main use was in making computations in the area of ballistics and aeronautics. By today's standards, ENIAC was slow and unreliable. It contained over 18,000 vacuum tubes and covered several hundred square feet of floor space, but ENIAC and Mark I represented a giant step in technological progress. They stand as silent testimony to the genius of men throughout history who have made contributions to the growing knowledge of man.

The first commercially available computer was another machine developed by Eckert and Mauchly, called UNIVAC (Universal Automatic Computer), which appeared in 1951. Eckert and Mauchly formed a corporation to develop the UNIVAC (now a Division of the Sperry Rand Corporation). UNIVAC stood more or less alone in the field of commercial computers for approximately three years, but since 1954 many companies have introduced their competitive models. The largest of these companies is the International Business Machines Corporation (IBM). Others include National Cash Register (NCR), Honeywell, Burroughs, Control Data, General Electric, Radio Corporation of America (RCA), and Raytheon.

REVIEW QUESTIONS

11. Name the man who can be credited with conceiving the basic principles of present day computers. Write a brief summary covering his ideas and achievements.

12. The base-10 system utilizes what numbers?

13. What is an abacus? How does a slide rule differ from an abacus?

Development of Punched-Card Machines

One of the most influential developments for the processing of mass data is that of the punched card. The use of the punched card for processing data was not effected until about 1890, but the method had been used as early as 1728 in the process of weaving. Jacquard, a French engineer, had invented an automatic loom which used cards with appropriately punched holes to "instruct" the loom in its operation.

Dr. Herman Hollerith, an American engineer and statistician, was placed in charge of the tabulation of data gathered in the census of 1880. The completion of this job was not accomplished until 1888, and it was apparent that improvements would need to be made in the system if succeeding decennial censuses were to be processed within the 10-year period. After all, the population was increasing and actually gained 13 million (from 50 to 63 million) between 1880 and 1890. By 1890 Dr. Hollerith had developed a tabulating device utilizing the concept of entering data in the form of holes in strips of paper tape. He used this system to process the 1890 census, and the job was completed in only 3½ years despite the increase in the amount of data. Today's punched-card machines are, for the most part, descendants of Dr. Hollerith's machines. Dr. Hollerith formed the Tabulation Machine Company to market his machines after leaving the Census Bureau at the completion of the 1900 census. The company was later merged with the International Time Recording Company and the Dayton Scale Company and by 1924 had been renamed the International Business Machines Corporation with a very capable executive, Thomas J. Watson, at its helm. Replacing Dr. Hollerith at the Census Bureau was a statistical engineer named James Powers. Powers developed machines which were also based on the punched-card principle. He stayed with the Census Bureau from 1905 to 1911, when he left to form the Powers Accounting Machine Company. Through a series of mergers, the Powers' machines and ideas are now incorporated into the UNIVAC Division of the Sperry-Rand Corporation.

It is not possible to include all the factors in the development of such an inclusive area as data processing. Each major development depended on a series of supporting developments. For example, ENIAC could not have succeeded without the vacuum tube, and more recent computers could not have been devised without access to supporting developments, such as the transistor and core memory devices. In turn, each of these supporting developments was dependent upon some more basic development, invention, or discovery.

REVIEW QUESTIONS

14. Line up the developments in column 2 to match the correct name in column 1 (make no change in column 1; simply rearrange the letters preceding column 2).

1	2
a. Smathers	a. Mark I computer
b. John Napier	b. Game theory
c. Blaise Pascal	c. Calculus
d. Isaac Newton	d. Math. theory of electricity
e. Karl F. Gauss	e. Electric typewriter
f. George Boole	f. Logarithmic tables
g. John Von Neumann	g. ENIAC computer
h. Luca Paciolo	h. Special form of algebra
i. Howard G. Aiken	i. Bookkeeping
j. Eckert and Mauchly	j. Mechanical adding machine
k. Jacquard	k. Tabulate the census
l. Herman Hollerith	l. Punched cards

15. What were the principal contributions of Dr. Herman Hollerith? What company evolved from his basic inventions?

16. The inventions of Dr. James Powers led to the forming of another well-known company. What is the name of this company, and what were Dr. Powers' major accomplishments?

2 THE DATA PROCESSING PROBLEM

NEED FOR PROCESSED DATA

The need for processed data is universal. An advanced culture survives and progresses on the basis of processed data. Without it the wheels of commercial and scientific activity would halt and society would immediately revert to a system of individual self-survival. Notwithstanding the occasional irrational act, the actions of man are based on assimilated information, data which have been processed.

But these are generalities and, if we were unaware of them before, their truth becomes immediately apparent. More specifically, the need for processed data can be analyzed from the standpoint of two general areas, business and scientific.

Business Needs

The needs of business for processed data are of an *external* and *internal* nature, i.e., the requirements for the data may originate from outside the company or organization, or they may originate within the business or organization.

External Needs

External needs for processed data include, among others, legal requirements. The demand from governmental agencies for data pertaining to the many facets of a business operation are many. Not the least of these requirements is the annual filing of the income tax return, but there are many more areas of taxation and control which require accurate and complete reporting, e.g., state sales and use taxes, federal excise taxes, social security taxes, etc. Statistical information is also required by government agencies for compilation of various analyses, indexes, and summaries of manufacturing and distribution activities.

Besides the need to furnish data in the form of reports to governmental agencies, business enterprises are called upon to furnish information to their customers, creditors, suppliers, owners, and the general public. Customers will require receipts, statements, price quotations, acknowledgments, invoices, and bills of lading. Creditors will require checks and remittance advices, and suppliers will require purchase orders. In the corporate enterprise the owners expect an annual stockholder's report and a quarterly dividend check. And even the general public will anticipate hearing and reading of the activities of business, and it behooves each business enterprise to make this information available through the various communication media.

Internal Needs

Demands for processed data which originate internally include those necessary for routine operations, management control, process control, project management, and simulation.

Document Origination. The catalyst of a business operation is the paper documents which cause things to happen. Except for the very small business enterprise, each action and transaction must be documented. Documents and reports are the "product" of the business office. There is always the danger that an office will overproduce the product, but elimination of the product is not the solution. The chide to "put it in writing" is valid enough. In order for the purchasing department to write a purchase order, they need a written purchase requisition. If the accounting department is to pay for the goods received, they will need written verification of receipt of the goods and written evidence of the purchase contract. If the employees are to be paid, checks must be written and can only be written if proper evidence and authorization has been written in the form of time sheets or time cards. The shipping department cannot ship unless they have a written shipping order, etc. Document origination, then, is a formidable task of any business.

File Maintenance, Materials Records. In addition to the creation of written documents, certain data files must be maintained. Information regarding men, materials, and money must be current and accurate. Except in rare circumstances a "book" inventory is essential. As business operations bring about changes in the physical inventory, the books should reflect these changes and the shorter the time differential between actual physical change and book change the better. Proper maintenance of the inventory records will aid in the provision for better customer service, better control over inventory items, and generally better distribution procedures with resultant improvement of the company image, as well as company profits. In some cases it is more than either an image or profit which is at stake. The massive job of supplying our military personnel throughout the world from supply depots is basically one of distribution and inventory control, once the supplies are produced. In cases such as these, when supplies are needed, knowing what supplies are available and where they are located is of utmost importance. Knowing what was on hand yesterday or having records that reflect what might be on hand today is not good enough for the needs of tomorrow.

File Maintenance, Personnel Records. Just as with materials, men and their abilities also need to be accounted for. In smaller organizations this need is not so apparent, but in larger organizations proper inventorying and updating of the personnel records will keep men from becoming numbers. The current, accurate, and inclusive knowledge of the available abilities represented in the total working force of a company will provide the basis for placing the right person in the right position. Assignments, promotions, and placements can be made on the basis of fact rather than fancy or whim. Or let us consider the task of maintaining proper records for the social security program and other similar large-scale programs involving millions of records which must be kept to administer this vast program adequately. And then between the levels of the single company and the federal government lie many other areas where processed data, as they concern individuals, are paramount. These areas would include the state and local license bureaus, police departments, other criminal investigation bodies, welfare departments, credit bureaus, etc.

File Maintenance, Monetary Records. Wherever credit is involved, and it certainly is involved in most business transactions today, accurate accounting for amounts owed and amounts due is essential. Accounts receivable and accounts payable require continual current updating to reflect dollar status. The essential nature of the banking operation is concerned with reflecting the dollar and cents changes in depositors' accounts. In fact, file updating in terms of monetary units is basic accounting and therefore has universal application wherever business is done.

The areas of file maintenance are legion. There are property record files as kept by individuals and companies, motor vehicle records, real estate and motor vehicle ownership records, insurance policy records, stock and bond ownership records, membership files, library book files, student records, and telephone directories, just to name a few.

Management Control. Document origination and file maintenance require a large part of the total data-processing time and effort. Yet, another aspect of the need for processed data is of equal significance. This is the internal need for analysis of the various operations of the business. Management, if it is to "run the shop" effectively and efficiently, must be properly informed. Each segment of the operation, as well as the over-all picture, must be presented in the form of summarized, processed data. For example, sales data need to be presented in various ways for management analysis and decision. A report could give sales with subtotals by salesman or region or district. Or sales data could be presented as an analysis by product or department. The reports could also include comparison data so that current operations might be compared with last month's or last year's operation.

Likewise, data pertaining to the cost of operations need to be processed and reported for management analysis. In a manufacturing operation these reports might be in the form of efficiency reports from which management might evaluate the operation. But even with revenue and expense items fully reported and analyzed, management will have further needs for processed data (data on markets, data on product acceptance and advertising effectiveness, data on raw materials and price structure, and so on ad infinitum). This data must be gathered, processed, and reported also.

Importance of Current and Accurate Reporting

It is readily observable that, if management is to make effective use of the reports which have been listed as necessary, these reports must be accurate and current. Management decision can be no better than the data and the resulting reports made available to management personnel. In the past, "historical" reporting, information on activity which took place months, weeks, and days before the appearance of the report, was considered satisfactory. Today these time lapses are intolerable. Information needs to be up to the minute literally. The ultimate in processing and reporting is instantaneous reflection of business transactions in the form of output on a *real-time* basis. Real-time processing is possible with the use of computers and will be discussed later in conjunction with computer applications.

REVIEW QUESTIONS

1. The need for processed data by businesses takes on two forms. What are these two different types of needs, and what causes the generation of documentation in each?

2. What is the objective of file maintenance?

3. Name three general areas requiring file maintenance in a business.

4. Name three areas of reporting required by the management of most companies.

5. What is historical reporting? Why is it no longer practical?

Scientific Needs

The usage of the term *scientific* here is possibly a pseudo usage but still best describes the remaining areas of processed-data needs. Although data processing is usually broken down into two general areas, business and scientific, from a data-processing point of view the scientific area is closely associated with business. Actually, the main differentiating factor is the complexity of the mathematics involved. Scientific data are stated in terms of mathematics, and scientific data processing is processing this data according to mathematical principles. It is not record keeping, nor is it mass information handling as is typical of business data processing. Scientific data processing is problem solving, and the problem might very well be one of significance for business. The first of these areas is production and process control.

Process Control and Automation

Production Control. Production control is the regulating of a manufacturing process, which requires the coordination of men, materials, and machines. A typical example would be the scheduling of an assembly line so that the right component parts are at the right place at the right time with the right men or machines to make the assembly. This is not a small task, as illustrated by a General Motors advertisement which states that hundreds of a particular model of Chevrolet automobile could be produced with no two cars being exactly alike.

Process Control. Process control is closely related to production control. A processing plant, such as a chemical plant, must be controlled at various steps in the process so that the end product will meet specifications. Changes in the product are continuous, and the data are new and different at each point from which they are gathered. On the basis of data gathered and processed, corrective action must be taken to keep the product up to standard. The operation can be simple or complex. It can be as simple as taking a temperature reading or drawing off a sample and checking its color and then adjusting a valve. Or it can be the analysis of a variety of factors via a complex procedure that results in corrective action involving a series of technical adjustments.

It is of significance to note that, until recently, the conventional method of operation has required *manual processing* of the data and *manual operation* of the corrective controls based on the *manual collection* of data. If, instead, a high-speed data-processing system is used and is fed the input data directly from the manufacturing process and subsequently returns the processed data so as to control the manufacturing operation *automatically,* the whole process is called *automation.* The automatic control of a manufacturing process is automation in the strictest sense of the word. The data-processing system used is a computer, and it is an integral part of the total manufacturing process in an automated plant. The need for data in an automated plant is so great and so critical that there is a continuous flow of that data between the manufacturing process and the data-processing system, resulting in a continuous cycle of data. Technically it is called a *closed-loop feedback system.*

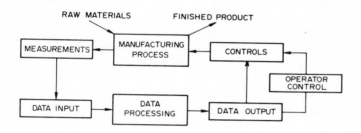

Fig. 2-1. Data flow in an automated process.

The diagram (Fig. 2-1) shows the data flow in an automated process. This example shows the data flowing counterclockwise. Data originate out of the manufacturing process by means of measuring mechanisms such as temperature and pressure gauges. These data are forwarded to the data-processing unit as input, where they are analyzed with reference to prescribed standards. The output from the data-processing unit is in the form of directions to the controlling mechanisms, which take the corrective action called for. Then the process is repeated again and again as a continuous operation.

Project Management and Simulation

The era of scientific management has made its debut, and today, in the more progressive organizations, management planning is based on such sophisticated techniques as project management and simulation. These techniques and others of a similar nature draw heavily upon the mathematical approach to problem solving. They are an attempt to reflect what will happen before it happens.

In project management, techniques called *PERT* (Program Evaluation and Review Technique) or *CPM* (Critical Path Method) are commonly used. Their major use is in conjunction with the planning of large-scale engineering and construction projects. Exhaustive data are gathered and processed via the PERT or CPM technique, and the results provide management with detailed scheduling information for the project.

Simulation, or model building, is another area in which mass data and extensive processing are called for. Simulation is an attempt to reproduce a physical condition in symbolic form. A person, a firm, or even an economy is reduced to, and described in, mathematical terms. Relationships between and among the various component segments are expressed in algebraic form, and this complex expression becomes the model of that which it purports to represent and describe. What is the purpose? Suppose a valid mathematical model is "built" of a particular company or firm. Then certain decisions could be tried out before any real commitment is made. Many such decisions could be tested, and only the ones showing the greatest potential for the firm's success would be implemented. Similar applications of model building, or simulation, can be made to a large variety of situations including war "games," management games, air and surface traffic control, community planning, manufacturing processes, etc.

REVIEW QUESTIONS

6. In general terms, explain how scientific data processing differs from business data processing.

7. Define the terms *production control* and *process control*.

8. What is the special terminology that describes an automated plant that has a continuous flow of data between the manufacturing process and the controlling system?

NEED FOR AUTOMATED DATA PROCESSING

In discussing the need for processed data, the corresponding need for faster and more efficient methods of processing the data was usually evident. The very volume of data and the encompassing dependence upon its being processed dictates that machines be harnessed to do the job. The Industrial Revolution of the 18th and 19th centuries brought machines to relieve man of physical work and to be an extension of man's muscle. It gave him mobility and power. The continuing technological revolution of the 20th century has brought and is bringing machines to relieve man of mental work. These new machines are an extension of man's mind. The machines of the 20th century give us speed and accuracy in our mental work never before attainable.

Business Needs

The causes of the business need for improved methods of processing data can be included in three general headings: (1) the increased volume of data, (2) the shortage of clerical workers, and (3) business competition.

Traditionally, the office function has received only token consideration in the total picture of goods and services production. During and after the Industrial Revolution the major considerations by industrial management were typically those areas directly concerned with production. In the early 1900's, techniques of production including standardization of products and parts, specialization of labor, and mechanization of operations were readily received and implemented in the plant. Considerable attention was bestowed upon assembly lines, time and motion study, and other techniques aimed at efficiency in the plant. However, the attitude of management toward the office and its problems was generally one of indifference. The office was not looked upon as an integral part of the over-all objective of the company, namely, that of producing the product, but was rather regarded as a necessary evil. The office and its function were things to be tolerated. Only recently has the function of the office come to light as a contributing factor in a total productive operation. This evolving concept, coupled with the pressures exerted upon the data-processing facilities as enumerated above—data volume, worker shortage, and competition—and simultaneous revolutionary technological advancement all converging at a common point in time, has truly brought about an information explosion.

Increased Volume of Data

In noting the need for data in the foregoing discussion, some of the reasons for an increasing volume of data were listed. But what are the underlying reasons for these demands from government, customers, et al.? It is simply growth, population growth and its offspring, business and commercial growth. More goods and services are being produced for more people. And, because of the increased complexity of our society and economy, the volume of data tends to grow at a much steeper rate than in direct proportion to the growth. A familiar example of the increase in complexity of business procedures is the simple but widespread use of credit and checks in lieu of cash in the sale and purchase of merchandise at the retail level. Billions of checks are processed through the banks each year, and additional billions of credit transactions are processed. The problem of processing checks is in itself an awesome, if not impossible, one unless some type of automated system is employed to cope with it. The banking industry has adopted a system which is currently working satisfactorily. This system, magnetic-ink character recognition, will be discussed later.

Clerical-Worker Shortage

The white-collar labor situation has also contributed to the trend toward automated data processing. Perhaps, however, this section should have been headed "Inadequacy of Clerical Worker" or "Human Weakness" or some similar heading, for the problem is as much human nature as it is actual shortage of human beings.

At first the logical answer to the increased office work load was to add more people to the staff, more people to do routine clerical work. This answer was satisfactory up to a point, but people tend to get in each other's way. People cannot always tolerate other people. People get bored with routine work. People must have coffee breaks, vacations, and maternity leaves. People get disgruntled, dissatisfied, distraught, and people quit. This is not to say that people are not important. It does indicate that people are too important to do routine nonchallenging work. In fact, at a certain point, the adding of more clerical workers would not result in getting more work done and might even cause a decrease in output. Even before this point, however, the problem would have to be resolved in another way. Data-processing machines can overcome some, if not most, of these human problems.

Furthermore, in theory, if business were to process all of the data it generates without machines, there would soon not be enough people available to do the job. We say, theoretically, because on a practical basis the forces which generate the data, business activities, would have slowed or chugged to a stop long ago because of the processing bottleneck, if human processing were the only alternative.

Competition

Competition as a factor contributing to the need for automated methods of processing data is based on the inference that competition forces the production of the most desirable goods at the least possible cost. In a private enterprise system, where there is free consumer choice, the firm must produce what the consumer wants and offer it at a price which he will accept.

If a producer cannot do this, he will not stay in business. Of course there is wide latitude in this statement. A firm may be able to influence the choice of the buyer, or consumer, through advertising and promotion even to the point of convincing the buyer to pay a higher price, but there is a limit to this influence. The facts are that, if a firm cannot produce or merchandise at a competitive price, his competitor will get the business. It is also a fact that all of the costs of a business must be recovered in the price of the goods offered for sale before any profit is registered. Costs must be kept to a minimum.

The two factors of the increasing volume of data and the clerical-worker shortage, however, both result in higher costs. For, in addition to needing more clerical workers, clerical salaries gradually become higher as the demand for the workers becomes greater. More efficient methods of processing data then become necessary.

Efficiency in the processing of data involves more than simple reduction of absolute costs. It means getting the most out of a given amount of expenditure. In data processing it means providing the best information system commensurate with the needs of the organization. The needs will include *accuracy, more current reporting, more comprehensive reporting,* and *economy.* A company's competitive position may well depend upon how well it meets these needs.

A data-processing system cannot tolerate errors. An improved system must be one which is more accurate. Machines are more accurate than humans, many times more so. Machines are, therefore, particularly desirable for the repetitive type of jobs. If a machine is set up to do an operation correctly, it will continue to grind out correct answers hour upon hour, whereas a human would tend to make more and more errors as he becomes fatigued. Data-processing machines are, then, a logical fulfillment to the need for accuracy. A computer can make billions of calculations without error.

We have mentioned the need for current reporting and records which are up to date. From a competitive standpoint, business cannot afford to operate on out-of-date information. Business moves fast, and decisions need to be made before it is too late. The speed of a data-processing system is an important element. Machines again are many times more efficient than human beings. Electronic data-processing systems make computations in terms of millions per second. Preparation of printed output, one of the slowest operations of an automated system, is measured in hundreds and thousands of lines per minute.

Because of the outstanding processing speeds of automated systems, more comprehensive reporting is possible. Businesses with more meaningful analytical data will have the competitive advantage. The business management which has an electronic data-processing system at its disposal has a powerful tool with which to make soundly based managerial decisions.

Automated data processing (ADP) can also provide for better customer service through more comprehensive reporting, a definite competitive advantage in the battle for customers.

Economy is often thought of first in analyzing the comparative advantages of a manual and an ADP system. The fact is that automated systems are not generally more economical if thought of in terms of reducing the absolute cost of producing a given amount of data output. A company will not likely reduce its data-processing cost if a system is automated merely to do the same job. An automated system costs and can only be economical if its abilities are fully realized. A computer fully and properly used is more likely to make money than save money for its user.

REVIEW QUESTIONS

9. Give three reasons why business organizations had to devise advanced methods of processing data.

10. In what ways are machines more effective than human beings?

11. What type of work can an automated system do particularly well?

12. Name some of the reasons why an organization needs efficient data-processing methods.

Scientific Needs

Whereas business needs for automated methods of data processing resulted from the data volume-clerical worker shortage squeeze, scientific needs are based on man's surge for progress. Man has been greatly limited by his inability to interrelate sufficient volumes of data to base his scientific hypotheses on or to prove them. Brilliant scientific minds have been wasted on routine calculations. Early astronomers and mathematicians have spent lifetimes manually processing the data gathered from their observations, lifetimes of calculating which can be done today in a matter of minutes.

Scientific Investigation

Scientific needs spawned the computer, and the power of the computer has opened up a limitless vista of scientific investigation. Today the computer is an indispensable tool of the scientist. It is as essential as the test tube or the telescope once was. The computer affects every appendage of the body of scientific study from pure mathematics through the physical and life sciences to the area of social science. It then reaches down to the next level, the level of developmental research.

Developmental Research

Here again the need for processed data has been met by automated processing methods. The rate of progress in the development of new and better products has been greatly increased by the power of the electronic computer. It is rapidly displacing the slide rule and the drawing board. The computer can build simulated models of a product in infinite varieties and select the one with optimum utility. The significance of such an application of automated methods of processing data are apparent when we take note of the fact that more men were lost in man's endeavor to fly a few miles than have been lost in his endeavor to explore outer space.

Present-day accomplishments of man, from nuclear development and space travel to the daily used products of necessity and luxury, would not be remotely possible without ADP and its chief contributor, the computer.

REVIEW QUESTION

13. What is the most basic advantage of automation in scientific research?

THE LANGUAGE OF AUTOMATED DATA PROCESSING

It takes little more than a casual observation to be aware that data are universal and are created in immeasurable quantities. Also, the sources of data are widespread and divergent, ranging all the way from the sale of a licorice stick in a candy store to a seismographic reading of an underground atomic blast.

Let us for the present, however, direct our attention somewhere in between these two extremes. Let us examine the sources of business data. Data originate with business activity. Goods are sold, purchased, ordered, received, moved, manufactured, and destroyed. Men are hired, fired, promoted, classified, reclassified, assigned, reassigned, paid, and retired. Money is received, paid out, loaned, borrowed, lost, and stolen. As each activity takes place it creates data with potential importance to record and process.

Source Documents

The original recording of a business transaction is done on a source document. Source documents take the names of that which they record. Sales orders record a sale, material receiving reports record the receipt of merchandise or materials, etc.

Source documents are then the evidence of data for processing. They are the written documents from which the processing cycle begins. They are written in conventional language for human understanding. If, however, the data are to be processed by machine, a secondary recording of the data must usually be made in a machine-readable language or code. Some of these languages will now be described.

Machine-Language Recording

The IBM Punched Card

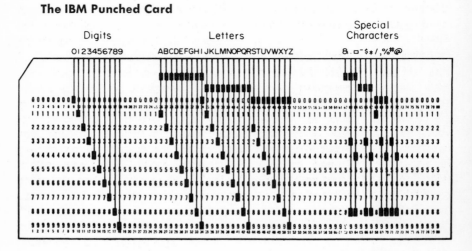

Fig. 2-2. An IBM punched card—a machine-language document.

One example of a machine-readable document is the IBM punched card in which data are recorded in coded form. (See Fig. 2-2) The code is the Hollerith code. Dr. Hollerith was the inventor of the code that bears his name. The card is 7⅜ inches long and 3¼ inches wide. Interestingly, this size was selected because it was the size of the dollar bill of 1890 when the card was designed.

The IBM punched card has 80 vertical columns, or spaces, across the card. Each column can have recorded in it one character of data, either a numeric character from zero through nine or an alphabetic character, a through z, or a special character such as a plus sign (+) or dollar sign ($). The horizontal positions, or rows, are used in the coding scheme. There are 12 rows. Each row represents a particular punching position, and, by punching holes in the proper positions of any column, a character of data can be recorded. Numeric characters require only one punch per column. For instance, the number 6 can be recorded in any one of the 80 columns by simply punching a hole in the "6 row." Any number can be recorded in any column.

An alphabetic character requires two punches per column. One of these two punches is a digit punch (rows one through nine), and the other is a zone punch (rows zero, eleven, or twelve). The two top rows are known as the 12 (or Y) row and the 11 (or X) row, even though they are not generally so indicated on the card, and these two rows plus the zero row are known as the *zone positions.* So an alphabetic character is written in Hollerith code by combining one zone punch and one digit punch in a single column. For instance, an "A" could be recorded in any column of the card by punching a combination of a 12 punch and a 1 punch (12-1 = A). A combination of a 12 and a 2 punch is the code for the letter B (12-2 = B). This procedure continues until the letter I is coded with punches in the 12 and 9 (12-9) positions. At this point the 11 row is used in combination with the nine digit positions to form the letters J through R. You can remember this by associating it with the quip "Junior is 11" (J-R is 11).

Using the zero-zone punching position now in combination with the nine digit punching positions would provide for a total of 27 different combinations. Since there are only 26 letters in the alphabet, it was originally determined that the zero-one (0-1) combination would be the one not used. Therefore, the letter S is coded with the combination of a zero and a two (0-2) punch, which makes the Z coded zero-nine (0-9).

Special characters usually require three punches per column. Learning the coding for special characters is not generally necessary, but being able to decode numeric and alphabetic codes is helpful. The machines used to record the data into the cards will automatically provide the proper punches to form the desired character.

The UNIVAC Card

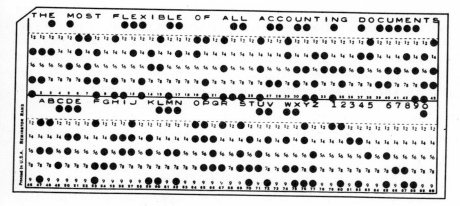

Fig. 2-3. The UNIVAC 90—column punched card.

Another machine-language document is the UNIVAC punched card (Fig. 2-3). Its size is the same as the IBM card, but the coding scheme is different. The UNIVAC card has 45 columns but is divided into two sections, an upper section and a lower section, so that effectively there are 90 columns into which data can be recorded. It is often called the *90-column card,* whereas the IBM card is known as the *80-column card.* The holes punched into the card are round, which is different from the rectangular holes of the IBM card. There are six rows in each section. The positions, or rows, are the 0, 1-2, 3-4, 5-6, 7-8, and 9. In numeric coding, odd numbers and the zero are coded with only one punch per column, but the even numbers require two punches, one in the row bearing that number combined with a punch in the 9 row. There is no pattern to the alphabetic code in the UNIVAC system.

James Powers, who, you may remember, succeeded Dr. Hollerith at the Census Bureau, developed the code now used in the UNIVAC card. The code is therefore known as the *Powers code.*

REVIEW QUESTIONS

14. What is a source document?

15. What punches or combinations of punches would form the following letters in 80-column card code: E, H, J, N, T?

16. A punch in the 11 row is often referred to as ———————

Punched Paper Tape

A data medium similar to the punched card is punched paper tape (Fig. 2-4). Paper tape as commonly used is a long strip of specially processed

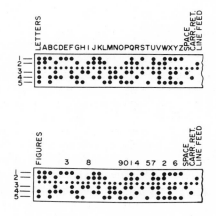

Fig. 2-4. Paper tape—five-channel code.

paper, approximately 1 inch wide. Data is recorded in coded form by punching the tape with a machine appropriately called a *paper-tape punch*. The positions in which the holes can be punched across the tape are called *channels*. Different coding systems require a different number of channels. There are five-, six-, seven-, and eight-channel codes.

Since eight-channel tape (Fig. 2-5) is one of the most commonly used, the coding system used in it will illustrate the nature of punched paper-tape coding. The eight-channel code is similar to the Hollerith code used in the IBM card. As in the card, there are digit punches and zone punches. All nine digit rows (channels) are not present, but with the combination of assigned values all of the digits can be represented. The values assigned are 1, 2, 4, and 8. A single hole can then represent any one of these digits, but the digits 3, 5, 7, and 9 require two or three punched holes.

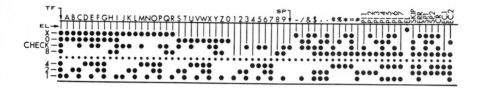

Fig. 2-5. Paper tape—eight-channel code.

The zero channel and the X channel are used for alphabetic coding just as the zone rows on the IBM card. Remember how the letters J through R were coded with a punch in the 11 (or X) row combined with a digit punch. A J was coded with an 11 (X) -1. In the eight-channel code the J is again an X-1. An R was coded with a combination of 11 (X) -9 and is so coded in the tape, except now an 8 and a 1 must be punched to form the equivalent of the 9. In Hollerith code the combination 0-2 decoded to be an S. In eight-channel code a 0-2 is again an S. Rather than use an extra channel, the equivalent of the 12-zone punch is represented on the tape by punches in both the zero and X channels. So an A is coded with the X, 0, and 1 channels punched. The other two channels are used for machine control and checking.

Magnetic Tape

Magnetic tape is very similar to punched paper tape in concept and coding system, although the substance, or medium, itself is quite different. The tape is a familiar one since it is the same type of material as that used in home and office tape recorders, a plasticlike substance on which an iron-oxide coating has been placed on one side. The coating provides a medium on which magnetic spots can be placed. The magnetic spot on magnetic tape is a

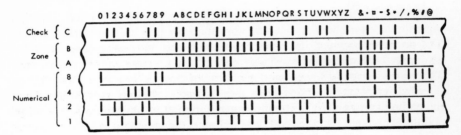

Fig. 2-6. Magnetic tape—seven-bit alphameric code.

counterpart of the hole in the punched paper tape. A commonly used magnetic tape code is the seven-bit code, which means that there are seven channels (Fig. 2-6). The designation and values of the numeric channels are the same as on eight-channel paper tape with the zero and X channels now being designated A and B. Their use in alphabetic coding, however, remains the same. The seventh channel is for machine checking purposes.

The Unit-Record Principle

The unit-record principle is basic to the various automated methods of processing data. Fundamentally the principle refers to the idea of recording all the information about a single unit or item on a single document (Fig. 2-7). What is determined to be the unit is a matter of definition. A customer could be defined as a unit, or a particular sale to a customer might be defined as the unit, or each type of merchandise that the customer purchased on a

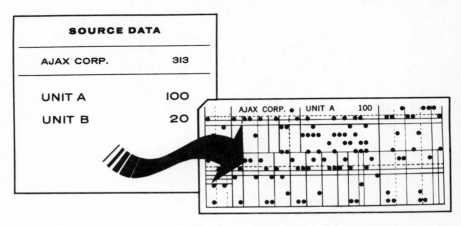

Fig. 2-7. Application of the unit-record principle. One card for each item in source document.

particular transaction could be defined as the unit. In the first instance, the information pertaining to the customer would be recorded on a single document in keeping with the principle. In the second example, a separate document would be required for each sale and would have recorded on it information applicable to the single sales transaction. In the third case, each item included in the sale would require a separate document and would include the detail information peculiar to the merchandise item, i.e., color, quantity, stock number, etc.

The purpose in utilizing the unit-record principle is to facilitate some of the processing steps, especially sorting. Automated data-processing systems are based on the unit-record principle. The punched card is a unit record, and the punched-card machines are often called *unit-record machines.* These machines are described in the following chapter.

REVIEW QUESTIONS

17. What is a channel in paper tape?

18. Since there are only two zone channels on an eight-channel paper tape, what replaces the 12-zone punch of the 80-column card code?

19. Relate the 12, 11, and 0 punches of an 80-column card code to the equivalent codes on both paper tape and magnetic tape.

3 ELECTRIC ACCOUNTING MACHINES (EAM)

WHAT IS EAM?

The term *EAM* is a common one in the data-processing business. It is used to describe machines, operators, methods, systems, and even supervisors. So let us examine what it means. Immediately it must be said that EAM is the abbreviation for electric accounting machines, but this tells us little, and the term must be examined still further.

Electric Accounting Machines

EAM, or electric accounting machines, refers to the type of equipment which grew out of the ideas of Dr. Hollerith and James Powers in their individual work with the United States Bureau of the Census, developing systems for tabulation. EAM refers to a family of machines using the punched card (either the IBM card or the UNIVAC card), exclusively in their operation (Figs. 3-1 and 3-2). Their language is the holes punched into the cards in coded form, either the Hollerith code, as used in the IBM card, or the Powers code, as used in the UNIVAC card. Each of the members of the family of EAM equipment is designed to perform one or a combination of the data-processing functions—recording, sorting, calculating, and reporting through the medium of the punched card. The two remaining functions, classifying and communicating, are performed manually. Classifying is accomplished by assigning codes, generally at the time the source document is created. Communication of data from one function to another is done by physically transporting the cards from one machine to another.

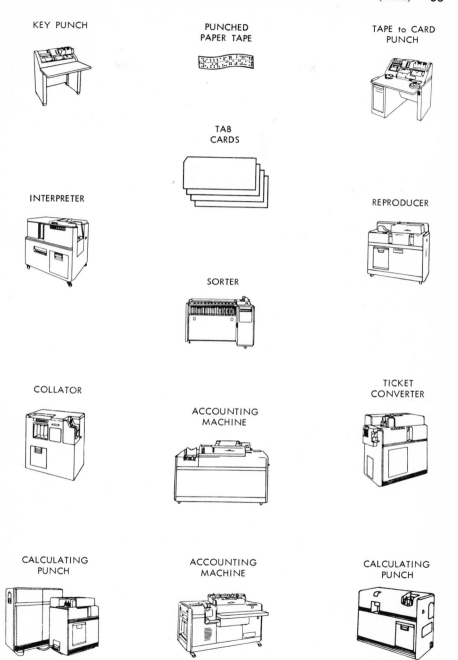

Fig. 3-1. IBM punched card machines.

KEY PUNCH

CARD to TAPE
CONVERTER

ELECTRONIC
SORTER

COLLATOR

REPRODUCER

ALPHA
TABULATOR

TAG
REPRODUCER

CALCULATING
PUNCH

TAB
and
SUMMARY
PUNCH

Fig. 3-2. UNIVAC punched card machines.

Punched-Card Machines

The importance of the punched card as the medium through which data are transported from one machine to another is the basis for EAM equipment's being known also as *punched-card machines.*

Unit-Record Machines

As has been explained previously, the card is a unit record (a separate document with data about a particular unit), and, since the EAM equipment is specifically designed to process data via cards, the machines are commonly known as *unit-record machines,* as well as EAM and punched-card machines.

Tabulating Machines

One of the EAM family of machines is often referred to as a tabulator. It is the machine that prepares the output report, and, because of the tabulator's functional importance, its name is applied to the entire group of machines. Thus, these machines are also called *tabulating machines.*

The Nature of Electric Accounting Machines

EAM Equipment Operates Mechanically. Now that it has been shown why these machines are identified by such a variety of names, it is appropriate that a closer examination of their nature follow. These machines are not electronic; they are electromechanical in operation. In order to be classified electronic, the form of the data would have to change for processing. In the EAM equipment, the form of the data does not change. In these machines, the data are processed by actually manipulating (processing) the card itself. Electronic data-processing systems (computers) process the data in the form of electronic impulses. A computer is *not* classified as EAM.

EAM Equipment Reads Electrically. The data, which are in the form of holes in the card, must, however, be recognizable to the machines. The machines must be able to read the card. Reading is accomplished by sensing the holes in the card electrically, hence the descriptive adjective *electric* in electric accounting machines.

EAM Equipment is Suited for Accounting. EAM equipment is particularly useful in the statistical and accounting type of applications, and, therefore, the word accounting is also used to describe the machines. Electric describes how EAM equipment works, and *accounting* describes what it does best.

Functions of Electric Accounting Machines

As indicated above, the punched-card machines are a family of machines. Each machine has its own function to perform, and one machine in the EAM family is of little value by itself. These are the things they can do, using the card as the data medium: The machines can *punch* holes in cards and *sort* cards. They can *add, subtract, multiply,* and *divide* data punched in cards and punch or print the results. They can *print* the punched data on cards or paper reports. They can *convert* data on punched cards to punched paper tape or from punched paper tape to punched cards. That is, they, the machines, can do all of these things if they are properly set up and operated by a human operator.

EAM Describes a System

Although EAM more logically describes machines, it also has general usage in describing a method, or system, of processing. Its use in identifying a system separates the EAM method from mechanical or electronic methods. A reference to an EAM system implies the exclusive use of electric accounting machines in the data-processing operation. Electronic computers may use the punched cards as input media and be called punched-card systems, but they are not classified as EAM. Instead, a system utilizing a computer would be referred to as an *electronic data-processing system,* or *EDP system.*

EAM Describes Auxiliary Equipment

The punched card has proven a very useful and versatile machine-language document since its initial usage as a data medium roughly 75 years ago. The machines using the punched card have continually been improved by giving them greater abilities and speeds, but the card itself has not changed since alphabetic coding was added early in its development. Tabulating, or EAM, equipment has been gradually made more versatile, an example being the development of a machine that could multiply and divide. With the advent of the computer these same machines are being used to support computer systems.

EAM Complements EDP

Many companies, large and small, installed EAM equipment and oriented their data-processing procedures to the use of the punched card and EAM equipment. Subsequently, as the commercial computers were designed and built, it was logical that they be made compatible with the EAM equipment. By so doing, the potential user could more easily make the changeover to EDP. A card-system computer will replace several of the machines in the EAM system. Undoubtedly, however, there will be some functions which EAM will perform more efficiently or economically than does the computer. Thus, EAM equipment is often used in a supporting role with computer systems. In this role EAM is often referred to as peripheral, or auxiliary, equipment.

Significance of Understanding EAM

The fact that punched-card (EAM) machines are in such widespread use as peripheral equipment and the fact that EAM systems continue to perform so satisfactorily in areas where computers are not currently practical make the study of them imperative. Even for those whose major data-processing interest is computer oriented or those who are scientifically inclined, a basic understanding of unit-record, or EAM, equipment and methods is of considerable value.

For those who intend to make data processing their career, whether it be as a machine operator or a systems analyst, the thorough knowledge of EAM and its concepts is important for proper performance on the job.

REVIEW QUESTIONS

1. What are some of the other names used for EAM?
2. Why is EAM called electromechanical?
3. What is the basic input tool of EAM?
4. What is the primary difference between EAM and computers?
5. Name some of the general functions of EAM equipment.
6. What are some of the specific operations that can be accomplished with EAM?
7. What do the letters EDP represent?
8. Is a punched-card system necessarily an EAM system? (If your answer is no, explain.)

THE PUNCHED CARD

Characteristics of the Card (Figs. 3–3 and 3–4)

As a matter of review it should be recalled that the punched card is a standard-size document of high-quality card stock. It must be manufactured

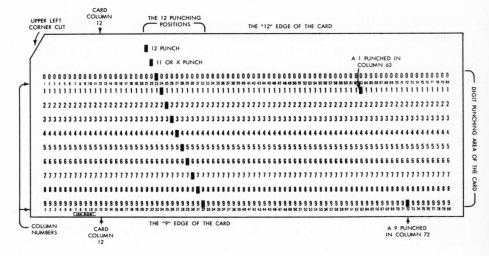

Fig. 3-3. An IBM card.

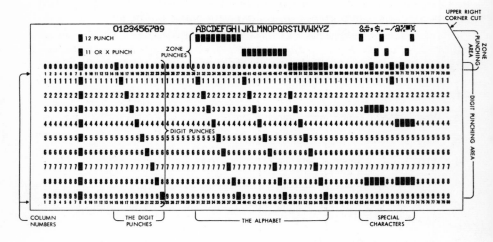

Fig. 3-4. Punching.

to exacting specifications for high-speed handling through the machines. Its size is 7⅜ by 3¼ by 0.007 inches. The 80 columns across the card provide for the recording of 80 characters of information and the 12 rows provide for the system of coding any numeric or alphabetic character and many special characters. Holes are punched in the appropriate row or rows in accordance with the established coding system.

40

Card Terminology

The top edge of the card is known as the *12 edge* and the bottom as the *9 edge*. This terminology is used in indicating the manner in which cards are placed in the various machines. In some machines the cards are entered with the 12 edge leading and others with the 9 edge leading. The front of the card is called the *face,* and this terminology is also used in describing how the cards are put into the machine, i.e., 9 edge leading, face down, or 12 edge leading, face up, etc.

Card Identification

The machines need only the properly punched holes for proper interpretation of the data in the cards, assuming that the human operator has entered the proper cards in the proper manner. So, further identification of cards is not necessary for the machines. However, the operator does need some visual evidence for card identification. *Color* is a convenient method, and cards are available in a variety of colors. The cards can be a solid color, or they can have a color strip across the face.

Another method of card identification to aid the operator is the *corner cut.* The cut is referred to as *upper right, upper left, lower right* or *lower left.* The corner cut serves two purposes. First, if cards for a particular procedure all have the same corner cut, then, a "foreigner" would be recognized by the presence of the corner. Also, in a deck a card which is upside-down or face backward is quickly spotted by the corner which appears from the deck.

Besides the corner cut and color identifications, cards can be especially designed with *printed identification* to meet the user's needs. The printing would show the card as an accounts receivable card or a sales analysis card or whatever application is intended for the card.

Organization of Data on Card (Fig. 3–5)

Importance of Card Design. Since the machines only understand the punched holes in the card, the organization of the card is of utmost importance. The items of data to be recorded on the card and the location on the card for each item of data must be determined before the machines can be set up to perform their individual processing functions. The design of the card is the critical phase in the over-all problem of setting up an EAM application. Once a card has been designed and the application built around it, a change in the design of the card results in a whole series of adjustments to machines and procedures.

Card Design Considerations

In card design the first step is a *consideration of the proposed output*. An analysis is made of the output report to determine what data are necessary to accomplish the objective. The second step is a *consideration of the available data* and a determination of what data are necessary to produce the desired output. After determining which of the items of available data are to be included on the card, the next consideration is the *order* in which the data are to be placed on the card. The *card format must be planned*.

Card Fields

The areas of the card designated for certain items of data are called *fields*. More specifically, *a field is a column or columns reserved for the punching of data of a specific nature*. A field can be from 1 to 80 columns, depending on the needs of the data item for which the area is reserved. An "amount field," for instance, would need only be an area of four adjacent columns if it is certain that no amount will ever exceed four significant digits such as $99.99 or 9999. If there is a reasonable chance that amounts may exceed four columns (four digits), the field should be planned as a five-column field or for whatever the maximum need might be.

In the example (Fig. 3-5), the fields have been identified. Card columns 1 through 5 have been set aside for customer number. It is not intended that any customer number will be larger than five digits. Twenty columns, 6 through 25, have been set aside for customer name. Month, day, and year are subfields of the invoice date field. The date is coded in the familiar manner and thus requires six columns.

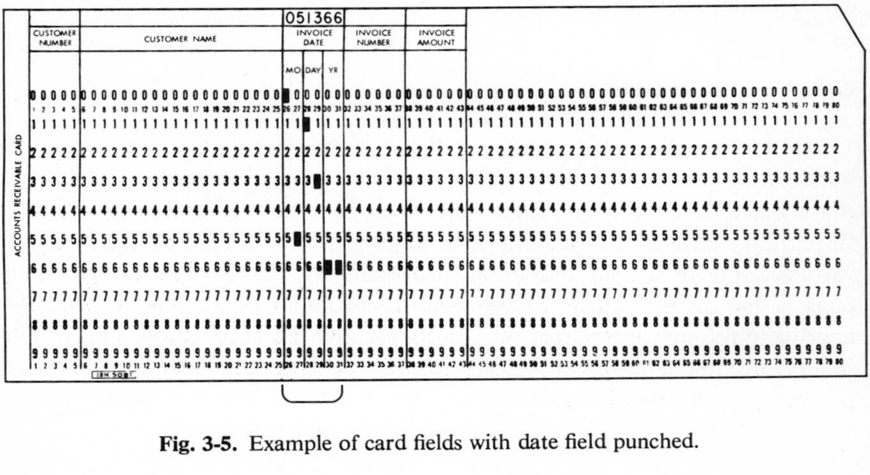

Fig. 3-5. Example of card fields with date field punched.

Invoice number is recorded in columns 32 through 37, and invoice amount in a field, columns 38 through 43. No space is necessary or desirable to separate fields. Appropriate setup of the processing machines will provide the necessary spacing on the output reports. Also, punctuation marks such as commas, decimal points, and dollar signs are not ordinarily punched into the card. Where necessary, these symbols are provided on the output report, sometimes by the machines and sometimes as a part of the preprinted report form.

Punching Practices (Fig. 3–6)

Recording Numeric Data

Numeric data, such as the customer number in the figure, are punched into the field with the units digit in the rightmost column. This practice is called *right justification.* Right justification of numeric data, when the data do not require all the columns of the field, leaves some unused columns in the left-hand position of the field. These unused columns to the left of the significant digits are usually punched with zeros, and, because the leftmost column is called the *high-order column,* the zeros placed in the unused columns are called *high-order zeros.*

Expanding the terminology used above, it is to be noted that the rightmost column of a field is known as the *low-order column,* or the least-

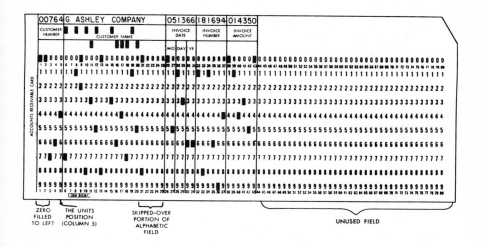

Fig. 3-6. Examples of punching practices.

significant digit column, as well as the units column. The columns to the left of the units column are identified as the *tens column, hundreds column, thousands columns,* etc., until the high-order column is reached. Notice the high-order zero in both the invoice date and invoice amount fields. The six digits in the invoice number field require all the columns of the field; consequently no high-order zeros are necessary.

Recording Alphabetic Data

The customer name field is an example of an alphabetic field. Compare it with a numeric field. It is *left justified.* The unused portion of an alphabetic field would, then, be in the low-order columns. The prevailing practice is to leave these columns blank. Notice that *within* an alphabetic field, such as the name field, spacing is provided. The spaces are actually a part of the recorded data, in this case, the customer name.

REVIEW QUESTIONS

9. Define the following terms as they relate to punched cards:
   a. Twelve edge
   b. Nine edge
   c. Face

10. What means are used to identify cards quickly?

11. Explain the meaning and use of card fields.

12. What are the meanings of the following terms?
    a. High-order position
    b. Low-order position
    c. Right-justified field
    d. Left-justified field

13. Numeric fields are usually _____ justified.

14. Alphabetical fields are usually _____ justified.

BASIC EAM

A Minimum EAM System

Just three punched-card machines will provide the machine capability to accomplish a complete data-processing application via the punched-card method. These three machines, called a *card punch,* a *sorter,* and an *ac-*

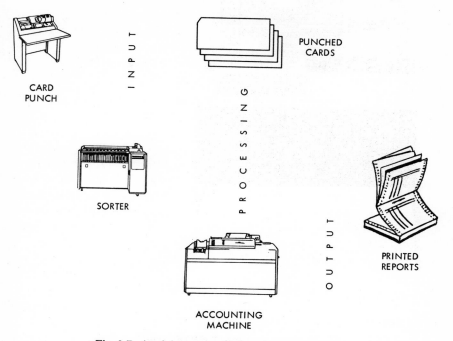

Fig. 3-7. A minimum punched card machine system.

counting machine, essentially cover the full data-processing cycle of input, processing, output. For this reason these three machines (Fig. 3-7) will be introduced first. It is, however, quite unlikely that any EAM installation would long remain a *minimum* installation. There are definite improvements which can be made in the processing procedure with the addition of other machines. These machines and their functions will be related to the *basic three* in the next chapter. IBM machines will be presented since they are the most widely used.

The Card Punch

The function of the card punch (Figs. 3-8 and 3-9) is to record data in the form of punched holes in the card. It is a manually operated machine and requires an operator to read the data from a source document and key the data via a keyboard similar to a typewriter. The data will then be encoded in punched-hole form on the card.

In the IBM line there are three basic models of card punches. They are the 024, the 026, and the 029. Their basic functions and features are similar, so we need only look at one in any detail. Let it be the Model 026.

Fig. 3-8. IBM 029 card punch.

Fig. 3-9. IBM 026 card punch.

Operation of Card Punch, Manual Control

Cards are placed in the card hopper with the nine edge down (see Fig. 3-10) and are fed down onto the card bed by depressing the *feed key* on the keyboard (see Fig. 3-11). The depression of the feed key a second time will cause another card to be fed while the first card is being registered at the punching station. *Registering* simply means locking the card into position with column 1 under the punching mechanism called the *punching station.* The card is now in a position to be punched. Depression of a *character key* will cause the character to be punched in coded form in column 1, and the card will automatically space to column 2. Punching and spacing takes place *serially*, i.e., one column at a time from 1 through 80. If a column is to be left blank, the space bar is used.

After column 80 has passed the punching station, the card is automatically released and moved across the card bed to the *reading station* where it is registered. Simultaneously, a third card is fed from the hopper, and the second card is registered at the punching station. Punching of the second card can now proceed in the same manner as the first. The cards at the reading station and the punching station travel through their respective stations *in phase*, i.e., they move simultaneously, column for column. In this way, at any time the same column of each of the cards is under its respective station.

Duplication. Reading a card at the reading station merely means that the holes, present in the card, can be sensed. With this ability to read and the fact

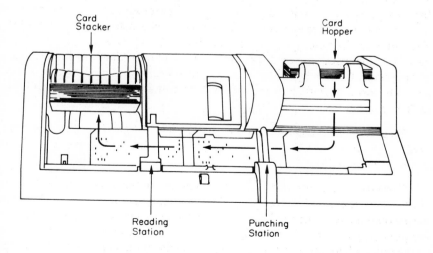

Card
Stacker

Card
Hopper

Reading
Station

Punching
Station

Fig. 3-10. The path of the card through the punch.

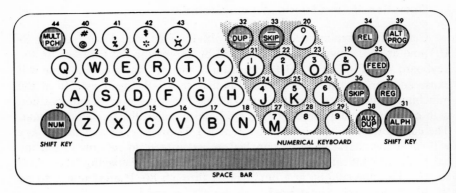

Fig. 3-11. Combination keyboard chart.

that the cards are positioned in phase, any data in the card at the reading station can be duplicated into the card at the punching station by simply depressing the *duplication (DUP) key.*

Four cards will move simultaneously, now that three are on the card bed, when the cards are released from the reading and the punching stations. The card at the reading station will be stacked in the stacker, the card at the punching station will be registered at the reading station, the card waiting on the card bed will be registered at the punching station, and the fourth card will be fed.

Alphabetic and Numeric Shift Keys. There is, of course, no upper and lower case to punched-hole-coded letters. The shift key is, then, not needed for this purpose as it is on a typewriter. Therefore, the use of the shift function allows a combination of two different characters on the same key. The numeric characters have been combined with alphabetic characters and have been arranged in a manner similar to a 10-key adding machine for ease in operation. Certain special characters have been combined, two to a key, also. The top designation on each key will be punched if the numeric (NUM) shift key is held down.

Purpose of the Release Key. The *release (REL) key* is used to advance cards to the next station without having to move the cards a space at a time through column 80.

Correction of Error Cards. Cards would be immediately released by the card-punch operator in case a conscious punching error is made. The error card would move to the reading station and a new card would be registered at the punching station. The new card is then duplicated from the error card up to the point where the error was made and then key punching from the source document is resumed.

If a special *correction* (*CORR*) *key* is available on the machine, the depression of this key upon recognition of an error would cause release and duplication up to the error column to be performed automatically. The correction key is a special feature on the Model 026. It provides the operator with real assistance in error correction.

Purpose of the Register Key. The *register* (*REG*) *key* is used to register cards at the reading station or punching station without having to feed additional cards as is done when the feed key is used.

REVIEW QUESTIONS

15. What are the three basic *electric* accounting machines?

16. How many cards can move simultaneously when cards are being keypunched?

17. Define the following terms:
   a. Registering
   b. Serially punched
   c. Cards travel in phase

18. What is the purpose of the release key?

Operation of Card Punch, Program Control

Although the card punch is basically a manually operated machine, there are certain functions which can be caused to occur automatically. A regular punched card with an especially designed instruction code punched in it

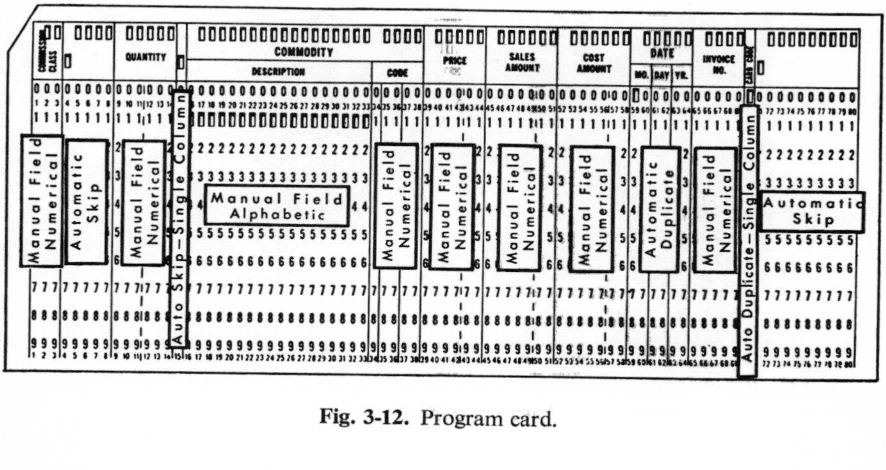

Fig. 3-12. Program card.

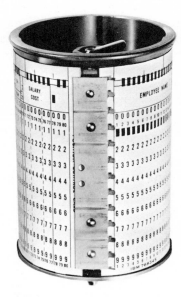

Fig. 3-13. Program drum with program card in place.

Fig. 3-14. Card punch showing location of program unit.

instead of data, wrapped and secured around a cylinder and placed in the machine, can serve as a program for the card punch to follow. The card is called a *program card,* the cylinder is referred to as a *program drum,* and the entire assembly is the *program unit* (*see Figs. 3-12, 3-13,* and *3-14*).

The Automatic Functions. Program control can provide for *automatic skipping, automatic duplication,* and *automatic shifting* between alphabetic and numeric modes. Program control affords a more efficient operation of the card punch. Unused portions of a card can be skipped very quickly on signal from the program unit with no action necessary from the operator. Likewise, duplication of punched data from the preceding card, when data are repetitive, can be accomplished rapidly and automatically. When the card-punch machine is switched to program control, the keyboard transfers to numeric mode. Therefore, in order to get alphabetic punching, the alphabetic shift key has to be depressed manually *unless* the program card calls for an automatic shift to the alphabetic mode. The program card, properly punched with the instruction code, will schedule the automatic functions.

Method of Coding Instructions. The instruction coding for a program card is simple. The first thing in which the machine needs to be instructed is the location and size of the fields in the data cards to be punched. This instruction is furnished the machine by punching a program card in the top row (12 row) *in all the columns except the first column* of every field. An unpunched column in the 12 row will, then, indicate to the card punch the beginning of a field, and punched columns in the 12 position will indicate the continuance of a field. A punch in the 11 position of the program card will cause *skipping* to be started, and skipping will continue as long as there are successive 12 punches. An *11 punch is thus placed in the first column* of a field to cause automatic skipping of the entire field. Automatic duplication of a field is accomplished by punching a *zero punch in the first column* of any field to be automatically duplicated. Instructing the machine for alphabetic shifting is done without regard for fields. *The one row is punched in every column* of the program card where the data card is expected to have alphabetic data.

Example of Program Card. (*Figs. 3-15* and *3-16*). Using the same data card as shown earlier, let us develop a program card to be used on the card punch to ease the burden of the card-punch operator.

There are six fields to be defined, so the 12 row is punched in all columns except the first in each field, columns 1, 6, 26, 32, 38, and 44. The unused (blank) field, columns 44 through 80, is to be skipped automatically, so the program card is punched in the 11 row of the first column, column 44. Since all of a given batch of source documents from which the data cards are being punched will likely have the same invoice date, this field is programmed for automatic duplication with a zero punch in

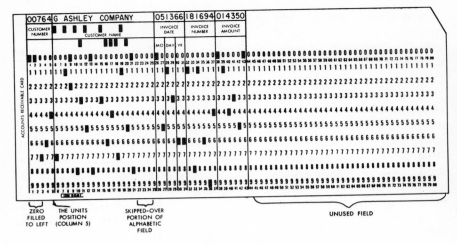

Fig. 3-15. Example of data card.

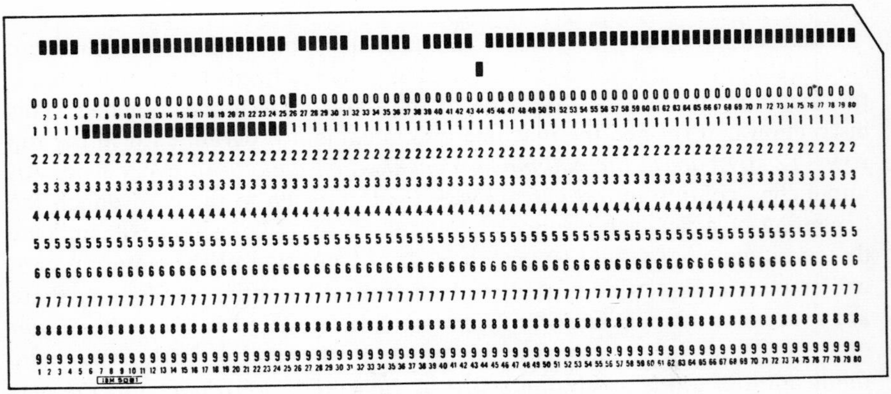

Fig. 3-16. Program card for data card in Fig. 3-14.

column 26. Names of companies are not likely to include numeric data, so each of the columns in the customer name field has been programmed alphabetic by punching the 1 row in all columns. Should a company name include a numeric character (such as The 88 Market), the numeric shift key would be held down to override the alphabetic-shift program instruction.

Uses of the Card Punch

The primary purpose of the card punch is to provide an efficient way to translate *human-language* documents into *machine-language* documents, in other words, to *translate source documents into unit records.* Most card punching is the recording of data. However, as in the preparation of a program card, punched cards can be used to instruct machines. By the same token, punched cards are used to record instructions for a computer. Computer programs are very often entered into the memory of a computer via punched cards. The considerable detail with which the card punch has been covered is with this in mind. Some readers of this text may very well find it necessary to "punch up" their own computer programs. Furthermore, it is certain that those primarily interested in EAM will find an understanding of the card punch of considerable value even though they are not destined to become card-punch operators. Card-punch operators, of course, will need to know even more than what has been included here.

REVIEW QUESTIONS

19. What type of operations can be performed by the keypunch machine under program control?

20. What causes the keypunch machine to operate in a programmed manner?

21. On a program card, which punch indicates the beginning of a field, and which punch indicates the balance of the field?

22. Which punch is used for automatic duplication of a field on the program card?

The Sorter

If data are to be summarized and reported, they must first be organized. Organization of data means bringing data of like classification together or, in other words, grouping data with similar characteristics. Data must be sorted if they are to be processed into meaningful output. In an EAM system, sorting is done by machine. The data are in cards, and cards can be machine sorted very efficiently.

Punched-card sorters are marketed by many companies. IBM manufactures sorters (Fig. 3-17). The UNIVAC Division of the Sperry Rand Corporation has a full line of EAM equipment including the sorter, and The National Cash Register Company (NCR) has their own model of a card sorter (Fig. 3-18). Sorting techniques, however, are basically the same for, and applicable to, almost any machine. The IBM Models 082 and 083 will be used here as a basis for discussion where reference to machines is necessary.

Fig. 3-17. IBM Models 082, 083, 084 sorters.

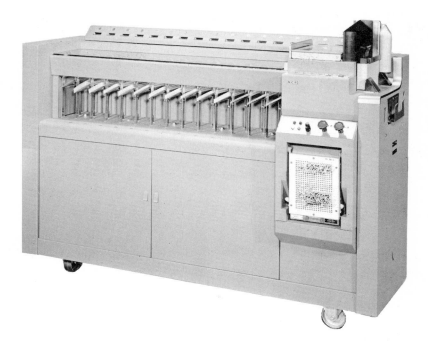

Fig. 3-18. NCR 406 sorter-comparator.

Methods and Types of Sorting

Sorting, or grouping, can be accomplished in either of two ways, by *sequencing* or by *selection*. The numeric (coded) and alphabetic (descriptive) data punched in the cards provide the basis for sorting. In *numeric sorting,* cards are grouped according to a common numeric code or value, whereas *alphabetic sorting* groups the data according to a common descriptive classification. When sorting into sequence, alphabetically or numerically, *all* like names or *all* like numbers will be grouped. When sorting by selection, only the selected items are grouped.

EXAMPLE:

File of numbers: no order   8, 6, 9, 3, 8, 8, 9, 3, 6, 8, 4, 3, 9, 6, 3, 8
        in sequence   *3, 3, 3, 3, 4, 6, 6, 6, 8, 8, 8, 8, 8, 9, 9, 9*
        one group selected   6, 9, 3, 9, 3, 6, 4, 3, 9, 6, 3, *8, 8, 8, 8, 8*

Ascending and Descending Sequence. In sequence sorting, data may be put in ascending or descending order. Ascending numeric order simply

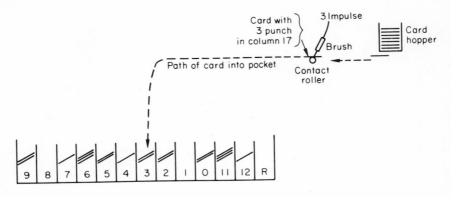

Fig. 3-19. Diagram of sorter operation.

means an order running from low to high, while ascending alphabetic order runs from A to Z. Descending order is just the opposite, high to low and Z to A.

Sorter Operation. The diagram in Fig. 3-19 represents either the IBM 082 or 083 sorter. There are 13 pockets, one for each row on the card and a reject pocket. Cards travel from the hopper across an electric contact roller and then into the proper pocket. The reading device consists of the contact roller and a small wire brush. The brush is small enough so that it can be set to read a single column of the card, and it is movable so it can be easily set on the desired column. The contact roller is charged with electric current, and the brush, falling through the punched hole, picks up the impulse. The position of the hole in the card determines the timing of the impulse, which in turn controls the selection of the pocket into which the card is sorted.

Single-Column Numeric Sorting (Fig. 3-20). Since the machine has only one brush, only one column of the card can be sorted at a time. If numeric sorting is being done on a *single-column* field, the cards would be in order after the first pass of the cards through the machine. If there are nine salesmen with codes 1 through 9 and the salesman code field is column 17, sorting on column 17 would cause all of the cards for salesman number 1 to fall into pocket 1, if there are any. All cards punched with salesman code 2 will fall in pocket 2, etc.

Multiple-Column Numeric Sorting (Fig. 3-21). Sequence sorting of cards when the field to be sorted is larger than one column, requires as many passes as there are columns in the field. Following certain sorting procedures will enable the operator to sequence the cards no matter what the size of the field.

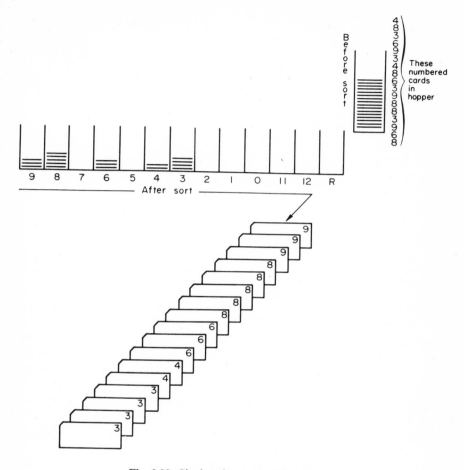

Fig. 3.20. Single-column numeric sorting.

Sorting is accomplished by using the *reverse-digit method*. The reverse-digit method can be used in manual sorting of documents, but, in sorting large volumes of card documents by machine, its use is essential. The reverse-digit method simply means that the least significant digit is sorted first. In sorting a multiple-column field, then, this means that the units, or low-order, column is sorted first. After the cards are in groups on the basis of the units column, they are assembled (picked up) into one deck and sorted on the basis of the tens column, etc. After the cards have been sorted on the high-order column, the deck will be in sequence.

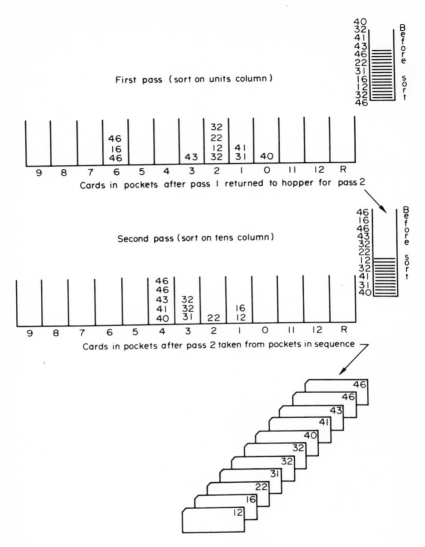

Fig. 3-21. Steps in a two-column field sort.

Sorting Alphabetic Data. Alphabetic-sequence sorting is accomplished on the sorter using the same reverse-digit method when the size of the field is more than one column. But on each individual column, since there are two punches in a column where alphabetic data is recorded, the sorting procedure must be modified. On the Model 082 sorter each column is sorted twice (Fig. 3-22). The first pass sorts the cards on the basis of the digit portion of

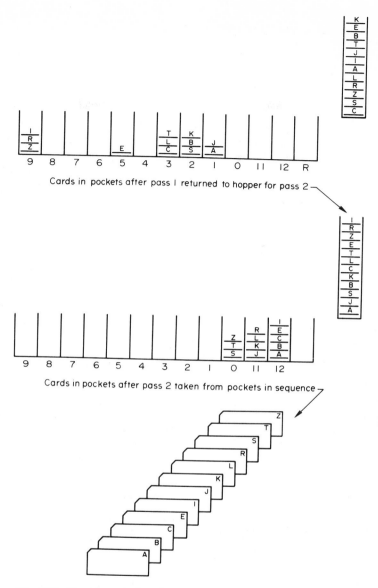

Fig. 3-22. Steps in a single column alphabetic sort (IBM 082 sorter).

the "alpha" code, and the second pass sorts on the zone portion of the Hollerith-coded letter.

Besides having a higher-rated speed than that of the 082 (650 cards per minute), the 083 (1,000 cards per minute) accomplishes alphabetic sorting more efficiently (Fig. 3-23). On the first pass the cards are sorted by the zone portion of the letter code. Letters J through R are sorted into the 11

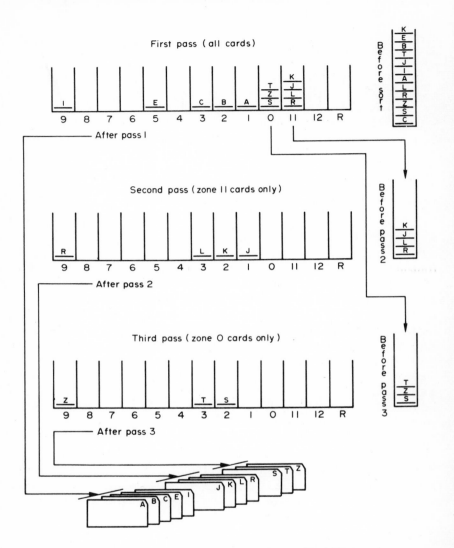

Fig. 3-23. Steps in a single-column alphabetic sort (IBM 083 sorter).

pocket, and letters S through Z are sorted into the zero pocket. Letters A through I, having the 12-zone punch, are sorted directly into the pockets corresponding to the digit punch used with the 12 punch. Therefore, approximately one-third of the cards are alphabetized (on one column) on a single pass. After the A through I cards have been taken from the pockets, the cards from the 11 pocket are sorted on the basis of the digit punch. They are taken from the pockets, assembled behind the A through I group, and then the cards in the zero pocket are sorted by digit. This procedure must be followed for each column of the alphabetic field.

Disadvantages of Alphabetic Data. The rather cumbersome procedures which must be followed in sorting cards on the basis of alphabetic data points out the advantage of assigning numeric codes to people and things. In addition, consider that an alphabetic name or description might require from 10 to 20 columns, whereas an assigned numeric code might not require over 5 columns. To sort a 20-column alphabetic field would require 40 passes on the Model 082, but a 5-column numeric field could be sequenced in 5 passes. It is nearly always easier to process numeric data than to process alphabetic data. Sorting is a good example.

Block Sorting. Although the sorters can handle cards at quite high speeds (2,000 cards per minute for the 084) and the basic operation of a sorter is simple, the very volume of cards can cause a sort job to be long and fraught with procedural-error possibilities. In order to minimize the ill effects of a mistake (human) or a malfunction (machine) and to provide better machine utilization, a procedure called *block sorting* is used. The procedure allows the operator to break a large volume of cards into smaller, more easily handled blocks. Unless the block-sorting procedure is used, even a 100,000-card file must be sorted a column at a time from beginning to end on one sorter. With block sorting, the job can be divided up. The procedure calls for sorting the cards according to a major consideration first. For instance, cards sorted on the first pass on the high-order column of a numeric field will be broken into 10 blocks. Each block can then be sorted separately and in accordance with standard procedures, i.e., from low-order column to high-order column. Individual blocks could be sorted on separate machines, or block 1 could go on to the next step in the total procedure immediately after it is sorted, and thus other available machines could be utilized. The entire sorting job would not need to be completed first. In addition, if a sorting error is made, it will affect only the single block being sorted and thus corrective procedures will be minimized.

Multiple-Field Sorting. Sorting on more than one field is necessary if cards are to be used to prepare reports which include *levels of totals*. If a report is to show total sales for each region within which several salesmen are selling, the cards must be arranged by region and, within region, by salesman. In the actual sorting, the reverse-digit method is applied; the least-significant data are sorted first. The salesman field would be designated the minor field, and region, the major field. The sort would start with the low-order column of the minor field and continue to the high-order column of the major field. If there were intermediate fields such as districts within regions, the intermediate field would be sorted after the minor field was sorted.

Sorting by Selection. Extracting from a file of cards only the cards falling into a certain classification is called selection. Selection procedures allow cards of a certain classification to be extracted from the larger group without disturbing the original order of the remaining cards.

EXAMPLE:

If a file of cards is in employee code number order and it becomes necessary to secure from the sequenced deck all cards representing men who are assigned to Department 6, it could be done in either of two ways. The cards could be sorted into sequence on the department-code field, and all the departments would be grouped, including Department 6, but the original order (employee code number order) would have been destroyed. On the other hand, if cards for Department 6 are merely selected out, both resulting decks will remain in employee code number sequence. Sorters can be used in card selection.

Uses of the Sorter. Wherever punched cards are used to record, store, and communicate data, the sorter will almost certainly be a part of the data-processing installation. A strictly EAM installation could hardly exist without one or more sorters, for the sorter is a machine which can efficiently group cards. Many procedures and machines depend on the input data's being in a prescribed order upon entry of the data into the system. Even EDP systems (computers), especially those using cards to receive data, will often be programmed to operate on input data that are in order. Although computer systems have recently been tending toward random processing, which eliminates the need for presorting of input data, the sorter is not likely to lose its position of importance for some time. No matter what data-processing interest the reader may have, knowledge of sorters and sorting techniques will be of particular value.

REVIEW QUESTIONS

23. What two types of data require sorting?

24. In what two basic ways is sorting accomplished?

25. Why is it easier to sort cards on the basis of numeric data?

26. Name several methods of sorting.

27. What is block sorting, and what are some of its advantages?

28. If you wished to sort a deck of cards first on the contents of column 6, then, on columns 1 and 2, and finally on columns 29 through 32, how would you describe this to the EAM operator?

The Accounting Machine

The ultimate objective of processing data is to produce new summary data in some understandable form. The most typical method of reporting is the printed form. In an EAM system the accounting machine performs this function.

Data fed to the accounting machine via punched cards can be *read* and *printed* on continuous or cut forms. Besides this, the accounting machine has the ability to *accumulate* quantitative data. Amounts from cards can be *added* and *subtracted* in counters to produce summary totals. The accounting machine thus becomes the focal point of an EAM system, for it is here where some finished product is produced—where some results are obtained. The accounting machine represents the output stage of the processing cycle.

Accounting Machine Characteristics

The accounting machine is also known as a *tabulator*. The ability of the machine to produce reports in tabular form accounts for its second name. The two most widely used models are the IBM 402 and the IBM 407 (Fig. 3-24). The 407 has a great deal more internal ability, but the external differences and the differences in function and purpose are not major ones. Both machines read data from cards, list the data from each card, and ac-

Fig. 3-24. IBM accounting machines.

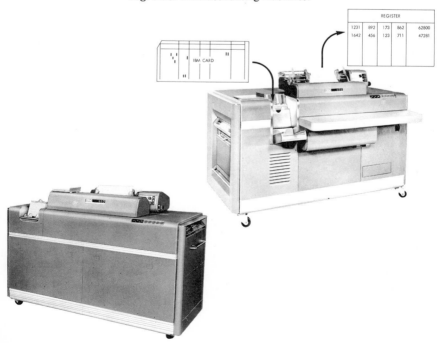

cumulate and print totals or accumulate totals for groups of cards and print only the totals for each group. The printing of the detail from each card is called *detail printing* or *listing*. The printing of group totals with the identification data for each total is called *group printing*.

The Model 402 has 88 typebars, which provide for printing in any one of 88 different print positions across the report. However, only about half of the typebars—43 of the 88—have both alphabetic and numeric characters. These are the 43 on the left-hand side and are called the *alphameric typebars*. There are 45 *numeric typebars* on the right. The important aspect of the limitation of alphameric typebars is that a report must be limited to alphabetic printing on the left-hand side only.

The Model 407 has 120 type wheels, and each wheel has all the numeric and alphabetic characters plus 11 special characters. The 407 thus provides greater flexibility in printing and greater variation in the design of forms.

PURCHASE ANALYSIS BY VENDOR				
Vendor No.	Vendor Name	Invoice Amount	Discount	Amount To Pay
1179	ABBOT BRASS	98.13	1.96	96.17
1179	ABBOT BRASS	25.00	.50	24.50
		123.13 *	2.46 *	120.67 *
1180	ABRAMS COAL	277.35	8.31	269.04
1180	ABRAMS COAL	300.00	10.50	289.50
		577.35 *	18.81 *	558.54 *
1181	ACE INS CO	18.50		18.50
1181	ACE INS CO	118.02		118.02
		136.52 *	*	136.52 *
1281	AMER STEEL	82.35	1.65	80.70
1281	AMER STEEL	182.34	3.62	178.72
1281	AMER STEEL	27.25	.55	26.70
		291.94 *	5.82 *	286.12 *
2179	APAL LUM CO	224.00	4.48	219.52
2179	APAL LUM CO	143.30	2.87	140.43
		367.30 *	7.35 *	359.95 *
3076	BARR MACH	3015.27	150.77	2864.50
		3015.27 *	150.77 *	2864.50 *
6195	BR WILLIAMS	276.65		276.65
6195	BR WILLIAMS	104.51	3.15	101.36
6195	BR WILLIAMS	37.65	.75	36.90
6195	BR WILLIAMS	310.52	6.21	304.31
		729.33 *	10.11 *	719.22 *
19285	COVTRY OIL	180.15	3.60	176.55
19285	COVTRY OIL	83.44	1.67	81.77
		263.59 *	5.27 *	258.32 *

Fig. 3-25. A detail printed report.

An examination of the types of reports that are produced on accounting machines will best illustrate their functions.

Functions

Detail Printing. The accounting machine can be used for printing data from cards with no accumulation of totals. This function, called listing as well as detail printing, as previously noted, is the simplest function of all those which the machine can perform. Usually data are being accumulated, however, as the cards are being listed, and totals for groups of cards can be printed. These functions are shown in the "Purchase Analysis by Vendor" report in Fig. 3-25.

Group Printing. Fig. 3-26 shows the "Purchase Analysis by Vendor" report as a group-printed report. Note that only the totals are printed for each vendor. This is the nature of group printing. Identification information is printed from the first card of each group, and the quantitative data are accumulated until the last card of that group has been processed. The totals are then printed on the same line as the identification.

PURCHASE ANALYSIS BY VENDOR

Vendor No.	Vendor Name	Invoice Amount	Discount	Amount To Pay
1179	ABBOT BRASS	1 2 3 1 3	2 4 6	1 2 0 6 7
1180	ABRAMS COAL	5 7 7 3 5	1 8 8 1	5 5 8 5 4
1181	ACE INS CO	1 3 6 5 2		1 3 6 5 2
1281	AMER STEEL	2 9 1 9 4	5 8 2	2 8 6 1 2
2179	APAL LUM CO	3 6 7 3 0	7 3 5	3 5 9 9 5
3076	BARR MACH	3 0 1 5 2 7	1 5 0 7 7	2 8 6 4 5 0
6195	BR WILLIAMS	7 2 9 3 3	1 0 1 1	7 1 9 2 2
19285	COVTRY OIL	2 6 3 5 9	5 2 7	2 5 8 3 2
29521	EL TRUST CO	2 0 5 5 0		2 0 5 5 0
36512	HASK SUPP	1 3 3 4 3 4	2 5 7 3	1 3 0 8 6 1

Fig. 3-26. A group printed report.

Programming. The word *programming* as applied to the accounting machine refers to its ability to identify the end of one group and the beginning of another group of cards. The purchase analysis report utilized this ability of the machine. Through the use of a comparing device the machine can "watch" for a change in the group identification. On the basis of this *control break* the machine will then follow its program instructions, which are primarily the printing of the totals. The accounting machine was programmed to take totals by vendor in the "Purchase Analysis by Vendor" reports.

NET SALES BY CUSTOMER			
Customer Number	Commodity		Amount #
	Cl.	Number	
2 1 7 9	2	3 7 0 2	2 1 0 9 0
		6 1 0 4	1 0 2 4 8
			3 1 3 3 8 ✿
	3	2 1 0 5	6 6 0 0
		3 2 0 4	6 8 7 5
		5 1 0 4	8 2 8 0
		5 1 0 5	1 3 1 2
			2 3 0 6 7 ✿
	4	4 1 0 5	1 1 0 4 9
		6 1 0 7	1 2 2 1 0
			2 3 2 5 9 ✿
	5	1 1 0 5	8 2 2 0
		3 2 0 8	4 6 0 7 5
		3 6 0 4	2 2 8 6 0
		3 6 0 5	2 6 4 5
		4 1 0 7	9 9 6 0
		5 7 0 6	9 7 6 5
			9 9 5 2 5 ✿
	6	2 1 0 8	3 1 8 1 5
		2 1 0 9	3 2 6 2 5
		2 1 1 0	1 8 1 2 5
		3 3 0 6	3 3 4 1 7
		5 1 1 2	8 3 7 2 0
			1 9 9 7 0 2 ✿
			3 7 6 8 9 1
2 2 8 3	1	6 1 0 2	1 5 3 0
			1 5 3 0 ✿
	2	3 7 0 2	7 7 7 0
			7 7 7 0 ✿
	5	3 2 0 8	1 2 1 2 5
		5 1 0 8	7 2 0 0 0
			8 4 1 2 5 ✿
	6	2 1 1 0	4 3 5 0 0
			4 3 5 0 0 ✿
			1 3 6 9 2 5
3 0 7 6	1	1 1 0 2	1 5 1 8 CR
		1 2 0 2	3 3 2 0
		4 2 0 2	1 7 6 0 CR
		4 7 0 2	1 0 8 0 CR
		5 1 0 2	9 0 7 5 CR
		7 2 0 3	8 1 0 CR
			1 0 9 2 3 CR ✿

Fig. 3-27. A multi-level programmed report.

The "Net Sales by Customer" report (Fig. 3-27) illustrates a further application of programming. In this case cards have been grouped and totals taken on three different levels. The *major* level is customer number with commodity class as the *intermediate* level and commodity number the *minor* level. The report, therefore, shows the $3,768.91 as total sales to customer no. 2179 with an analysis of that amount by commodity class and commodity number. Such a breakdown could be of real value to a sales manager in planning his sales effort.

The Skipping Feature. The first three reports reviewed have been *internal* reports. The statement, however, is an *external* report (see Fig. 3-28). It will be sent out and thus should take a different form from the

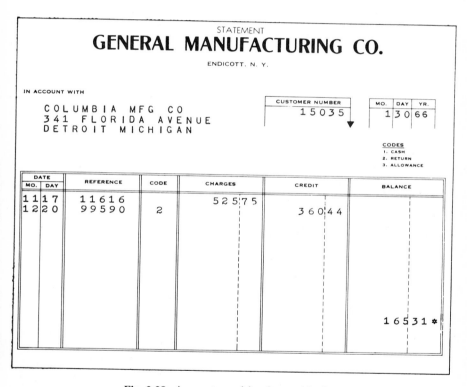

Fig. 3-28. A report requiring forms skipping.

analytical type of reports prepared for internal use. To meet this need, the major additional function required of the accounting machine is *automatic skipping* to predetermined lines of the form for the various parts. The parts are typically the heading and the body sections of the form.

Instructing the Accounting Machine

The accounting machine can do all things illustrated. It can *read, print, add, subtract, total, compare,* and *skip,* but not without specific instructions. These instructions come principally from a wired control panel (see Fig. 3-29).

For each report to be prepared, a wired control panel must be inserted in the rack on the end of the machine and locked into position. A control panel functions much like a telephone switchboard. It is a board with holes called *hubs* which are merely connected with wires to form the connections between the operating features of the machine. Reading brushes can be connected to typebars, any reading brush to any typebar, or counters can be assigned and wired to add or subtract the data from the proper card fields. Every function to be performed must be *wired* on the control panel. Control-panel wiring on EAM is somewhat analogous to the programming of computers. Each is a method of machine instruction.

Significance of the Control Panel

The wiring of a complex control panel requires a complete knowledge of the machine for which it is intended if the full potential of the machine is to be

Fig. 3-29. Wired control panels.

realized. With the exception of the card punch and the sorter, electric accounting machines employ the control-panel technique for machine instruction. The wired control panel provides the flexibility which the machines possess for adaptation to new and varied data-processing tasks.

REVIEW QUESTIONS

29. What is the primary function of the accounting machine?

30. What is another name for the accounting machine?

31. What is meant by detail printing?

32. What is meant by group printing?

33. What must be accomplished if skipping is required in the preparation of a report?

4 SUPPLEMENTARY EAM EQUIPMENT

A BASIC EAM APPLICATION

The three machines that have now been examined can be used to process data from input through output in limited applications. Some efficiencies must be sacrificed with only a minimal installation, but many procedures can be accomplished. The procedure presented here is developed around the three machines—key punch, sorter, and accounting machine.

Flow Charting

A step-by-step chart of the procedure to be followed, presented in the form of diagramming symbols, is called a *flow chart*. The flow chart is the standard tool of data processing. The use of standard symbols and techniques enables data-processing personnel—systems analysts, programmers, machine operators, supervisors, etc.—to communicate in an efficient manner. A simple procedure with a supporting flow chart will serve as an example of the flow-charting technique, which will be covered in more detail in Chap. 8.

The flow chart presented in Fig. 4-2 shows the steps to be taken to process incoming invoices into the finished "Cash Requirements Statement" report in Fig. 4-1. Machine processing starts at step 1 where the data on the source document are converted to punched cards. A certain amount of processing was necessary, though, before the document arrived in the EAM department. Incoming invoices from vendors requesting payment for goods shipped will be of varying sizes, shapes, and design. Some will have more information on them than others, and none can have all that is needed. In any event, the input data must be organized.

70

The Unit Record

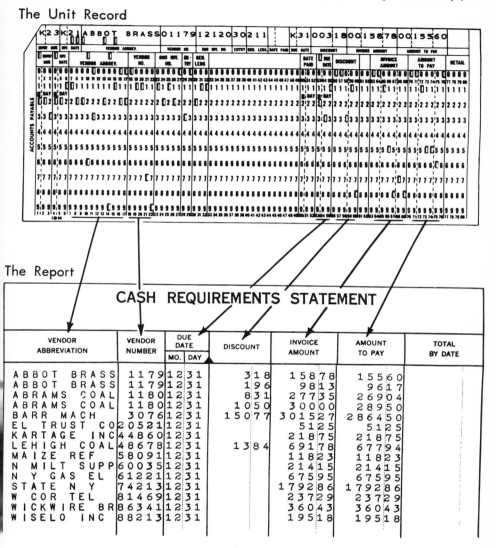

The Report

CASH REQUIREMENTS STATEMENT

VENDOR ABBREVIATION	VENDOR NUMBER	DUE DATE		DISCOUNT	INVOICE AMOUNT	AMOUNT TO PAY	TOTAL BY DATE
		MO.	DAY				
A B B O T B R A S S	1 1 7 9	12	31	3 1 8	1 5 8 78	1 5 5 6 0	
A B B O T B R A S S	1 1 7 9	12	31	1 9 6	9 8 13	9 6 1 7	
A B R A M S C O A L	1 1 8 0	12	31	8 3 1	2 7 7 35	2 6 9 0 4	
A B R A M S C O A L	1 1 8 0	12	31	1 0 5 0	3 0 0 00	2 8 9 5 0	
B A R R M A C H	3 0 7 6	12	31	1 5 0 77	3 0 1 5 27	2 8 6 4 5 0	
E L T R U S T C O	2 0 5 2 1	12	31		5 1 25	5 1 2 5	
K A R T A G E I N C	4 4 8 6 0	12	31		2 1 8 75	2 1 8 7 5	
L E H I G H C O A L	4 8 6 7 8	12	31	1 3 84	6 9 1 78	6 7 7 9 4	
M A I Z E R E F	5 8 0 9 1	12	31		1 1 8 23	1 1 8 2 3	
N M I L T S U P P	6 0 0 3 5	12	31		2 1 4 15	2 1 4 1 5	
N Y G A S E L	6 1 2 2 1	12	31		6 7 5 95	6 7 5 9 5	
S T A T E N Y	7 4 2 1 3	12	31		1 7 9 2 86	1 7 9 2 86	
W C O R T E L	8 1 4 6 9	12	31		2 3 7 29	2 3 7 29	
W I C K W I R E B R	8 6 3 4 1	12	31		3 6 0 43	3 6 0 43	
W I S E L O I N C	8 8 2 1 3	12	31		1 9 5 18	1 9 5 18	

Fig. 4-1. Report printed from IBM cards.

Preparation of Input Data

The preliminary manual processing starts with the separation of invoices (bills) from the incoming mail and routing them to the accounts payable department. Here, a clerk processes each invoice. The processing includes checking the invoice for authenticity and accuracy, plus assigning necessary

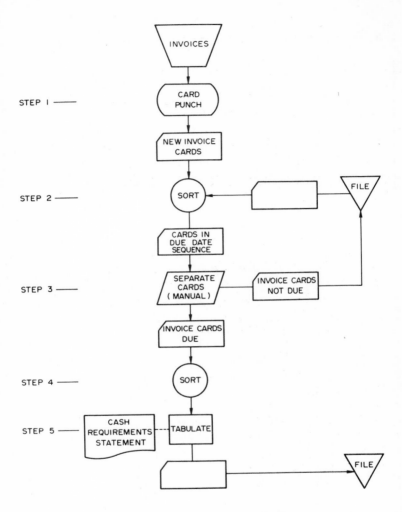

Fig. 4-2. Flowchart of EAM procedure.

classification codes. If the vendor is not a new one, he will have a code number by which we know him. Abbot Brass is *vendor number* 01179, as can be determined from our code chart. This number is written on the invoice by the accounts payable clerk. The invoice number is assigned by selecting the next number in our system of sequential numbering of incoming invoices. In addition, an account number (general ledger number) for accounting purposes is assigned. The *due date* and *cash discount* are determined from the stated terms on the invoice, and an *amount to pay* is calculated. The invoice is entered on a control register where an entry number and an *entry date* are assigned. After this manual processing has been completed, the invoices are now ready for machine processing.

Card-Punching Step

Batches of invoices are routed to the card-punch department. Here, the data are translated into machine language. In this case the unit record is the invoice, and, therefore, the cards are punched one card per invoice. Card punching should proceed very routinely since all the data were placed on the source document in a prescribed form so that it can be easily read by the card-punch operator.

Need for Verification

However, even the best operator makes an occasional error. The procedure, as represented by the flow chart, would seem to be lacking, then, since it does not provide for any type of checking or verification to determine that the data have been correctly transferred to the machine-language document. It is apparent, too, that punching errors, errors in the card, cannot be tolerated. Accuracy is of paramount importance in all input data, for the output can be no better than the input no matter how good or expensive the machines might be. The accounts payable cards being prepared in the application will obviously be used for additional purposes besides the preparation of the cash requirements statement. They will be used, for instance, to prepare the checks to the vendor, and errors on checks would hardly be desirable. There are several methods of *verification*. One of these methods uses a machine. The various methods of verification will be discussed along with the *verifier* later in the chapter.

Analyzing Procedural Steps Required

Now that the punched cards are shown created and available for processing, the steps needed for creation of the report can be determined. An observation of the report form indicates that five fields of the card are to be listed. The report is issued daily and includes only those payments due on the day following the issuance of the report. The listing is organized in vendor-number sequence, and, since the vendor numbers have been assigned on an alphabetical basis, there is also an alphabetic sequence. Required, then, will be a procedure which will: (1) group cards according to due date, (2) separate the next day's payment cards, (3) arrange them by vendor number, (4) list each invoice, and (5) accumulate a total of the amount-to-pay field.

The total represents the cash needs for the next day. Assuming this to be a branch office operation, a teletypewriter message to the home office will bring the needed cash in time for the next day's disbursements.

Sorting

Step 2 of the flow chart shows the combining of the cards from the unpaid file with the newly punched cards. The sorter is used, and, by sequence sorting on the due-date field, the cards on the front of the sorted deck are those due for payment on the next day (December 31). They are manually separated in step 3. Those payment cards not due are returned to the file, and those due continue through the procedure.

Reporting

In the next step, step 4, the cards are sorted by vendor number and are now ready for the accounting machine. At step 5 the report is run.

Next, the cards are placed in a file to await use in another procedure.

SUPPLEMENTARY MACHINES

As previously indicated, a punched card system is not likely to remain at a three-machine level, even if it starts as such. There are too many places where card handling and card processing can be expedited with the addition of other machines to limit the installation to the basic configuration. There will be the need to supplement the key punch with automatic punches under certain conditions. The sorting function can be facilitated with the addition of a collator to supplement the sorter. The accounting machine can be augmented with a calculating punch to accomplish the calculation function more fully. In addition, data punched into cards must be checked for correctness, or verified.

Each of these machines (which are likely to be added to the system) will now be discussed. Their characteristics and functions will be presented. It should be recognized that some of these supplementary machines will be found supporting a computer installation as well as performing their individual functions in an expanded EAM system.

The Reproducing Punch

Once data have been initially recorded in cards, it should not ever be necessary to record the data manually again. The system should be integrated so that any data needed for continuance of the processing cycle are maintained in punched-card form. An integrated system requires that machine-language recorded data be rerecorded automatically by machine, not manually. It requires that summary data, as accumulated by machine, be captured in machine language (punched cards) before they are lost. These needs are served by the functions of the reproducing punch, functions such as *reproducing, gangpunching, mark-sense punching,* and *summary punching.*

Models and Features

A look at two machines will serve to illustrate the machine functions. They are the IBM 514 and the IBM 519 (Fig. 4-3). These two machines are basically alike, so what applies to one generally applies to the other.

Fig. 4-3. Reproducing punch and document originating machine.

The basic ability of the reproducing punch is to read a card and punch what is read into the same or a different card. Therefore, its principal features are sets of reading brushes and a punching mechanism. The machine has two units which can be operated either independently or in combination as a single machine. The function to be performed determines how the units will be used. The units are the read unit and the punch unit (see Fig. 4-4).

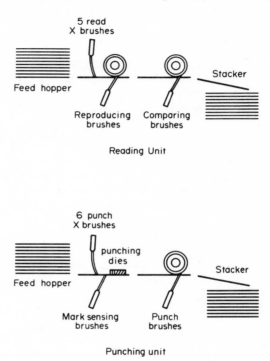

Fig. 4-4. A schematic diagram of 514 reproducing punch.

Refer to the machine schematic in the figure. The read unit has two sets of reading brushes. They are identified as the *reproducing* brushes and the *comparing brushes.* Each set is made up of 80 brushes so that, as the card passes over them, all 80 columns can be read. The punch unit has two stations also, namely, the *punch dies* and the *punch brushes.* Just as in the key punch, the cards pass through the respective units of the reproducing *in phase.* There is a difference, however. In the key punch the cards traveled through the machine and were punched serially, one column at a time. In the reproducing punch the cards are read and punched laterally, row by row in a parallel fashion. The cards are fed into the machine with the 12 edge leading.

Reproducing Function

Reproducing means duplicating. More specifically, reproducing means duplicating one or a deck (file) of cards. The deck to be reproduced is placed in the read-unit hopper, and blank cards are placed in the punch-unit hopper. Through panelboard wiring the machine is instructed to read the columns of the card at the reproducing brushes and transmit the impulses to the punch dies for punching. Because the cards pass the respective stations synchronized (in phase), a punch sensed in any row will be punched in the same row in the card passing under the punch dies.

The entire card can be reproduced with no changes of field location in the reproduced card, or, through panelboard wiring, certain fields of the punched cards may be selected and punched into any desired area of the reproduced deck (Fig. 4-5). (Figure 4-6 shows a form of reproducing in which data recorded in a ticket is converted into punched-card form. The function is performed on a modified reproducing punch called a *Ticket Converter*.)

Cards are reproduced for rather obvious reasons. Decks which are continuously used and reused need to be duplicated when they become worn and dog-eared. In addition, data cards needed for another application can be reproduced, and the duplicate deck made available for processing.

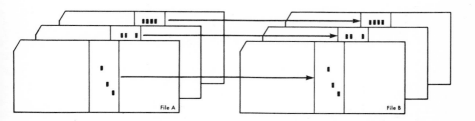

Fig. 4-5. Example of reproducing.

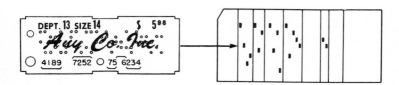

Fig. 4-6. Ticket converter.

Gangpunching Function

Gangpunching is duplicating like information into a series of cards. For instance, if the same date or the same code number is to be placed in an entire file of cards, the job can be accomplished by gangpunching (Fig. 4-7). A chain reaction is the best description of gangpunching.

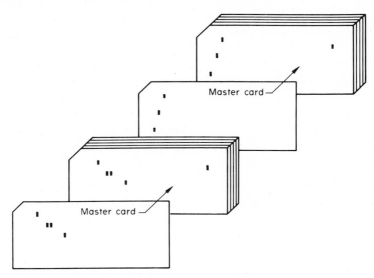

Fig. 4-7. Gangpunching with interspersed master cards.

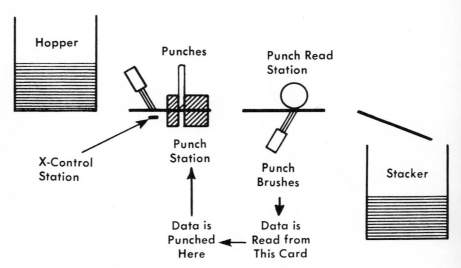

Fig. 4-8. Schematic of gangpunching.

Only the punch unit of the reproducing punch is used. A *master card* is prepared on the key punch and placed on the front of the deck of cards to be punched. The cards are then entered into the punch hopper face down so that the master card is the lead card. As the master card is read at the punch-brush station, the impulses are carried through panelboard wiring to the punches at the punch station (Fig. 4-8). The first detail card is punched and moves on to serve as the master card for punching the following card. This procedure continues until the entire deck has been punched. Master cards may be interspersed throughout the deck if multiple decks are to be punched.

Mark-Sense Punching Function

The conversion of data recorded in the form of marks on special mark-sense cards to punched-hole form is called *mark-sense punching* (Fig. 4-9).

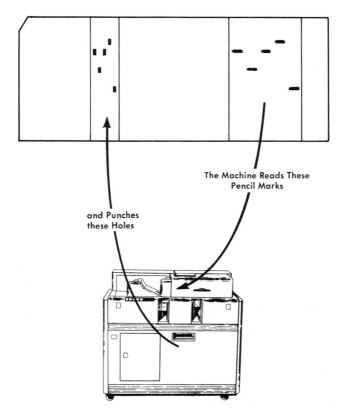

The Machine Reads These
Pencil Marks

and Punches
these Holes

Fig. 4-9. Mark-sense punching.

The mark-sense card is one printed with "bubbles" identifying the positions to be marked for coding numeric and alphabetic data. The mark is made with a special marking pencil so that the mark can be sensed electrically. The reproducing punch is equipped with special mark-sense brushes on the punch side (punch unit) of the machine which reads the marks. The impulses are transmitted via panelboard wiring to the selected punches where the card is punched.

Mark-sense cards are used when it is desired to record data in a machine-readable language at the data source. Gas-, electric-, and water-meter readings are good examples. Student-attendance reporting and the recording of physical-inventory counts are some other possible applications of mark sensing. The primary advantage to be gained is the elimination of the card punch operation. The data can be recorded at the source and quickly converted to punched-card form for processing.

Summary-Punching Function

The EAM system is basically an accounting system, and accounting is typically cyclical in nature. That is, balances are continuously adjusted by the net result of an accumulation of transactions in order to arrive at a new balance. The new balance becomes the old balance to be adjusted on the next cycle. The need, then, in a punched-card system is to capture newly created

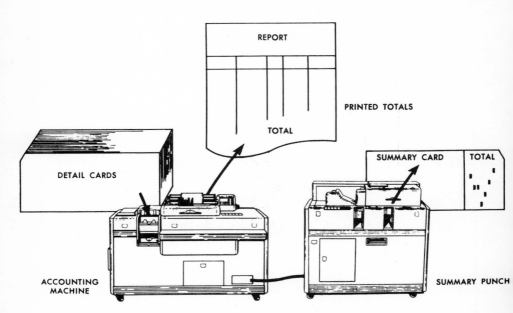

Fig. 4-10. Summary-punching operation.

data in a form which can be reentered into the system. This need is satisfied by having summary data recorded in punched-card form. This machine function is called *summary punching*. It is accomplished by connecting the accounting machine and the reproducing punch via a cable so that summary data (totals) can be communicated to the punch and these totals punched into a card (Fig. 4-10).

Uses of the Reproducing Punch

The reproducing punch is commonly included in an EAM installation. Reproducing and gangpunching can be done on the card punch, but the reproducer is more efficient since it operates at 100 cards per minute. Mark sensing and summary punching are techniques employed to better integrate a system. The alternative is to keypunch the data from the printed document with the inherent inefficiencies of decreased speed and decreased accuracy. In an EAM system the reproducing punch provides a solution to the problems of reproduction of recorded data.

The reproducing punch will undoubtedly pay its way also as a supporting machine in a computer system which uses punched cards. Computer time is too valuable to employ the computer on functions that can be done just as efficiently with EAM equipment—in this case the reproducing punch.

REVIEW QUESTIONS

1. What are the functions of the reproducing punch?

2. If identical information is to be punched into a deck of cards, what would be the best way to accomplish this?

3. What is mark-sense punching?

The Verifier

As was observed earlier, it is of extreme importance that data entering any system be absolutely accurate. The summary information reported can be no better than the entering data. In the vernacular of the profession this idea is often referred to as GIGO (garbage in, garbage out). Verification is any procedure for checking the accuracy of the data on the input document.

Methods of Verification

Different techniques may be used to verify the input data. These methods can be identified as (1) the visual method, (2) the batch-total method, and (3) the machine method. The machine method will be discussed first.

Fig. 4-11. IBM card verifier.

The Machine Method. Externally, the verifiers (IBM 056 and 059, Fig. 4-11) appear almost exactly like the card punches (IBM 026 and 029), and in operation they are also nearly identical. The operator of the verifier keys data via a keyboard from source documents. The documents are the same ones from which the card-punch operator punched the cards, and the cards put through the verifier are the same ones the card-punch operator punched. If the two operators read and key the data in the same way, it is assumed that the operation has been done correctly and that the punched card truly represents the source document.

The verifier does not punch alphabetic and numeric data codes but merely senses the holes by means of sensing pins at the verification station. If there is a discrepancy, i.e., if the verifier operator disagrees with what is punched in the card, the verifier automatically places a notch on the 12 edge of the card in the column in which the discrepancy has occurred (Fig. 4-12). The notch is known as the *error notch*. If the verifier operator agrees completely with the punched card, this is indicated with a notch on the right-hand end of the card. This notch is known as the *OK notch* and indicates that the card has been verified and is correct.

The Visual Method. Although machine verification is the most dependable, it does require additional machines at additional cost. The visual method can be used and would not require any additional machines. The procedure is simple. The card is converted to printed copy and the printed copy is compared visually with the source document. Error cards are identified and returned to the key punch for correction. The printing can be done by (1) using the print feature of the 026 key punch, (2) using an interpreter (a machine to be discussed later) to print on the card, or (3) preparing a listing on the accounting machine.

Batch-Total Method. The batch-total method employs the same principle that is used in a trial balance in an accounting procedure. In a trial balance it is assumed that the ledger is correct if the total debits equal the total credits. The batch-total method of verification assumes that, if a total taken from the source documents equals a total taken from the cards, then all of the cards have been punched correctly.

The procedure is as follows. Source documents are accumulated in the originating department until enough (a batch) are ready to forward to the card-punch section. Before they are forwarded, adding-machine tapes are prepared from the documents. The totals might be total dollar amounts, total of quantities, a total of the product number, or a total of any of the numeric

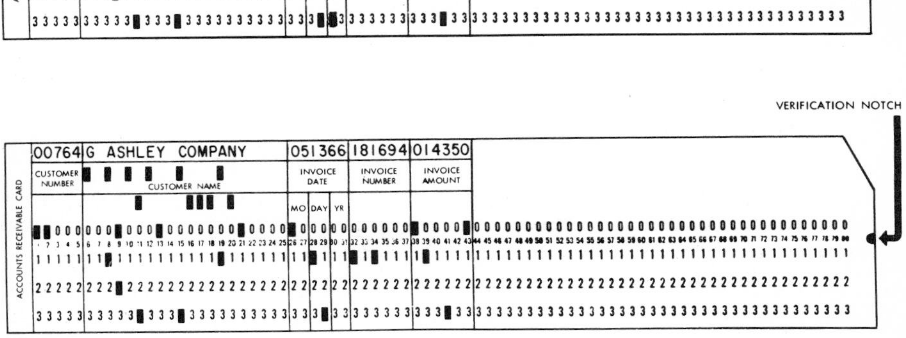

Fig. 4-12. Error and verification notches.

data items. After the cards have been punched in the card-punch section, the numeric data fields for which batch totals have been provided are added from the cards on the accounting machine and the totals compared with the totals from the tapes. If the totals agree, the cards are verified. If the totals disagree, another method (probably the visual method) must be used to locate the error card or cards.

Need for Verification

As long as data are not originally recorded in a machine language and it is thus necessary to translate the language of the source document to the language of the machine, verification will be necessary. This is so regardless of the type of system, EAM or electronic, used to process the data after recording and verification. Machine-language documents (punched cards) prepared for an EDP (electronic data-processing) system must also be verified before entering the system. No system can get correct results from incorrect input.

Because the need for verification is so critical when data are converted from one language (natural) to another (machine) and because these steps of recording and verification are slow, techniques have been developed to reduce or eliminate the need to translate from source document to machine-language document in some electronic systems. These techniques will be discussed in later chapters.

REVIEW QUESTIONS

4. There are three methods of verification. Name them and explain each method briefly.

5. Why is verification necessary?

The Interpreter

The Function

The EAM operator is the communication link between and among the machines in an EAM system. The data medium is the punched card, and herein lies an inconsistency, for the human operator is ill equipped to interpret the language of a machine (the punched card). An operator cannot read holes very efficiently. The answer to the problem is the *interpreter*. The interpreter's function is simply to translate machine language to human language (Fig. 4-13).

Fig. 4-13. Alphabetic interpreter.

Models and Features

The two most prevalent models are the IBM 548 and the IBM 557. The 557 is the better of the two insofar as speed and printing flexibility are concerned. Both, however, have just one purpose, to print on the card. The 557 will interpret cards at a rate of 100 cards per minute on any one of 25 lines on the card. The 548 (Fig. 4-14) operates at 60 cards per minute, and the printing is limited to two lines, one above the 12 punching position (row), and the other between the 12 and 11 punching positions (Fig. 4-15). The selection of fields for interpreting and the areas of printing (Figs. 4-16 and 4-17) are controlled by panelboard wiring.

Uses of the Interpreter

Wherever cards are being used, having the data printed on the card is helpful. But if non-data-processing personnel are to use the cards, interpreting them is mandatory. Cards being handled by bank tellers,

Fig. 4-14. IBM 548 interpreter and interpreted card.

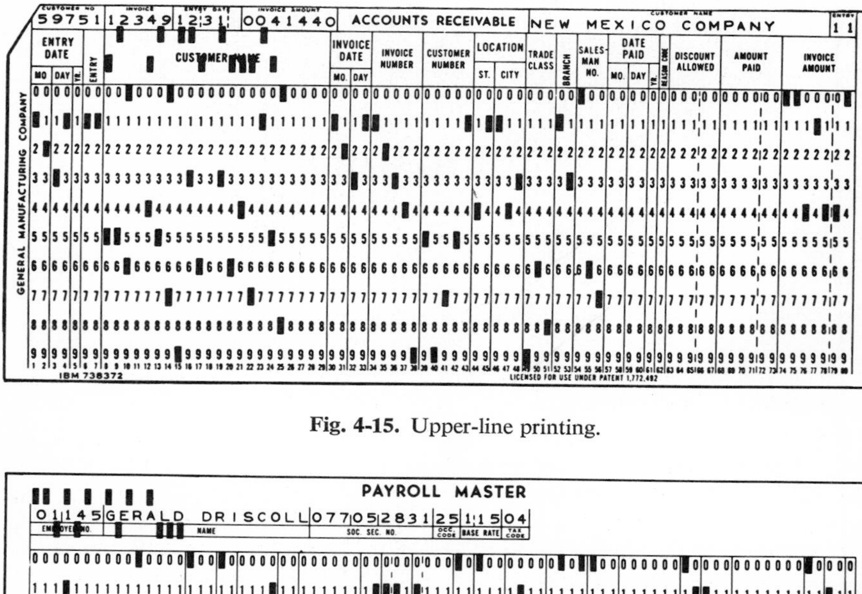

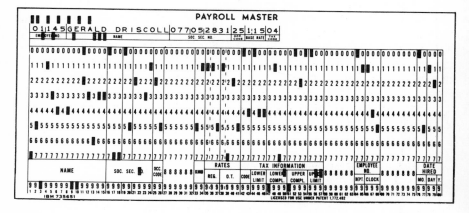

Fig. 4-15. Upper-line printing.

Fig. 4-16. Lower-line printing.

86

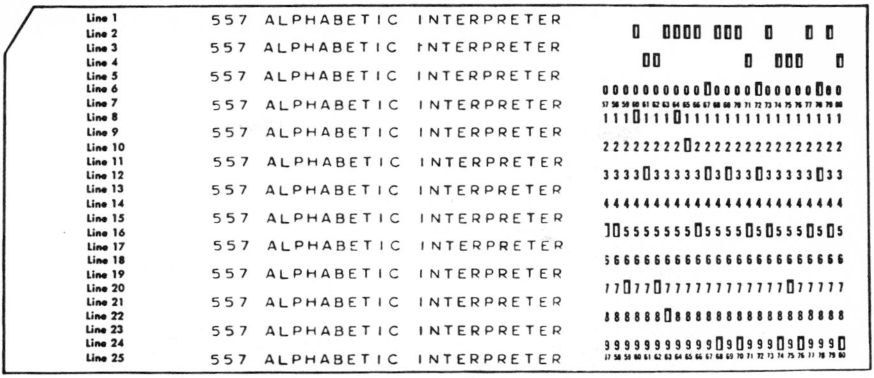

Line 1		557 ALPHABETIC INTERPRETER
Line 2		
Line 3		557 ALPHABETIC INTERPRETER
Line 4		
Line 5		557 ALPHABETIC INTERPRETER
Line 6		
Line 7		557 ALPHABETIC INTERPRETER
Line 8		
Line 9		557 ALPHABETIC INTERPRETER
Line 10		
Line 11		557 ALPHABETIC INTERPRETER
Line 12		
Line 13		557 ALPHABETIC INTERPRETER
Line 14		
Line 15		557 ALPHABETIC INTERPRETER
Line 16		
Line 17		557 ALPHABETIC INTERPRETER
Line 18		
Line 19		557 ALPHABETIC INTERPRETER
Line 20		
Line 21		557 ALPHABETIC INTERPRETER
Line 22		
Line 23		557 ALPHABETIC INTERPRETER
Line 24		
Line 25		557 ALPHABETIC INTERPRETER

Fig. 4-17. Interpreted card showing 25 print lines.

inventory clerks, customers, and others, by whom the card is being used as a reference document, must be interpreted.

REVIEW QUESTION

6. What is the function of the interpreter?

The Collator

The collator is used in an EAM system as an aid in accomplishing the sorting step in the total procedure. The collator supplements but does not replace the sorter. The collator is often compared to a filing clerk, for, just as a file clerk files and extracts printed documents in and from a file drawer, so the collator files (merges) and extracts (selects) cards in and from a file of cards.

Models and Functions

The most widely used collators are the IBM models 085 and 088. The basic capabilities are the same. These basic capabilities, or functions, are:
1. Merging
2. Matching
3. Selecting
4. Sequence checking

Fig. 4-18. IBM 088 collator.

To accomplish these functions the machines are designed with two hoppers and either four (Model 085) or five (Model 088) stackers (see Fig. 4-18). All of these functions are accomplished by the collator through its basic ability to compare. Data from cards can be read, remembered, and compared. When two numbers are compared, one of three conditions must exist. The two numbers are equal, or one number is either smaller or larger than the other. Based on this ability to detect and react to the conditions of *higher than, lower than,* or *equal to,* the collator can merge one deck of cards into another deck forming a single deck (merging), extract cards from a file on any of several different conditions (selection), select out cards from one file of cards which have no matching card in a second file (matching), and check to see if each card in a file of cards is in its proper place according to a sequential arrangement (sequence checking).

Merging. In the merging operation two files of cards, each sorted into order, are merged into one file which will also be in sequential order. The two decks of cards are placed in the machine, one deck to each hopper, and the decks are merged into a single stacker (see Fig. 4-19).

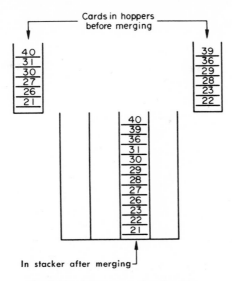

Fig. 4-19. Collator merging function.

Two decks of cards can be merged by use of the sorter simply by resorting all of the cards, but the collator can do the merging job in one pass of the cards. The collator is thus more efficient in most cases. Typical merging jobs include combining name and address cards with data cards or combining balance-forward cards with new-transaction cards.

Matching. The function called matching is actually the selection of unmatched cards. It assumes two decks of cards and requires that the cards in one deck be compared with the cards in the second deck to ascertain if a counterpart, or matching, card is there. As in merging, an assumption is made that the two decks are in the same order and in proper sequence. The decks are placed in each of the two hoppers and separate stackers collect the matched and unmatched cards (see Fig. 4-20).

An example of the use of the matching operation is bank account reconciliation when punched cards are used for both checks and check stubs. Returned checks are matched against the check-stub file. Unmatched stubs represent the outstanding checks.

Selection. The collator can select, or extract, cards from a file of cards on a wide variety of bases. Cards which have *X punches* in a certain column can be identified and selected into a different stacker from the non-X-punched cards (called *NX cards*). Likewise, cards punched with a *specified number* can be selected out. A number can be entered into, and "remembered" by, the machine, and cards which have a number equal to the

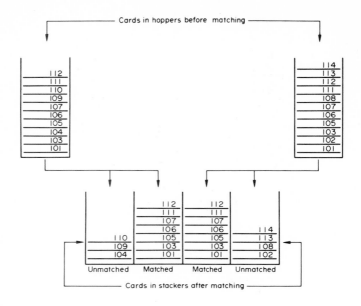

Fig. 4-20. Collator matching function.

"stored" number can be separated from the original deck (see Fig. 4-21). In fact, two values can be remembered by the collator, and cards which have values between the two stored numbers can be selected. This is referred to as *minimum-maximum selection.* Finally, cards can be selected on the basis of being the *first* or *last card of a group* of cards punched with equal values.

There are untold situations which call for selection, but a common need is to separate merged decks and thereby restore the file to two decks after having served their function as a combined deck. Selecting balance cards which show a zero balance is an example where the significance is apparent in the business relationship between the business and its credit customers. A paid-up account is a natural for some sort of action.

Sequence Checking. The merging and matching operations are dependent on the files, or decks, of cards' being in order. These functions cannot be accomplished unless this condition is met. Also, cards entering the accounting machine for report preparation must be in proper sequence. Sorters and sorter operators perform dependably, but neither are perfect. Therefore, a check on the sequence of files of cards is essential as a part of most procedures. The collator performs this function. The machine can be wired to feed the cards through, check the relationship between adjacent cards, and stop if an error-in-sequence condition exists. The function is simple, but

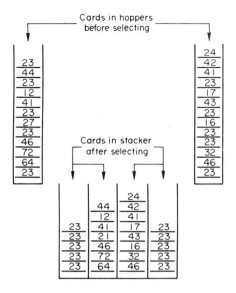

Fig. 4-21. Finder card selection. (Selecting cards with specific value.)

very important. Cards can be checked for ascending order or descending order on a numeric or alphabetic basis.

Collator Usage

The collator is a workhorse in both an EAM system and a card computer system. Its varied abilities and functions make it an indispensable machine in all but the smallest of installations. The collator is used extensively in organizing input cards for the computer. A great deal of computer time can be saved if the data are organized before entry into the computer.

The Calculating Punch

The calculating punch (Fig. 4-22) is what the name implies. It is a machine which will calculate and punch the result of the calculation into a card. The calculating capability of the various models includes addition, subtraction, multiplication, and division. The process can be as simple as reading two factors from a card, performing one of the arithmetic functions, and punching the answer into the card. On the other hand, the calculating punch can read several factors from one or more cards, perform a series of arithmetic operations, and punch intermediate and final results into a summary card. Thus, a calculating punch can calculate formulas similar to the following:

$$\text{Balance plus receipts} = \text{new balance}$$
$$A + B = N$$
$$\text{Balance minus issues} = \text{new balance}$$
$$A - C = N$$
$$\text{Balance plus receipts minus issues} = \text{new balance}$$
$$A + B - C = N$$
$$\text{Total cost divided by number of units} = \text{average cost}$$
$$A \div B = C$$
$$\text{Hours worked times rate of pay} = \text{gross pay}$$
$$A \times B = C$$
$$A \times B + C + C = R$$
$$\frac{(A + B)(C - D)}{X} = Y$$

Fig. 4-22. IBM calculating punched (602 - 604).

Types of Calculating Punches

The calculating punch represents a step toward the computer as a data-processing system. Some calculating punches have electronic calculating units and therefore perform in much the same manner as an electronic computer. However, the calculating punch does not qualify in other respects as an EDP system (computer). A major difference is the manner in which a calculating punch is instructed in its operation. The calculating punch utilizes the wired control panel, whereas a computer utilizes an internally stored program.

Uses of the Calculating Punch

The calculating punch is not always included in an EAM installation and would rarely be needed in a computer installation. Unless an installation has extensive calculating requirements, the cost of a calculating punch cannot be justified and procedures are designed to accomplish calculation in other ways. One way would be to perform the calculating with the aid of a desk calculator and then punch the results into summary cards via the card punch as a manual function. Furthermore, when the use of an installation grows to the point at which a calculating punch can be justified by the volume of calculating work, a computer can probably be justified. There is nothing that a computer does better than calculate (compute), so the calculating punch is immediately displaced by the arrival of the computer.

REVIEW QUESTIONS

7. What are the functions of a collator?

8. Basically, how does the collator accomplish its functions?

9. What is the function of the calculating punch?

5 NUMBERING SYSTEMS

BACKGROUND

Some sort of counting activity has been carried out by man since his earliest developmental days. In the very early days, sticks and stones were used as aids and counting devices. The fingers were also very handy and were

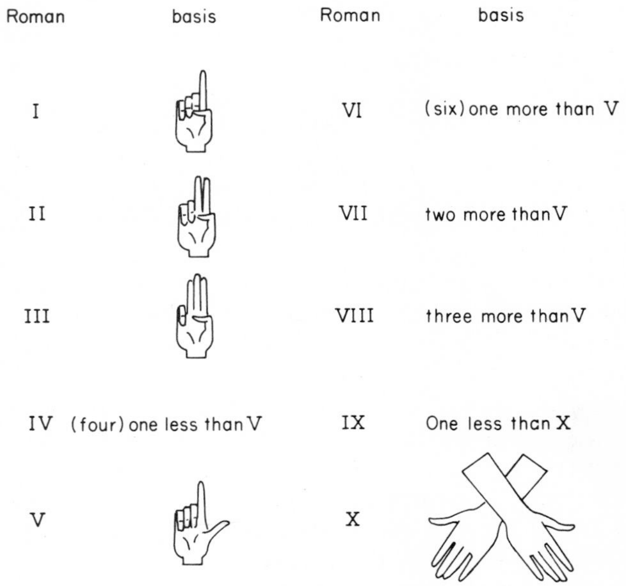

Roman	basis	Roman	basis
I		VI	(six) one more than V
II		VII	two more than V
III		VIII	three more than V
IV	(four) one less than V	IX	One less than X
V		X	

Fig. 5-1. Roman numbering system.

extensively used by early civilizations. The Pueblo Indians used the fingers of one hand only, creating a *base-five* number system, while the Maya Indians used both hands and both feet, creating a *base-twenty* system.

The Romans appreciated the 10-finger counting system so much that their entire method of counting was based on it (Fig. 5-1).

Many of our present concepts about numbers are based on Roman usage. For example, the word *digit* is derived from the Latin *digitus,* meaning *finger*. Our present day decimal system is based on 10 digits much as the early Romans based their numbering system on the 10 fingers of the 2 hands.

The greatest difference between our system and that of the Romans is that the Romans did not recognize zero as a digit. This forced them to develop a different symbol for every different number they wished to express in writing. (For example, 10 could have been expressed as I0 instead of X.)

REVIEW QUESTIONS

1. What was the basis for the Roman numbering system?

2. In what way did this differ from our present-day numbering system?

3. What is the first digit in the decimal numbering system?

4. What is the *base* of the decimal numbering system?

PRINCIPLE OF THE MODULUS

The modulus of a counter, or counting system, may be defined as the maximum number of different digits that it can represent in a single cycle. For example, a clock is a modulo-12 counter. Its modulus is 12 since it can count to 12 hours in one cycle. The minute and second hands have a modulus of 60.

Quantities may be represented by symbols. On this type of counter, the quantity that a symbol represents depends upon the number of cycles that have been counted. If there is a *common difference* between the assigned values of the counter, this will be its *modulus.*

Take, for example, the five fingers of one hand. If each finger is to have a value of 1, it would be a modulo-5 counter (maximum amount). This system is called a *unitary* (or one-for-one) system. If, on the other hand, it were determined that the value of each finger will be 4, then the progression would be 4, 8, 12, 16, 20 and the modulus would be 4 (the common difference between the series of numbers is 4).

There is no limitation to the codes that may be assigned to a counter.

Again, using the fingers as an example, each finger may be assigned a different number, as shown in Fig. 5-2. This would be a modulo-56 code: 10 + 9 + 8, etc., = 55; since zero is also a number in our counting system, it must be added to the total to make 56.

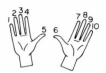

Fig. 5-2. Numbering based on fingers.

This code is somewhat wasteful as it is possible to express numbers in more than one way. For example, the digit four could be expressed by holding up the three and one fingers or by holding up just the four finger. The most efficient coding for 10 fingers will be shown in Fig. 5-3.

When trying to determine the modulus of a counter, two things must be examined: (1) Is it the type of system that has a fixed number of digits in a cycle (like a clock); or (2) are arbitrary values assigned to each position of the counter and, if so, what is the common difference between these values?

EXAMPLES:

1. The octal code consists of the digits zero through seven. This falls into category 1 (the number of different digits within a single cycle) and is a modulo-eight code.

0, 1, 2, 3, 4, 5, 6, 7

2. A five-position counter, each position having a value 5 higher than the previous position, would fall into category 2 (the common difference between the assigned values) and would be a modulo-five counter.

You will note that for this second type of counter, after the first time around the cycle, it will be necessary to keep a separate count of the number

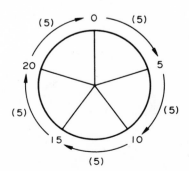

of times around the cycle to determine actual value. The first time back to the zero position, the value will be 25; the second time back to zero position, the value will be 50; etc. This has no bearing on the modulus and should not be a consideration in determining the modulus of a counter.

REVIEW QUESTIONS

5. What are the two definitions of modulus?

6. What is the modulus for each of the following counters?
   a. Given a five-position counter with values 3, 8, 13, 18, 23
   b. Given a five-position counter with values 6, 11, 16, 21, 26
   c. Given a five-position counter with values 4, 8, 12, 16, 20
   d. Given an eight-position counter with values from 1 through 8
   e. Given a two-position counter with values of 0 and 1
   f. Given a six-position counter with values 1, 3, 4, 7, 9, 14

7. What is the limitation to the codes that may be assigned to a particular counter?

BINARY NUMBERING SYSTEM

Some time has been devoted to counting on the fingers, but this has a definite bearing on the method of counting for computers. Since the fingers are a basic counting device, every principle that applies to the fingers also applies to more sophisticated counting devices.

To return to the 10 fingers, it can be mathematically proven that the most efficient code is one that doubles the value of each finger (Fig. 5-3).

This code is often called the *8-4-2-1 code* after the four lowest numbers in the sequence. This code can be used to count from zero to a maximum of 1,023, making it a modulo-1,024 counter (adding zero to the total).

$$512 + 256 + 128 + 64 + 32 + 16 + 8 + 4 + 2 + 1 = 1,023$$

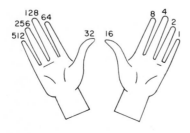

Fig. 5-3. The 8-4-2-1 code.

Modern digital computers also use the 8-4-2-1 code. Nearly all computers work in the *binary* mode. This is a base-two (or modulo-two) system utilizing only two digits, *zero* and *one*. This is most convenient for computers because an electrical field may be "on" or "off" and a magnetic device may be magnetized or not magnetized. These are also a modulo-two type of action. Since computers use binary circuits, the internal arithmetic of computers is binary in nature.

The importance of numbering systems other than decimal is not immediately apparent to most people. We are so accustomed to using the decimal system that it has become almost second nature to us, while other numbering systems seem strange and difficult. You will find that they are difficult only because they are strange.

In reality, the two systems to be discussed in this chapter (binary and octal) are quite important to computer programmers, and, after a bit of study, you will realize that each system is as simple as the decimal system. The new ground rules must be understood before the systems fall into place in a logical manner.

In the binary system, only two digits are used, zero and one. It requires the invention of a code (using only zero and one) that will cover all possible combinations of numbers to have a workable system. An arbitrary code could easily be devised, but we want a very efficient code and for this reason the 8-4-2-1 code will be utilized (Fig. 5-3). Details of this code and some of the methods for using it will be covered in the following pages.

REVIEW QUESTIONS

8. What is the most efficient code for a 10-position counting system?

9. The code referred to above is a modulo- ———————— counter.

10. Computers work in a modulo-two mode, which is usually called

————————.

11. Why is the modulo-two mode so convenient for computers?

12. What digits are utilized in the base-two numbering system?

Counting in the Binary System

The 8-4-2-1 code described on the previous pages is, in fact, the binary code. It utilizes just two digits, zero and one. In such a *two-state* code, the *one* is arbitrarily chosen as the *on* condition and the *zero* as the *off* condition. Therefore, only the *ones* will be counted in a sequence of binary numbers.

Code value →	512	256	128	64	32	16	8	4	2	1	Count only ones
	O	O	O	O	O	I	O	I	O	O	= 20 (16 + 4)
	O	O	O	O	I	O	O	I	O	I	= 37 (32 + 4 + 1)
	O	O	O	O	O	I	I	O	I	I	= 27 (16 + 8 + 1)

Fig. 5-4. Code values of the 8-4-2-1 code.

The location of each of the ones (based on the 8-4-2-1 code) is the key to its value, as shown in the table in Fig. 5-4. It is important to note that the values given to each binary position start from the *right* and progress to the *left*. (If this sequence were reversed, the results would be entirely different.) The rightmost position, then, is the position of the *least-significant* digit (LSD) and the leftmost position is that of the *most-significant* digit (MSD). Notice that this is exactly the same as in the decimal numbering system, in which the leftmost position is the most significant (Fig. 5-5).

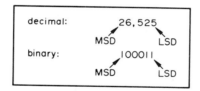

Fig. 5-5. Position significance of numbers.

A number of other codes based on the binary system are possible, and many such codes are used for computers. The 8-4-2-1 code described above is usually called the *pure binary code*.

REVIEW QUESTIONS

13. In the binary code, which digit represents the "on" condition and which digit represents the "off" condition?

14. What is the value of each of the following sequences of binary numbers?
   a. 001101
   b. 0001111100
   c. 001010000
   d. 001000111

15. Show the following numbers in binary notation:
  a. 48
  b. 27
  c. 13
  d. 128

16. What is the 8-4-2-1 code usually called?

17. Indicate the number of the MSD and LSD in the following groups of numbers:
  a. 010111
  b. 7,263$_8$
  c. 000110

Counting in Binary (cont'd)

Since binary numbers tend to be extremely long (roughly 3.3 times longer than decimal numbers), it is more convenient to group them in threes. This does not change the relative value of each position but simply makes it easier to read.

Counting in the binary system is as follows:

Decimal	Binary	Decimal	Binary
0	000	5	101
1	001	6	110
2	010	7	111
3	011	8	001 000
4	100	9	001 001

Since the binary system only contains 0 and 1, it is necessary to take the same "move" at 2 that is taken at 10 in the decimal system. This is to place a "1" to the left and start again (at the right) with "0." Therefore, a decimal 2 is a binary 10, 3 is 11, and then another shift must be made, adding 1 to the left and starting again with 0.

EXAMPLES:

Convert the following decimal numbers to binary:

1. $22 = 0\overset{\downarrow}{1}0 \qquad 1\overset{\downarrow}{1}0$

    $16 + 4 + 2 = 22$

In the 8-4-2-1 sequence, find the number just less than the value of the one to be converted. Start with this number, and continue adding until the required number is reached.

2. $76 = 00\overset{\downarrow}{1} \qquad 00\overset{\downarrow}{1} \qquad 1\overset{\downarrow}{0}0$

    $64 + 8 + 4 = 76$

Add zeros to the left of the MSD to complete this last (leftmost) group of three binary digits.

REVIEW QUESTIONS

18. Show the binary equivalents of the following decimal numbers:
   a.   6
   b.   9
   c.   15
   d.   32
   e.   73
   f.   426

19. Convert the following binary numbers to decimal:
   a.   011   101
   b.   010   001   101
   c.   111   111
   d.   000   011   001

Binary Arithmetic, Addition

Only a few rules need to be observed to accomplish simple arithmetic in binary form.

ADDITION:

> Rule 1: Zero plus zero equals zero.
> Rule 2: Zero plus one equals one.
> Rule 3: One plus one equals zero with a *carry* of one to the left.

EXAMPLES:

1. Add $15 + 7$

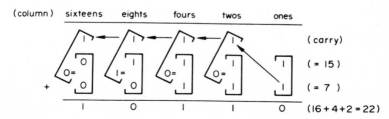

In the ones column, Rule 3 applies. In the twos column, Rule 3 applies again, but we must further add the carry, so the result is 1 with a carry. The same thing happens in the fours column. In the eights column, Rule 2 applies, but again we must add the carry; so now Rule 3 takes over, and we end up with zero and a carry. In the sixteens column, Rule 1 applies, then add the carry, which winds it up with a 1.

2. Add 3 + 3

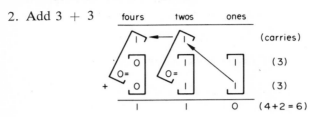

In the ones column, Rule 3 applies. In the twos column, two steps must be taken: First, 1 + 1 = 0 with a carry; second, the 0 (resulting from the first step) + 1 (from the previous carry) = 1. In the fours column, two steps must be taken: First, 0 + 0 = 0; second, the 0 + 1 (from the previous carry) = 1. Each time there is a carry, the second step must be taken.

3. Add 4 + 3

fours	twos	ones	
			(carries)
1	0	0	(4)
+ 0	1	1	(3)
1	1	1	(4+2+1 = 7)

4. Add 7 + 6

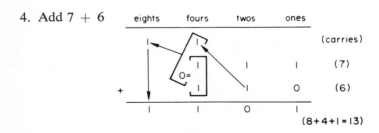

REVIEW QUESTIONS

20. State the three rules for binary addition.

21. Work the following problems:

a.

sixteens	eights	fours	twos	ones	
0	1	0	0	1	(9)
+ 0	0	1	1	0	(6)

b.

	sixteens	eights	fours	twos	ones	
	I	I	O	O	I	(25)
+	O	O	I	I	O	(6)

c.

	sixteens	eights	fours	twos	ones	
		I	O	I	O	(10)
+		O	I	I	I	(7)

Binary Arithmetic, Subtraction

The rules for binary subtraction are as follows:

SUBTRACTION:

> Rule 1: Zero minus zero equals zero.
> Rule 2: One minus one equals zero.
> Rule 3: One minus zero equals one.
> Rule 4: Zero minus one equals one, with one borrowed from the left.

EXAMPLES:

1. Subtract 15 — 7

(column)	sixteens	eights	fours	twos	ones	
						(borrows)
	O	I	I	I	I	(=15)
−	O	O	I	I	I	(= 7)
	O	I	O	O	O	(= 8)

Applying the rules above, in the ones column, Rule 2 applies, and also, in the twos and fours columns. In the eights column, Rule 3 applies. In the sixteens column, Rule 1 applies.

Similar but somewhat different rules are used for multiplication and division. They are nothing more than sequences of addition and subtraction, extremely cumbersome with paper and pencil, but very rapidly accomplished with the high speeds attained by modern computers. These examples demonstrate the way arithmetic is actually accomplished within the computer.

2. Subtract 12 — 4

	eights	fours	twos	ones	
					(borrows)
	I	I	O	O	(12)
−	O	I	O	O	(4)
	I	O	O	O	(= 8)

3. Subtract 12 − 7

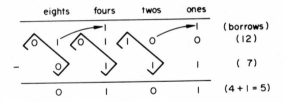

eights	fours	twos	ones	
				(borrows)
O	O	O	O	(12)
			I	(7)
O	I	O	I	(4 + I = 5)

In the ones column, Rule 4 applies; but, since there is no 1 to borrow in the twos column, we must get it from the fours column, changing the 1 to a 0 in the fours and the 0 to a 1 in the twos. In the twos column, Rule 2 applies. In the fours column, 0-1 causes a borrow from the eights column, leaving it a 0, which results in 0 for the final subtraction.

REVIEW QUESTIONS

22. State the four rules for binary subtraction.

23. Work the following problems.
　　a. Subtract:

	sixteens	eights	fours	twos	ones	
						(borrows)
	O	I	O	O	I	(9)
−	O	O	I	I	O	(6)
Result:						

　　b. Subtract:

	sixteens	eights	fours	twos	ones	
						(borrows)
	I	I	O	O	O	(25)
−	O	O	I	I	O	(6)
Result:						

　　c. Subtract:

	sixteens	eights	fours	twos	ones	
						(borrows)
		I	O	I	O	(10)
−		O	I	I	I	(7)
Result:						

OCTAL NUMBERING SYSTEM

We have said that the binary system is a *base-two,* or *modulo-two,* system. The octal numbering system is a base-eight system and is very convenient to use as a shorthand to binary.

Since it is a base-eight system, it will utilize only the numerals 0 through 7. Counting in this system is as shown in Fig. 5-6 (notice that 8 and 9 are never used):

DECIMAL	OCTAL	DECIMAL	OCTAL
0	0	8	10
1	1	9	11
2	2	10	12
3	3	11	13
4	4	12	14
5	5	13	15
6	6	14	16
7	7	15	17

Fig. 5-6. Decimal to octal conversion.

When writing a number in octal, it is usual to designate the system in the following manner: 376_8. The sub 8 indicates that 376 is an octal number.

As in the decimal and binary systems, the value of each digit in a sequence of numbers is definitely fixed.

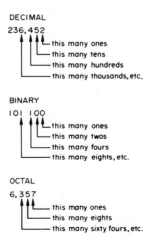

DECIMAL
236,452
— this many ones
— this many tens
— this many hundreds
— this many thousands, etc.

BINARY
101 100
— this many ones
— this many twos
— this many fours
— this many eights, etc.

OCTAL
6,357
— this many ones
— this many eights
— this many sixty fours, etc.

REVIEW QUESTIONS

24. What is the modulus of the octal numbering system?

25. Convert the following decimal numbers to octal:
  a. 6
  b. 8
  c. 12
  d. 17
  e. 20

26. What are the values of the three LSD's in:
  a. The decimal numbering system?
  b. The binary numbering system?
  c. The octal numbering system?

Conversion between Octal and Binary

The relationship between octal and binary is so simple that conversion may be made instantaneously. Consider every binary number in groups of threes (001010101 = 001 010 101). Now, each grouping of three binary digits is identified by ones, twos, and fours positions, and these are used to convert to octal.

fours	twos	ones	fours	twos	ones	fours	twos	ones
O	O	I	O	I	O	I	O	I

| octal | I | | octal | 2 | | octal | 5 | |

Conversely, each octal number is converted to three binary numbers as in Fig. 5-7. The binary representation of the octal numbers is often called *binary-coded octal*.

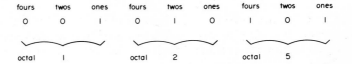

binary: O I I   I I I   I I O   I O I

OCTAL	BINARY
I	O O I
2	O I O
3	O I I
4	I O O
5	I O I
6	I I O
7	I I I

Fig. 5-7. Octal to binary conversion.

REVIEW QUESTIONS

27. Convert the following binary numbers to octal:
   a.   101
   b.   010   110
   c.   110   101   111
   d.   001   011   100

28. Convert the following octal numbers to binary:
   a. 27_8
   b. 450_8
   c. $1,267_8$
   d. $34,165_8$

Converting from Octal to Decimal

This is usually accomplished by looking up the number in a conversion table (refer to Appendix B). It may be accomplished manually in the following manner:

Multiply each octal position in turn by eight, starting with the leftmost position. Then add the next number to the result, multiplying the sum by eight, and continue until the last digit is reached. This one is not to be multiplied.

EXAMPLES:

1. $3327_8 = ?_{10}$

$$
\begin{array}{r}
3327_8 \\
\times\ 8 \\
\hline
24 \\
+\ 3 \\
\hline
27 \\
\times\ 8 \\
\hline
216 \\
+\ 2 \\
\hline
218 \\
\times\ 8 \\
\hline
1744 \\
+\ 7 \\
\hline
1751_{10}
\end{array}
$$

Result: $(3327_8 = 1751_{10})$

2. $426_8 = ?_{10}$

$$
\begin{array}{r}
426_8 \\
\times\ 8 \\
\hline
32 \\
+\ 2 \\
\hline
34 \\
\times\ 8 \\
\hline
272 \\
+\ 6 \\
\hline
278_{10}
\end{array}
$$

Result: $(426_8 = 278_{10})$

REVIEW QUESTION

29. Convert the following octal numbers to decimal notation. Do the first three problems manually, then look up the others in Appendix B.
   a. 17_8
   b. 56_8
   c. 133_8
   d. 560_8
   e. $1,407_8$
   f. $7,214_8$
   g. $10,000_8$
   h. $10,123_8$

Note: Use of the Octal-Decimal Conversion Table is explained on page 111.

Converting from Decimal to Octal

This procedure is also generally accomplished by checking a conversion table, but it may be done manually in the following manner:

Successively divide the decimal figure by eight, until no further division is possible. The *octal result* will be the last quotient figure, followed by each of the remainders, starting from the last and finishing with the first.

EXAMPLES:

1.
$$1751_{10} = ?_8$$

$$
\begin{array}{r}
218 \\
8\overline{)1751} \\
16 \\
\overline{15} \\
8 \\
\overline{71} \\
64 \\
\overline{7}
\end{array}
\qquad
\begin{array}{r}
27 \\
8\overline{)218} \\
16 \\
\overline{58} \\
56 \\
\overline{2}
\end{array}
\qquad
\begin{array}{r}
3 \\
8\overline{)27} \\
24 \\
\overline{3}
\end{array}
$$

Result: $1751_{10} = 3327_8$

2.
$$278_{10} = ?_8$$

$$
\begin{array}{r}
34 \\
8\overline{)278} \\
24 \\
\overline{38} \\
32 \\
\overline{6}
\end{array}
\qquad
\begin{array}{r}
4 \\
8\overline{)34} \\
32 \\
\overline{2}
\end{array}
$$

Result: $278_{10} = 426_8$

3.

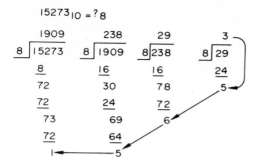

$15273_{10} = ?_8$

Result: $15273_{10} = 35651_8$

REVIEW QUESTION

30. Convert the following numbers from decimal to octal notation. Work the first three problems manually, then look up the rest of the answers in Appendix B.

a. 8_{10}
b. 29_{10}
c. 357_{10}
d. 579_{10}
e. 999_{10}
f. $3,003_{10}$
g. $4,096_{10}$

OTHER NUMBERING SYSTEMS

There are a large variety of computer codes in use today. In fact, two different computers seldom use exactly the same code in their internal operation. On the other hand, it is not practical for anyone to try to memorize dozens of different codes.

There are three basic categories of codes:

1. *Regularly weighted codes.* In these codes, each number has a weighted value which is regular and is based on a specific rule. If you know the rule, you can determine the weight of any number in the sequence. The 8-4-2-1 code is an example of this type of code. It increases progressively by a power of 2.

2. *Arbitrarily weighted codes.* In these codes, each number is weighted, but without a regular rule. The weights are arbitrarily assigned. For these codes, you must know the assigned values.

3. *Nonweighted codes.* In these codes, the numbers have no weighted values. Each one in the series is defined to represent a specific quantity. The Roman numbering system is an example of nonweighted codes.

The following are examples of different commonly used codes:

Decimal	Binary*	Binary-Coded Decimal (BCD)	7421 Code	Biquinary Code	Excess-3 Code (XS-3)
0	000	0000	0000	01 00001	0011
1	001	0001	0001	01 00010	0100
2	010	0010	0010	01 00100	0101
3	011	0011	0011	01 01000	0110
4	100	0100	0100	01 10000	0111
5	101	0101	0101	10 00001	1000
6	110	0110	0110	10 00010	1001
7	111	0111	1000	10 00100	1010
	(r.w.)†	(r.w.)†	(a.w.)‡	(r.w.)†	(n.w.)**

*This is identical with binary-coded octal for the first eight digits.
†r.w. = regularly weighted code.
‡a.w. = arbitrarily weighted code.
**n.w. = nonweighted code.

REVIEW QUESTIONS

31. Name the three categories of computer codes.

32. Identify the type of code represented by each of the following counters:
   a. A five-position counter with values 2, 4, 6, 8, 10
   b. A five-position counter with values 1, 3, 7, 9, 12
   c. A five-position counter with values as shown:
   0 = 000
   1 = 001
   2 = 011
   3 = 010
   4 = 110

USE OF THE OCTAL-DECIMAL CONVERSION TABLE

You will note, when examining this table, that the octal numbers are along the top and down the left-hand side of the table. Reading the table can most readily be explained with an example.

EXAMPLE:

Assume that the number to be converted is 154₈. Procedure: find 150 in the left column and 4 in the top column. The intersecting point is the decimal equivalent number (in this case, 108).

The numbers in the first column (under the octal 0) are the equivalent decimal numbers to the octal numbers in the left-hand column.

To convert in the opposite direction (from decimal to octal), simply find the desired number in the body of the table, then add the octal numbers in the left-hand column and top row for the desired answer.

OCTAL	0	1	2	3	4	5	6	7
0000	0000	0001	0002	0003	0004	0005	0006	0007
0010	0008	0009	0010	0011	0012	0013	0014	0015
0020	0016	0017	0018	0019	0020	0021	0022	0023
0030	0024	0025	0026	0027	0028	0029	0030	0031
0040	0032	0033	0034	0035	0036	0037	0038	0039
0050	0040	0041	0042	0043	0044	0045	0046	0047
0060	0048	0049	0050	0051	0052	0053	0054	0055
0070	0056	0057	0058	0059	0060	0061	0062	0063
0100	0064	0065	0066	0067	0068	0069	0070	0071
0110	0072	0073	0074	0075	0076	0077	0078	0079
0120	0080	0081	0082	0083	0084	0085	0086	0087
0130	0088	0089	0090	0091	0092	0093	0094	0095
0140	0096	0097	0098	0099	0100	0101	0102	0103
0150	0104	0105	0106	0107	0108	0109	0110	0111
0160	0112	0113	0114	0115	0116	0117	0118	0119
0170	0120	0121	0122	0123	0124	0125	0126	0127
0200	0128	0129	0130	0131	0132	0133	0134	0135
0210	0136	0137	0138	0139	0140	0141	0142	0143
0220	0144	0145	0146	0147	0148	0149	0150	0151
0230	0152	0153	0154	0155	0156	0157	0158	0159
0240	0160	0161	0162	0163	0164	0165	0166	0167
0250	0168	0169	0170	0171	0172	0173	0174	0175
0260	0176	0177	0178	0179	0180	0181	0182	0183
0270	0184	0185	0186	0187	0188	0189	0190	0191
0300	0192	0193	0194	0195	0196	0197	0198	0199
0310	0200	0201	0202	0203	0204	0205	0206	0207
0320	0208	0209	0210	0211	0212	0213	0214	0215
0330	0216	0217	0218	0219	0220	0221	0222	0223
0340	0224	0225	0226	0227	0228	0229	0230	0231
0350	0232	0233	0234	0235	0236	0237	0238	0239
0360	0240	0241	0242	0243	0244	0245	0246	0247
0370	0248	0249	0250	0251	0252	0253	0254	0255

EXAMPLE:

Convert decimal 254 to octal. Find 254 in the table. The number in the left-hand column is 370 and the number in the top row is 6, totalling 376 for the octal answer.

REVIEW QUESTIONS

33. Convert the following decimal numbers to octal:
   a.   67
   b.   199
   c.   104
   d.   133

34. Convert the following octal numbers to decimal:
   a.   70
   b.   117
   c.   344
   d.   278

6 ELECTRONIC DATA PROCESSING (EDP)

COMPUTER CHARACTERISTICS

Computer Capabilities and Limitations

A computer can perform repetitive operations hundreds, thousands, or millions of times without getting tired or careless. It never gets bored with an operation, therefore it never creates errors that would be normal for a human being under similar conditions.

A computer can be designed to be as flexible or specialized as desired. It can be designed to be a special-purpose computer to solve only a specific type of problem, or it can be designed to be a general-purpose computer which will solve many types of problems. There is a further breakdown even within the general-purpose computer class in that it may be specifically designed to serve as a scientific computer or as a business applications computer.

The computer can provide answers that are as accurate as desired, and it has the capability of checking itself to doubly assure accuracy of results.

The biggest computer limitation is that it cannot do anything that it is not ordered to do. It does its work exactly as it has been directed, making no independent judgments. It cannot assimilate new facts that have not been fed to it, and it does not have the capability of performing any creative activity. The one thing that it can do is to follow orders, and this it does marvelously well.

Although a computer gives the impression that it is extremely flexible and can do a vast variety of jobs, one of its major limitations is its inflexibility. Programming a problem may cost so much expended effort in both time and money that it may be impractical to make serious changes after the program has been completed.

It must also be understood that, although the computer appears to solve monumentally difficult problems, in reality it performs only basic arithmetic.

Therefore, a difficult mathematical problem must be broken down into simple step-by-step procedures, which may become a most laborious and time-consuming chore for the programmer.

In spite of the fact that computers work at fantastic speeds, there are certain applications for which the process is still not fast enough. In these areas, particularly in real-time situations, solutions and answers are required in seconds and the computer may take hours to achieve the desired results.

These limitations, although slightly exaggerated, are very real and will not be overcome until a low-cost, lightweight, extremely reliable digital computer is developed that will have the capability of providing instantaneous response without previous programming effort. It is not often understood by the layman that months, and even years, of programming effort has preceded the simple ease with which a computer accomplishes its given tasks.

In the final analysis, a digital computer is simply an arithmetic machine that receives individual digits, performs simple arithmetic, and produces answers consisting of individual digits. Special techniques can change the digits to alphabetic characters, but the computer handles all of its information simply as digits.

REVIEW QUESTIONS

1. In a brief paragraph, summarize the advantages of computers.

2. What are the major limitations of computers?

3. What is meant by special-purpose and general-purpose computers?

Comparison between Analog and Digital Systems

Computer systems are of two general types, digital and analog. Although it is the former with which we are concerned, it would be well to differentiate between the two. Analog computers will not be mentioned again. When we speak of computers, we shall be referring to digital computers.

The term *analog* is related to the word *analogous,* meaning *proportionate to or corresponding to something else.* Our factories, offices, and homes abound in different analog devices. An analog machine is any device in which two or more parts are intergeared at predetermined ratios. The relative size, length, etc., of each part is representative of one particular factor. A movement of one part actuates others to produce a final result. The automatic record player, the time-controlled oven, and the automatic lathe are all analog devices. If each variable in a problem were scaled to a given gear ratio and if all these gears were set into mesh on a basis of relatedness and finally if provisions were made for the output of final results, we should have the basic parts of a mechanical analog computer. These results are generally expressed graphically. For example, if we let one gear represent the rate of plant growth and another, the average hours of daylight, per season, then by turning either one of the gears we could determine the graphic relationship between seasonality and rate of plant growth. Enormous numbers of variables can be entered into an analog system. An intricate study can be made of their interrelationships by changing one variable and then observing the effects produced upon others.

For our purposes, the analog computer has several disadvantages. First, most conventional data are expressed by numbers or digits. Secondly, to introduce a new factor into the problem or to remove one from it, a new part must be built into the system or stripped out of it. This makes the system uneconomical for diverse data handling, and for this reason its use has been largely confined to the solution of highly complex and well integrated scientific problems. Thirdly, and quite obviously, the accuracy of the system is dependent upon the mechanical accuracy with which computers' representative parts are milled and fitted.

The general-purpose digital computer is a combination of relatively simple subassemblies. It is designed to carry out the simple fundamental processes of addition, subtraction, multiplication, and division. However, the machine has two advantages: (1) It can be set up to perform these arithmetic functions in a long sequence, or *program* as it is called, and (2) it is able to perform at amazing speeds and with extreme accuracy.

Unlike the analog computer, which is designed for more specific types of problem solving and is capable of complex manipulation of a small body of data, a digital computer is built to assimilate large volumes of data and to reduce them by carrying them through the foregoing basic arithmetic steps. Even in areas of specialized types of problem solving, the trend has been away from the pure analog computer and in the direction of a more-flexible general-purpose digital system.

The digital computer lends itself to a variety of problem-solving techniques with which changes in the problem may be met through appropriate changes in programming (giving the machine its instructions) rather than by a rearrangement of wiring or other physical changes in the internal mechanism. The digital computer is capable of a great sequence of programmed operation without human intervention.

REVIEW QUESTIONS

4. What are the two general types of computers?

5. Which of the following devices are analog and which are digital?

a. Oil-measuring stick
b. Cash register
c. Slide rule
d. Fuel gage on a car
e. Abacus
f. Hour glass
g. Adding machine

6. What are some of the disadvantages of analog computers?

7. What is the basic function of a digital computer?

Basic Components of All Computers

All digital computers are composed of the following five major components: (1) input devices, (2) memory unit, (3) control unit, (4) arithmetic unit, and (5) output devices. The block diagram in Fig. 6-1 shows the interrelationships of these components.

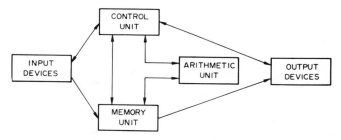

Fig. 6-1. Basic computer components.

If a machine is to carry out the function of a computer, it must be capable of performing arithmetic calculations. The arithmetic unit carries out this requirement. It is the operational portion of the computer, performing the actual work of calculation and comparison.

The work of the arithmetic unit must be controlled so that it will accomplish the desired tasks. The control unit carries out this requirement. It is the switching section of the computer, receiving incoming information and deciding what to do and when to do it. It also decides what to do with the results, and it controls the work of the arithmetic unit.

The memory unit (also referred to as the storage unit) performs the function of storing information until it is needed by one of the other components of the system. It provides information to both the arithmetic and control units. Although there are many types of memory units, they all perform the function of holding information until it is required.

Finally, input devices are used for people to communicate with the computer so that it will know what should be accomplished, and output devices are used to communicate with people regarding the results of the computer calculations.

These statements are highly generalized of course. The input and output devices will be covered in detail in Chap. 7, but the actual internal operation of the computer itself (the control, memory, and arithmetic units) is not usually of major concern to computer users. The details of wiring and methods of switching used are only of concern to the maintenance technician. These units will be covered only in sufficient detail to provide a basic understanding of their functions and interrelationships.

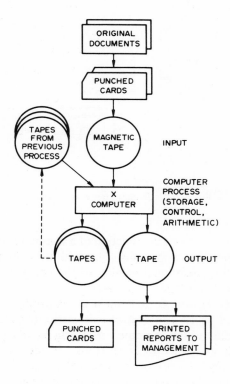

Fig. 6-2. Basics of EDP system.

Basics of an EDP System (Fig. 6-2)

1. Data are recorded in punched cards (by a card-punch machine from original documents or automatically by means of radio, telephone, telegraph, or typewriter).

2. They are (usually) transferred to magnetic tape. It may be fed directly into the computer.

3. The tape is processed by the computer along with tapes saved from previous processing periods (to compute, calculate, compare, check tables, and process the current data in accordance with the desires of management).

4. Outputs from this process are updated records on tape and printed reports or cards as desired. It is usual for the output to be on tape, and any additional outputs needed are accomplished away from the main computer (called *off line*).[1]

REVIEW QUESTIONS

8. Name the five basic components of all computers.

9. Describe briefly the function of each component mentioned in Question 8.

10. What would you suggest as the meaning of *on-line* processing?

THE CENTRAL PROCESSING UNIT (CPU)

Primary Storage

The three blocks in Fig. 6-1 labeled memory, control, and arithmetic are contained in the central processing unit (CPU) of the computer. Storage is often used as an alternate term to memory since this portion of the computer literally stores information in the form of *bits* (ones and zeros) and retains the information in readily accessible form until it is needed.

There are many types of storage devices, and more types are constantly being developed in an attempt to make storage more compact and less expensive. Some storage devices are:

Magnetic core	Magnetic tape
Drum	Paper tape
Disk	Thin film

---

[1]These processes are usually accomplished on a much smaller and less expensive computer.

When we refer to *primary storage,* we are referring to *magnetic core storage,* an integral part of the CPU. The other storage devices will be discussed in more detail in the chapter on input and output, since they also serve as input-output media.

There are two important terms to learn in connection with storage devices: (1) *Access time* refers to the speed with which stored data can be extracted from the storage device, and (2) *capacity* refers to the maximum amount of data that can be stored.

Access time is determined by the particular storage device. In magnetic cores, equal amounts of time are required to access any group of stored bits. Therefore, a core storage system is called a *random-access* system since any core can be selected for extraction and the data are available in the same amount of time (about a thousandth of a second) that it takes for data extraction from any other core.

This is not true of magnetic tapes, which must be read sequentially, or drums or disks, for which a fixed amount of time is required to read or write on the surface of the device and a certain additional amount of time to position the desired information under the *read-write* head of the device. Drums and disks are also *random access* equipment, but with the above stated limitations.

We have mentioned magnetic cores several times in this discussion. Now let us examine a magnetic core a little more closely. You will note a tie-in with the binary code discussed in the chapter on numbering systems.

A magnetic core is a tiny doughnut-shaped bit of ferromagnetic material capable of being magnetized in one direction or the other by the direction of flow of an electrical current passing through it. When it is magnetized in one direction, we may consider it to be "on" like a switch; when magnetized in the other direction, it is "off." Let us assume that each storage position in memory is composed of six magnetic cores. Each core may be called a *bit,* which is an abbreviation for *bi*nary dig*it,* and is a single character in a binary number or a single pulse in a group of pulses.

A code made up of the various combinations of these six cores (or bits) in on or off conditions tells the computer which character is stored at that position. A single storage position may be graphically represented as in Fig. 6-3. The A and B bits are known as *zone* bits, and the lower four bits are

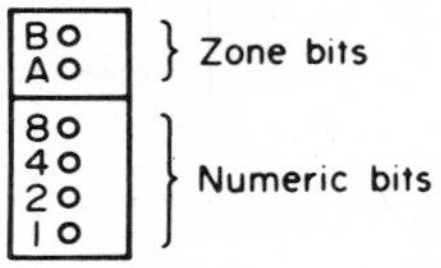

Fig. 6-3. Graphic representation of a storage position.

known as *numeric* bits. The numeric bits, singly or in combination, represent the digits from zero to nine. The numeric bits with one or the other or both zone bits added make up the alphabet and special characters.

The 80-column card is depicted and explained in Chap. 3. Note that the codes are identical with the codes shown in the Example below, with the exception that the zone bits take the place of the 12, 11, and 0 punches for alphabetic characters. There is no requirement to memorize these codes as they are merely the internal representations of the Hollerith card codes.

EXAMPLE:

When a bit is shaded, we shall consider it to be on.

Alphabetic characters:
A through I: Both the A and B bits are "on" with numbers 1 through 9.
A = 1, B = 2, C = 3, D = 4, E = 5, F = 6, G = 7, H = 8, I = 9
J through R: Just the B bit is "on" using numbers 1 through 9.
J = 1, K = 2, L = 3, M = 4, N = 5, O = 6, P = 7, Q = 8, R = 9
S through Z: Just the A bit is "on" using numbers 2 through 9.
S = 2, T = 3, U = 4, V = 5, W = 6, X = 7, Y = 8, Z = 9
Special characters such as the period (.), the slash (/), etc., are composed of various other combinations of the zone and numeric bits.

The close-up of a magnetic-core plane in Fig. 6-4 shows some of the thousands of metallic, doughnut-shaped cores that make up the central

Fig. 6-4. Magnetic core plane.

memory units of most electronic computers. The cores can be magnetized individually by energizing the tiny electronic wires on which they are threaded. Data are represented in each core by its "on" or "off" condition.

REVIEW QUESTIONS

11. Primary storage refers to what storage device?

12. What is the meaning of:
    a. Access time?
    b. Capacity?
    c. Bit?

13. Name three other storage devices.

14. In the following symbolic representations of storage units, darken the bits to spell out DEC25XMAS.

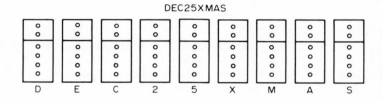

15. Read the following storage units, and place the letter or number each represents in the box below the figure.

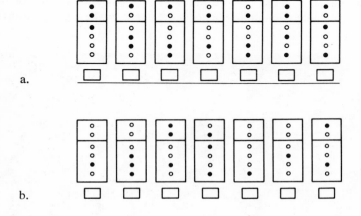

16. If the zone bit was removed from the letter P, the result would be _____.

17. If the zone bits were removed from the letter G, the result would be
_____.

18. If an A bit was added to the numeric 5, the result would be _____.

The Stored Program

The ability to store large amounts of data is not the only function of the
storage unit. The data referred to here are those which the computer will use
in its calculations or those which have been developed by the calculations.
Even more important is the fact that the *program* that instructs the computer
in its functions is contained within storage.

A *stored-program system,* then, is one that stores its instructions internally. A sequence of instructions to solve a problem is called a *program*. The
individual instructions are called *program steps*.

To follow the process through, refer to Fig. 6-2. The program steps are
converted from writing to punched cards,[1] which are *loaded* into the
computer (i.e., placed in the memory unit of the computer). When data are
fed into the computer, the stored program acts on the data to produce the
desired results.

EXAMPLE:

As a very simple example, let us assume that we wish to process a large
number of punched cards, and, among other things, every time we find a card
with the digit 5 in column 1, we shall want to print out the contents of this
card in a management report.

Our stored program will contain an instruction that says, "Look for a 5 in
column 1. If a 5 is found, this card is to be processed to produce a printed
report."

As data cards are fed into the computer for processing, each card will be
examined for a 5 in column 1 and the contents of the 5 cards will be printed
as desired.

After both the data to be operated upon and the program that instructs
the computer about the operations to be performed are in storage, the
computer proceeds to go through the necessary calculations to solve the
problem.

A program step (a single instruction) may cause any one of a number of
actions to be taken by the computer:

1. It may bring data into storage from some input device.

2. It may cause an arithmetic operation to be performed.

---

[1]This is one method, not the only method. Other methods will be discussed in the
chapter on input and output.

3. It may move data from one place to another in storage.

4. It may cause a logical test to be made to determine which of two or more paths in the program should be followed (the proper path to follow would depend on the results of the test itself).

5. It may send data from storage to an output device.

The details of these and many other things that an instruction can do will ›e covered in the chapter on programming.

REVIEW QUESTIONS

19. What is a program?

20. A program step is ―――――.

21. What is a stored-program system?

22. What two ingredients must be present in storage before a computer can solve any problem?

23. Name three functions of an instruction.

Arithmetic and Control Units

Arithmetic Unit

This unit contains the circuitry required to perform simple arithmetic and comparisons. It usually includes a small amount of storage to hold both the *operands* (the actual numbers to be added, subtracted, etc.) which are to be acted upon and partial answers.

The computer performs arithmetic by following sets of simple rules. The technique in many machines is primarily addition. It is possible to subtract by using complement arithmetic, which is a form of addition. Multiplication can be accomplished by a sequence of additions, and division can be accomplished by a sequence of subtractions. Therefore, rules for addition can solve all four types of problems.

It should also be emphasized that the binary numbering system is used in nearly all computers because of the simplicity of the system in comparison to the decimal numbering system. There are two basic types of computers, one operating directly in the binary system and the other in a system which codes decimal digits as binary numbers (known as *BCD-binary-coded decimal*).

Subtraction using nines complement. The rules for arriving at the nines complement are very simple. The nines complement is obtained by subtracting each digit of any sequence of numbers, separately, from nine.

EXAMPLE:

The nines complement of 607 = 392
The nines complement of 2,453 = 7,546

If the two numbers are added together, the sum will always be all nines.

607	2,453
392	7,546
999	9,999

To subtract, using nines-complement arithmetic, add the nines complement of the subtrahend to the minuend, then move the most-significant digit of the sum under the least-significant position (called *end-around carry*), and perform a second addition. This technique requires a small modification if the most-significant digit is not a one (1).

This is one manner in which the computer can perform subtraction by addition.

Control Unit

This unit is the heart of the computer. It serves as a switching unit and monitor to the computer. All program steps are decyphered here and instructions issued to carry out the required operations. It controls the functions of the arithmetic unit, causing data to move into it from storage and then issuing the instructions that perform the required calculations.

Often, the first operation to be performed is manually entered into the computer. The control unit then takes over and sequentially follows all instructions in the program until it is completed.

When the computer is operating under program control, the control unit brings in data, as required, from the input devices and it controls the routing of results to the required output devices. Usually, the last instruction in the program tells the computer to stop.

REVIEW QUESTIONS

24. What is an operand?

25. Show the nines complement of the following numbers:
   a.   28
   b. 359
   c.   9,999
   d. 17,680

26. Subtract the following numbers using nines complement arithmetic:

a. 254	b. 4,427	c. 256	d. 7,293
−103	−3,958	− 18	− 126

27. What are the basic functions of the arithmetic unit?

28. What are the basic functions of the control unit?

SURVEY OF DATA SYSTEMS

Types of Systems

Computer systems can be classified in three major types: (1) large-scale systems, (2) medium-scale systems, and (3) small-scale systems. Each of these types has its own place in the over-all scheme of data processing. It is important for any organization moving for the first time into the automatic data-processing field to survey their needs very carefully before deciding on the particular system to be adopted.

Size differences between various computers are rather difficult to describe, but basically the differences are in the size of memory and the speed of execution. Also, time moves very quickly in the computer business, and what may have been considered large scale five years ago would not be considered in that class today.

To simplify the explanation, pictures of one broad system have been chosen to reflect the differences between the large-, medium-, and small-scale machines. This is the IBM System 360, Models 20 (small), 40 (medium), and 65 (large). The differences range from a minimum of 4,096 core-storage positions with a speed of 200 nanoseconds per operation to a multicomputer complex that can add 2.5 million 32-bit words in 1 second and has a core-storage capacity of 524,000 positions.

Prices vary as much as machine capabilities, starting from a monthly rental of about $2,500 and increasing to a monthly figure of $115,000. Where this type of capability is needed, the price (although it sounds high) is not exorbitant. Many people think that computers are used to save money. This is not usually the case. The reason is primarily the speed, facility, and accuracy of the machines, giving the capability to perform computations in minutes that might otherwise take years of manual effort.

Figures 6-5, 6-6, and 6-7 show typical configurations of the IBM System 360, Models 20, 40, and 65. These three systems typify the small-scale (Model 20), medium-scale (Model 40), and large-scale (Model 65) computer systems.

Procedure For Data Processing

The preparation of data for an EDP system involves a number of steps and considerable time and effort.

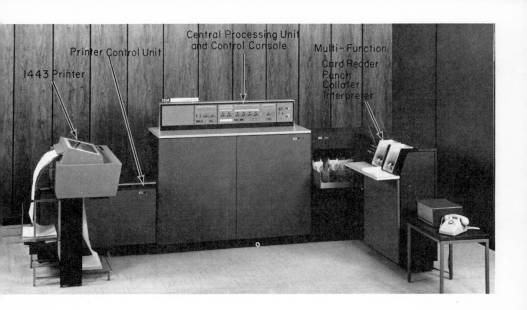

Fig. 6-5. IBM System/360 Model 20.

Fig. 6-6. IBM System/360 Model 40.

Fig. 6-7. IBM System/360 Model 65.

Analysis of the Problem

The first step in the process is the analysis and definition of the problem. The problem must be clearly defined with (1) a complete description of the types of data going into the problem, (2) the manner in which the business transactions or scientific calculations are to be processed and (3) the types and forms of data required in the final output. These three points must be completely clear before a problem can be prepared for solution by a computer.

During this analysis, it is often found that a procedure that has been taken for granted can be greatly streamlined at the same time it is being adapted to computer processing. Other procedures must be changed because of new requirements or the restrictions imposed by the computer. The important point is that each step in the problem analysis must be rigorously examined, carefully worked out, then documented in a clear and understandable form.

Flow Charting

As a result of the detailed problem analysis, the logical and arithmetic operations which must be performed by the computer should be made up into a flow chart (details in Chap. 8). Flow charting is a tool that is used very extensively by programmers. It helps to define the problem, shows up flaws in logic, and is an extremely valuable aid in writing the program, documenting the project, and making future changes and corrections in the program.

Writing the Program

The program must either be written in a language understandable to the computer or in a language that can be translated into computer language (details in Chap. 9).

Debugging

This term is meant to indicate "getting the bugs out of the program." In other words, the errors that invariably get into every program must be found and corrected. There are a variety of techniques used including the development of test data, operational checkout, desk checking, etc. These will be discussed in Chap. 8.

Documenting

Documentation seems to be rather anticlimactic after actively developing an operational program, but without proper documentation a program is rather useless if the author is no longer available to answer questions. It is very difficult for even the most expert of programmers to pick up an operational program developed by someone else and make changes or corrections in it. With good documentation, the job of servicing another man's program is, if not simplified, at least made easier.

REVIEW QUESTIONS

29. Name the three types of computer systems (from the point of view of size).

30. The size of the systems (mentioned in Question 29) is based upon what two factors?

31. Name five important areas of consideration in designing a program for automatic data processing. These should be named in the sequence in which they occur.

32. Explain the reasons for using each of the five areas mentioned above.

7 INPUT-OUTPUT DEVICES

GENERAL

The subject of input and output is very complex. It is possible to devote entire chapters to each facet of the topic, but this would not be practical in a basic text. This simplified explanation is meant to be suggestive and helpful rather than definitive.

Input and output are the terms used to describe the computer's method of communication with the outside world. Input units supply data to the computer and output units receive data from it. These units are generally called *peripheral equipment* to the computer. When they are connected directly to the main computer, they are considered to be *on line*. When operating independently from the computer, they are *off-line*.

Typical input devices are punched-card readers, paper-tape readers, magnetic-tape drives, operator console, and typewriters. There are also some special-purpose input devices such as radar sets, cathode-ray tubes, and directly coupled keyboards. Typical output devices are card-punch units, paper-tape punches, magnetic-tape drives, typewriters, and high-speed printers. Other special-purpose output units are display consoles, cathode-ray tubes, gun mounts, production machining tools, plotting boards, and a large variety of other devices.

Use of the input-output (I-O) devices is controlled by the stored-program. For example, an instruction to read a card would cause the card reader to start operating. It would feed in one card, read it, and transmit it to storage. The next card would not be read until the computer encountered the next instruction which specified the reading of a card.

CARD-HANDLING EQUIPMENT

Reading Devices

Card-reading devices are used to convert data from holes punched in cards to electrical impulses by which the data are transferred to computer storage. This may be accomplished in one of two ways: (1) by passing the card between a contact plate and electrical contact brushes that make contact with the plate wherever a hole has been punched in the card or (2) by photoelectric cells that are activated by a source of light below the card as holes in the card allow light to pass through.

Cards are mechanically moved from a card *hopper* through the card feeding unit to the *read station* (where the brushes or photoelectric cells are positioned). The sensing device converts the holes to electrical impulses, which are relayed to computer storage. Many card readers require the cards to move through a second read station which is used for checking purposes.

After reading has been accomplished, the cards are moved to a *stacker* in the same sequence in which they originally entered from the hopper. Some equipment allows selective stacking of cards (Fig. 7-1) based on the requirements of the stored program. On these machines there are several stackers available, and the program can specify that certain types of cards are to fall into specific stackers from either input (read) or output (punch).

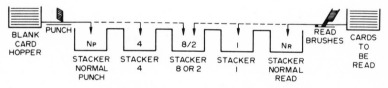

Fig. 7-1. Schematic of one type of selective stacker.

Punching Devices

Card-punching devices reverse the process of the reading devices in that they convert the electrical impulses as they are sent from storage to holes punched into cards. These machines contain a punching station, which accomplishes the punching specified by the program (Fig. 7-2). Cards move automatically from a blank-card hopper, under the punching mechanism, then through a checking station, and to the *stacker*.

The speed of card readers and card punches varies depending on the equipment used. Card reading can vary from 100 to 1000+ cards a minute, and card punching can vary from 100 to 250+ cards a minute.

Fig. 7-2. IBM card reader-punch unit.

REVIEW QUESTIONS

1. Define the following terms:
   a. On-line peripheral equipment   c. Hopper
   b. Off-line peripheral equipment   d. Stacker

2. What is the function of a card reader?

3. What is the function of a card punch?

4. List four input and four output devices.

TAPE AND TAPE-HANDLING DEVICES

Paper Tape

Tape of any type has obvious advantages over the conventional punched card. The fact that a tape can be rolled onto a reel makes for economy of storage. Punched cards are limited to 80 or 90 items of information per card, whereas enormous quantities of serial information may be entered onto tape.

Paper tapes carry information in the form of positional punches, and the paper-tape reader transmits the data to computer storage by feeding the tape past a reading unit where the presence or absence of holes is sensed and converted to electronic impulses. The rows capable of containing holes are called *channels*. Paper tape varies in width from five-channel to eight-channel size (Fig. 7-3).

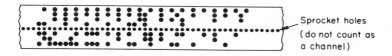

Sprocket holes (do not count as a channel)

Fig. 7-3. Sample 7 channel paper tape.

Paper tape is punched by the computer with an automatic tape punch. It is also punched on line or off line by a machine called a *Flexowriter*. Data from storage are converted into tape code and punched in blank tape as it passes through the punching mechanism. Not all computers are equipped to handle paper tape. One big advantage of paper tape is that it may be punched in teletype code that can be transmitted over commercial teletype lines allowing fast data transmission to any part of the country.

Magnetic Tape

A magnetic-tape unit (Fig. 7-4) is used as either an input device or an output device. Each unit carries two magnetic-tape reels, and it operates these reels in much the same manner as the reels on a movie projector or tape recorder, starting with one full reel and one empty reel and winding tape from one reel to the other. This unit accomplishes the actual reading or writing of information.

Magnetic tapes not only serve as the primary input and output agents but are also a practically unlimited means of external storage. They are capable of retaining information (data) for years, can be used in the storage of running accounts or end products, and may be erased and used over and over. Further, they provide a rapid method of putting information into, or getting it out of, the machine.

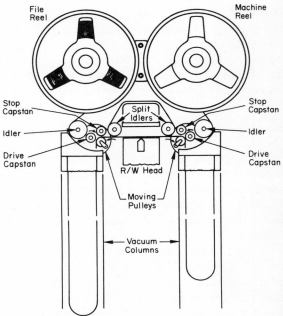

Fig. 7-4. IBM 729-IV magnetic tape unit.

Tape is mounted (*loaded*) on the unit and threaded through the moving mechanism (*feed*) with two long loops held by vacuum columns (or take-up arms, etc.) to permit high-speed starts and stops.

REVIEW QUESTIONS

5. a. What is a Flexowriter?
   b. Is it an on-line or off-line machine?

6. A paper tape contains how many channels?

7. Mounting a tape is called _____ and the mechanism that moves tape is called a _____ _____.

8. What are some of the advantages of magnetic tape over punched cards?

Terminology

There are a number of terms used in connection with magnetic tape with which the beginner must familiarize himself. Some of the terms are in wide enough use to warrant special description.

Tape Character: A tape character consists of the bits (discussed under Primary Storage, Chap. 6) that constitute one character stored across the longitudinal channels of the tape. Most tapes have seven channels, six to represent a single character and one used as a check bit. For example, assume that a computer word consists of 30 bits and that each character consists of 6 bits. The entire word can be stored in five sequential frames on tape.

Record: A record consists of a number of words which normally are needed in the computer at the same time. A tape record may be as long or as short as necessary and is often referred to as a *block* of data.

File: Each collection of records, of the same type, stored on tape is called a file. A file may be stored on one tape reel or more than one if it is a very large file.

Reflective Spot: A normal tape is about 2,400 feet long. It takes 6 to 8 feet on each end to wind on the tape drives. The tape has a little magnetic mark, called a reflective spot, near the beginning. This is the *load point* of the tape (where *read* or *write* will begin). There is also a reflective spot near the end of the tape beyond which writing should not be done. Checking for the reflective spot at the end of the tape must be done by the program.

Tape Mark, Interrecord Gap, End-of-File Gap: Figure 7-5 gives a symbolic representation of a tape which shows all of the areas named here. A tape record contains the same bits that we have been dealing with in computer storage except that they are stored on tape as magnetic spots. Between the groups of magnetic spots are blank areas of tape, approximately ¾ inch wide. These are called *interrecord* gaps (IRG). The gap after the last record on the tape is called the *end-of-file gap*. This last gap and the *tape mark* which precedes it constitute the end of the file (EOF), and, when this is reached, the tape may be rewound and unloaded from the tape drive. It must be understood that an end of a file (designated by the tape mark) is a record just like any other record on tape.

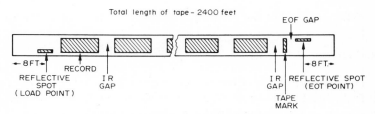

Fig. 7-5. Symbolic representation of magnetic tape.

Labels: Every tape reel should have three labels. One label is a sticker attached to the reel showing the name of the file. When we refer to a label in this text we shall refer to the second and third types. A *header label* should be written on the front of the tape in magnetic characters, just as records are written. This special record should provide identifying information about the file contained on the tape reel. Such information may include the file name, date the tape was written, reel number, etc. The programmer must provide for writing this data on each reel *before* he begins to write the data records.

Each tape reel should also include a *trailer* label. The *trailer* label is written at the end of the tape after all data records are on the tape. It should include such information as the number of records on the tape and whether the file is continued on another tape.

Tape Mark: When all the data are recorded on a tape, they may occupy only a small part of the reel. To avoid reading beyond the end of the data, the programmer must cause a tape mark to be written after the trailer. A tape mark is a one-character record, written as any other record, by the program. As the tape is read, the program continually tests for the tape mark. This symbol is not used with all computers, but, if it is required, it must not be forgotten.

REVIEW QUESTIONS

9.. Identify the following abbreviations and terms, and explain the meaning of each:
   a. IRG
   b. EOT point
   c. Load point

10. If a magnetic tape was unrolled from its reel and stretched out in a straight line, how many feet would it cover?

PRINTERS

The medium- and high-speed printers are by far the most practical output devices. The printed data that results from the printing operation can be photographed and reproduced to allow wide distribution of the results of the computer process. Punched cards, paper tape, and magnetic tape are excellent devices for use by the computer, but what is most frequently required is information that can be read by people. This must be in English words and Arabic numbers, which can be produced most effectively by the printer. (See Figs. 7-6 and 7-7.)

The printer may receive data directly from the computer, or it may operate in conjunction with a tape or card unit independently of the main computer. In other words, it may operate on line or (if it is direct tape-to-print or card-to-print conversion) off line.

Printers are of various types. One type uses the principle of the *typebar* and is quite similar in operation to a standard typewriter. Another type of printer uses the principle of a rotating *print wheel;* it actually contains 120 rotary print wheels, each containing a fixed number of characters (e.g., 48, 64, etc.). At the time of printing, all 120 wheels are correctly positioned and strike the paper nearly simultaneously, delivering the entire line of print practically at one blow. Another type is the *wire-punch* printer in which a five

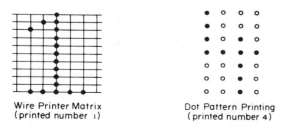

Wire Printer Matrix   Dot Pattern Printing
(printed number 1)   (printed number 4)

Fig. 7-6. Sample types of printing.

Fig. 7-7. IBM high speed printer.

wire by seven wire matrix of stiff wires is used in the printing process. By using the proper combination of wires, it is possible to punch any character or number. Another type of printer is called the *sliding bar* printer. It contains a sliding bar with segments (or sets) of characters along the bar. The bar is positioned by moving horizontally so that the proper character is positioned for printing. The segments are 13, 39, 52, and 63 character sets. The final type of printer we shall mention is the *chain printer*. The chain is built into a complete circle containing 5 sections of 48 characters. As the chain travels, each desired character is printed as it is positioned against the paper. Up to 132 positions can be printed in one line with this type of printer.

At the present time, the chain type of printer is the most popular and most commonly used. It can print at the rate of 800 lines per minute, with a maximum printing speed of 1,000 lines per minute.

REVIEW QUESTIONS

11. Why is printing the most practical form of computer output?

12. Name four types of printers.

13. Which of the printers is the most commonly used, and what is its maximum printing capacity?

OTHER INPUT-OUTPUT DEVICES

Operator Console and Typewriter

This unit may be compared to the engineer's control panel on a locomotive. It is a control keyboard containing a typewriter and a number of keys and indicator lights (Fig. 7-8). It is used by the operator to control and monitor the job being run by the computer system.

Through this unit, the computer can be:
1. Started and stopped
2. Given new operating instructions
3. Instructed to change the selection of I-O devices
4. Given the proper substitution for erroneous data
5. Reset when error conditions cause it to halt

Its basic purpose is that of a monitoring device, which is used by the operator to redirect the program at critical points and to control the input and output devices.

The typewriter attached to the console is an on-line device. The stored program may cause it to type instructions to the operator at various times

Fig. 7-8. Operator console and on-line typewriter.

during the running of a program. Through this unit, it is also possible to put either instructions or data directly into computer storage, to alter what is already there, or to add new information. While the operator's console may be used for general input purposes, it is not advisable to use it in this manner because that greatly decreases the speed of the machine's operation.

Data Synchronizers

Most input and output devices operate at slower speeds than the computer. Also, these I-O devices require many externally supplied control signals. Further, it is necessary to keep the CPU (central processing unit) of the computer running at full capacity, otherwise the maximum efficiency of the entire system is not maintained. To overcome these difficulties, data synchronizers are sometimes used.

To achieve maximum efficiency, the operations of the CPU and the I-O units must be so arranged that they overlap or occur simultaneously. Data synchronizers act as *buffer* storage units between the computer and the I-O units. They can also perform the function of selection and control of the I-O units based on the instructions in the stored program.

These units are usually special-purpose devices with their own control and memory units containing fixed programs (Fig. 7-9). They can also be used to increase the I-O capability of the computer. By utilizing a number of data and control channels, the contents of a large number of buffer memories can be transferred to and from the computer at different time increments. The important feature is that the CPU does not stay idle during I-O operations and that the time differential is overcome without any time lag. In some computers, the buffering action is allocated to predesignated areas of core storage rather than to special equipment.

Fig. 7-9. Simple schematic of buffering concept.

REVIEW QUESTIONS

14. What is the basic purpose of the operator console?

15. Is the on-line typewriter an input or an output device?

16. Is it a good idea to enter instructions to the computer via the on-line typewriter? If not, why not?

17. Explain briefly the functions of a buffer.

Cathode-Ray Tubes

Cathode-ray tubes are familiar to all of us in the form of the picture tubes of home TV sets. These tubes are electrostatic devices which, although they operate on somewhat different registration principles, are known as cathode-ray tubes (CRTs) and serve a single purpose, that of displaying information in understandable form and with extreme rapidity (Fig. 7-10). In many display units, the face of the tube is laid out in a grid pattern.

An illustration of one type of operation may make the principle behind the use of these tubes a little clearer. Let us use a dot-circle representation as an example. In this example, the face of the tube has two patterns. The first of these is a storage pattern. When power is turned on, in the computer, the grid

Fig. 7-10. Cathode ray tube display unit.

shows up on the face of the tube as discrete dots of low electrical potential. This is the storage pattern before registration begins.

The information is fed in as binary zeros (0) and ones (1). Wherever a one is *registered*, the dot becomes surrounded by a circle, raising the potential of the bit (dot) and giving it a significant output pulse. On the other hand, entering binary zeros makes no change in the grid. Information once entered into the tube can be drawn upon repeatedly and is only lost when the power is turned off or new information erases it.

Usually, a second CRT is attached in parallel with the original display tube. This second tube is connected to a camera which provides a permanent record of the displayed data on film.

In recent years these tubes have become extremely versatile. For example, an engineer can (with the aid of a light pen) work directly with the computer in original design development, which makes the tube into a very useful *input* device. He can draw his design in a rough manner on the face of the tube with a light pen and insert necessary data with the aid of a small console equipped with coded keys. The computer will smooth his drawing, display any portion that he desires in enlarged form, and make adjustments based on data being fed to it by the engineer.

One of the major functions of the CRT is the presentation of data, graphs, and charts for immediate visual display and analysis. As computers increase in speed and multiple programs are processed in a time-sharing mode, it becomes more and more imperative that data be presented to engineers or management in the fastest possible manner. Printouts (fast as they are) are not fast enough for some applications. The answer in such cases is the CRT, which can produce nearly instantaneous response and immediate displays upon request.

A large number of other special-purpose devices could be mentioned, such as optical scanners, plotting boards, microfilm readers, etc. Special-purpose devices will continue to be added to the periphery of computers as the need arises and human ingenuity can develop devices that will answer the need.

REVIEW QUESTIONS

18. What does the word *registration* mean in connection with CRTs?

19. If a CRT display is used, how can you keep a record of what is displayed?

20. What is the major function of the CRT?

21. Would you call a CRT primarily an input or an output device? Amplify a little on your answer.

Secondary-Storage Devices

Magnetic Tape

A magnetic-tape reel can be used not only as a means of input or output of information, but also as a storage device. An output tape, loaded with data, can be placed in a storage rack (called a *tape library*) and kept there until it is needed again. The storage devices that we shall discuss in this section also have the capability of interacting directly with the computer and of storing data for future use. In fact, all secondary-storage devices are used primarily to increase the memory capacity of the computers to which they are connected.

Drum Storage

There are several types of magnetic drums, but their basic construction is similar. All of them have magnetized regions on their surfaces. Around the circumference of the drum are bands which are essentially like pieces of magnetic tape. As an example, we shall describe one type of drum system. It can accommodate as many as 30 drums. Around each drum there are 10 bands. Each band is divided into 10 sections each of which will hold 200 characters of information. With 30 drums, it would have a total capacity of 1,800,000 characters.

Reading and writing is usually accomplished by having the drum cylinder rotate at a fixed speed under rows of reading heads, which are usually staggered around the drum. External switching circuits select the proper head and proper operation.

Access time to information is slowed by the necessity for mechanical rotation of the drum. On the other hand, the drum may be used for either permanent or temporary storage, and it adds a huge amount of extra storage to the basic storage capacity of the computer. This type of storage has a definite advantage over magnetic-tape storage in that sections of the drum may be addressed directly without reading through record after record as on tape.

Disk Storage

This is another form of external storage device that is like the drum in that it is slower to get information from disk storage than from computer memory, but it is much less expensive. Again, it adds a fantastic amount of memory capacity to the computer.

Disk files are constructed much like the coin-operated phonographs (juke boxes). Access to the disk surfaces is provided by read-write heads on both sides, like the two sides of a phonograph record. As an example, a disk file may have a maximum of 4 modules with a single module containing 6 disks, making a total of 24 disks. To get an idea of the total storage capacity, this number can be multiplied by 8 (4 modules per disk file, 2 files), netting over 175 million characters.

Other Devices

Secondary-storage devices, such as disks and drums, can add a great deal of capacity and flexibility to a computer installation. These devices can supplement, but not replace, core storage. There is a continuing, constant search for devices capable of storing information. These devices must be inexpensive, must have the capability of storing information for long periods of time, must be reusable, and must be readily accessible.

Thin-film memory was developed by a process of depositing magnetic film on a nonconductive base. This evolved into large-scale memories using magnetic films. Film planes may be mounted inside and outside around a U-shaped holder, and access for this type of memory is much faster than for either of the other two systems.

All of these systems are called *random-access* systems because it is possible, by program instruction, to go directly to a specified location in these auxiliary storage devices in the same manner that primary storage is accessible.

REVIEW QUESTIONS

22. Can a magnetic-tape reel be called a random-access device? If not, why not?

23. What is the major purpose of secondary-storage devices?

24. Why is access time slower on most secondary-storage devices?

Magnetic Character Reader

A growing variety of devices is constantly being developed to aid the computer in doing a better job. As many as 300 new inventions directly or indirectly oriented to computers are put on the market every year.

Many of these devices are developed for special-purpose uses with computers. The magnetic character sorter-reader pictured in Fig. 7-11 is

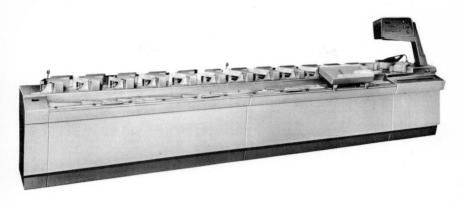

Fig. 7-11. Pitney-Bowles National Cash Register magnetic character sorter-reader.

one such special-purpose device. It was designed and developed as an aid to the automation of the banking industry. It does a variety of sorting jobs, and it has the ability to read magnetically encoded data, such as is now used by most banks on customer checks. The sorter-reader shown has the additional ability of sorting intermixed documents of various lengths, widths, and thicknesses.

8 FLOW CHARTING

PRINCIPLES OF FLOW CHARTING

Flow charting is an important part of problem analysis and programming. Programmers use flow charts for many reasons, a few of which are listed below. They are useful in:

Defining the problem

Developing the program

Determining that no areas are left uncovered

Coding the program

Documenting the project

Debugging (eliminating the program errors)

Once a good flow chart has been developed, the rest of the job is comparatively simple. Developing a good flow chart is not an easy thing to do, especially for a beginner. It is particularly difficult because there is no absolute right way to do it. If two different programmers are given the same job to do, the chances are 100 to 0 that they will not do it in exactly the same manner.

Even flow-charting symbols are not uniform. It is an unfortunate fact that each computer manufacturer provides its customers with flow-charting templates, all of which are different in some respects. The template and symbols selected for use in this book are those of the IBM Company. A picture of the template and the meanings of the various symbols are shown on the following pages.

It is not important that everybody accept these particular symbols as the standard, but it is important that all programmers within a given organization use a standard set of rules and symbols for flow charting. This will improve the readability and interpreting of flow diagrams in the organization.

144

The direction of flow should usually be from left to right or from top to bottom of the page. It is better not to cross over lines, but to use *connectors,* if a return to an earlier part of the chart is desired. Arrows *may* be used to show the direction of flow, but they *must* be used if the flow is in any direction other than from left to right or top to bottom.

The purpose of a flow chart is to show *what* is to be accomplished, not *how* it is to be accomplished. Also, there are many levels of flow charts, from those depicting total systems, through rather general flow charts, to the extremely detailed charts. Each of these types has its own particular use and function. The main point to remember is that any process that can be

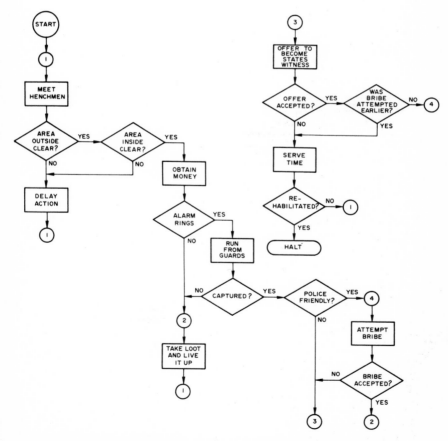

Fig. 8-1. Sample flow chart. (*Courtesy of F. Trignor and H. S. Englander.*)

performed can be flow charted. Although the little sample flow chart in Fig. 8-1 is meant to be humorous, it does show the step-by-step procedure required in developing a flow chart.

FLOW-CHARTING SYMBOLS

A typical flow-charting template (Fig. 8-2) and a description of commonly used symbols are shown on this and the following pages.

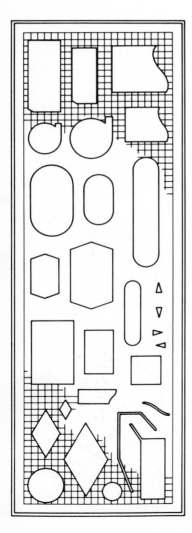

Fig. 8-2. Flow charting template.

FLOW CHART SYMBOLS   DESCRIPTION

Decision block. Use to illustrate a logical choice made while processing a problem. Both forms are acceptable, but not interchangeably. Use one or the other.

Switch and branch. Do not confuse with decision block.

Operation (action statement) other than in auxiliary equipment (generally known as a *processing block*).

Operation in auxiliary equipment.

Manual operation.

Closed subroutine or library subroutine.

Stop, program halt, end-of-job halt. Use the oval for end-of-job and the triangle for temporary halts, or use either one for all halts.

Start. Some installations prefer the triangle for both start and stop symbols.

Connector or step identification (left).
Variable connector (right).

Communication link for any type of data transmission.

Line of flow with arrow to denote direction. Arrowhead is required if flow is not from left to right or top to bottom.

The following symbols are used primarily in *system charts* to denote input, output, and equipment to be used.

FLOW CHART SYMBOLS	DESCRIPTION
	Data card or card file. Symbol may be used to represent I-O (input-output) operation.
	Printed document. Symbol may be used to represent I-O operation.
	Magnetic tape. Symbol may be used to represent I-O operation.
DRUM DISK	Mass storage media such as drum or disk. Symbol may be used to represent mass-storage-media operation.
	Paper tape. Symbol may be used to represent I-O operation.
	Display device. Special I-O device such as plotter, video display, or inquiry unit.

REVIEW QUESTIONS

1. Name three reasons for using flow charts.

2. What is the proper direction of flow?

3. What should be used if a return is to be made to an earlier part of the flow chart?

4. Name three levels of flow charts.

5. Identify the following symbols:

a. ▭   c. (magnetic tape symbol)

b. ◇   d. (rounded rectangle)

EXAMPLE:

Flow-charting problem statement: The annual inventory for a company is punched into cards with the following format:

Card Columns	Description
1–10	Stock number
11–15	Quantity counted
20	Order code

If the quantity counted is 0 or if the order code is X, only the stock number is to be punched on a card. Otherwise, all 20 positions of information are to be punched on a card.

The first step is to read a card into memory.

Next, the quantity area must be examined for zeros, and the order code checked for an X.

At this point, the computer must make a decision:

1. If the quantity is zero, the stock number must be moved to an area away from the rest of the data so that it may be punched out by itself.

2. If the information passes the quantity check, the order code must be examined for X ,and, if X is there, the same action must be taken as in point 1.

3. If there is neither zero nor X, all the data are punched on a card.

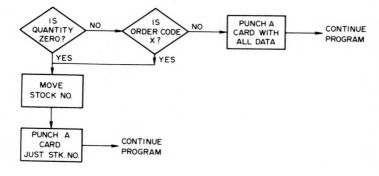

4. Then the next card is read and processed, followed by all other cards. When the last card has been processed, the job is done and the machine is stopped.

A flow chart for this process is shown in Fig. 8-3. It is not really complete and, of course, the problem itself is very insignificant, but it should give the student an idea of how a problem is analyzed and flow charted.

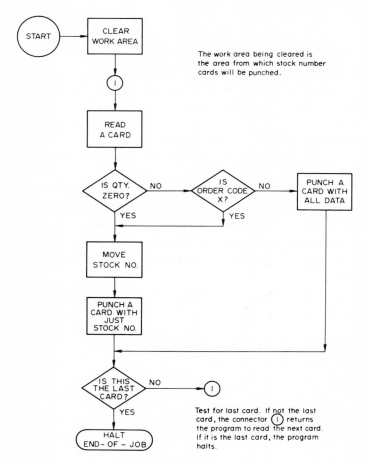

The work area being cleared is
the area from which stock number
cards will be punched.

Test for last card. If not the last
card, the connector ① returns
the program to read the next card.
If it is the last card, the program
halts.

Fig. 8-3. Flow charting example.

GENERAL FLOW-CHARTING INSTRUCTIONS

Flow charting, as shown previously, is an extremely useful programming tool. Besides helping to define the problem and to code and document the program, it is an aid in program modification. It is a means of visualizing the sequence of operations and the relationship of the various program segments, one to another. The following instructions apply to all flow charting:

1. Only symbols that are acceptable at your installation are to be used, but the size of any particular symbol may vary depending on the need.

2. Each page of the flow chart shall show the job title, job number, chart title, page number, programmer's name, and date prepared, in the upper right corner of the page.

3. Use a soft pencil, and make all erasures complete.

4. Direction of flow should be, for the most part, from top to bottom and from left to right. An arrowhead is required if the flow is in any other direction.

5. Do not cross over lines. Use connectors wherever necessary.

6. When writing the operation to be performed within a symbol, print legibly and keep it brief.

7. Each terminal point should be labeled with a meaningful title which should be the same as that used in coding.

8. An off-page connector shall contain the chart identification (ID) and the block to which it goes or from which it is coming.

9. Only one line of flow may enter each block. All other entry lines shall be connected to this line.

10. A margin of 1 inch shall be maintained on the left side and top of each page for binding purposes. One-fourth-inch minimum margins shall be maintained on the other sides.

11. For general flow charts and short jobs, 8½- by 11-inch paper should be used. For large jobs, 18- by 11-inch paper may be used; the page can then be folded in half and bound on the 11-inch side.

REVIEW QUESTION

6. Enumerate the errors in the accompanying sample (partial) flow chart. (How many errors are there, and what are they?)

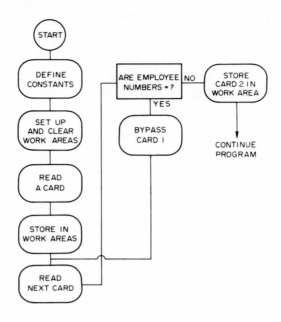

SYSTEM FLOW CHARTS

Flow charts of this type depict the broad picture of what is desired from the program. They show the expected inputs to the system and the desired outputs from the system.

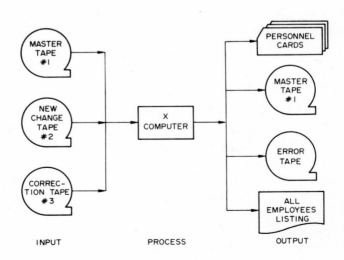

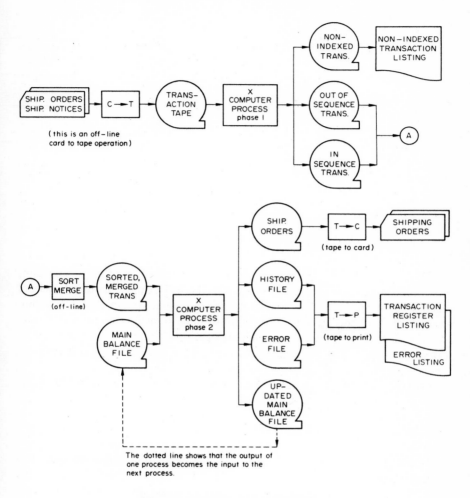

Fig. 8-4. System flow chart example.

The system chart, opposite, shows that input to the system will be three magnetic tapes (1, 2, and 3). The process is not shown in this type of chart, but is merely indicated by a block labeled with the name or number of the computer that is expected to process the job. The output of the process will be a deck of personnel cards, two magnetic tapes, and a printed management report.

General flow chart   Detailed flow chart

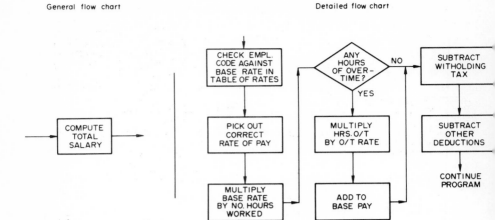

Fig. 8-5. Example of general and detailed flow chart.

The system flow chart is designed to present the flow of data from their source through each processing routine to the ultimate use or disposition of each file and product. It depicts all elements of each system segment: input, output, file sequence, and the treatment of data in each operation. It should clearly portray the desired sequence of operations and the relationships of operations one to the other. The intended use of the output of one or more operations as input to other operations must be recognized.

An example of a fairly large scale system segment is shown in Fig. 8- 4.

GENERAL AND DETAILED FLOW CHARTS

Flow charting may be general or detailed or a combination of both. The larger the problem, the more detailed the flow chart should become. On extremely long and complex problems, flow charting should be done in great detail. A generalized flow chart should be developed first to assure that there are no large *system holes* (errors). The final step, before proceeding to the writing of instructions, is to develop a detailed flow chart from the general chart, showing the *procedure* step by step. This is not to imply that every instruction should have a corollary flow-charting block. It is possible to overdo the detail work.

Developing a detailed flow chart from a general flow chart is almost impossible without having some knowledge of what is to be accomplished by the program. The general chart may contain a block which simply says,

"Compute total salary." This would involve a number of steps which should be shown in the detailed flow chart, and this would be impossible to do without extensive knowledge of what is involved. An example is shown in Fig. 8-5.

Consider the flow chart to be a map. How the map is drawn is not really important as long as it is understandable to anyone who looks at it. This is the only reason that a certain degree of standardization is attempted in the diagrams that constitute a flow chart.

Another purpose of flow charting is to provide the programmer with a means of visualizing the sequence of logical and arithmetic operations and the relationship of one portion of a program to another.

For program modification, flow charting is useful to the programmer, who is usually responsible for any program he writes even after a considerable length of time has elapsed. If changes need to be made at a later date, he can insert them more easily by understanding just where in the program they should go.

The final and perhaps most important purpose of flow charting is to prove the logic of the application. A flaw in logic will show up very quickly in a flow chart, whereas it might be completely overlooked if flow charting were not accomplished.

REVIEW QUESTIONS

7. Problem statement: Input cards contain four *integers* (whole numbers). The first two integers are to be added together. The fourth integer is to be subtracted from the third integer. Output cards are to be produced containing only the sum and difference figures.

Input Card Format

Card Col.	Description
1 – 7	1
11 – 17	2
21 – 27	3
31 – 35	4

Output Card Format

Card col.	Description
1 – 7	Sum of first two integers
11 – 17	Difference between integers 3 and 4

Note: For addition and subtraction, the fields to be worked on must be the same size. Field 4 is smaller than field 3, therefore it will have to be expanded until it is equal in size to field 3.

Remarks

Assume that the sum will be in field 1 and the difference in field 3. It will be necessary to move these to a special output area prior to punching a card because nothing else is needed in the output card. It would be possible to leave field 1 alone, move field 3 to positions 11 through 17, and clear the rest of the data out of the work area, but this would be much more complicated and time consuming.

There will be no decision required in the program except a test for the last card prior to a return to read the next card.

8. Problem statement: This is a *trigger* routine to compare stock levels with the quantity on hand in the levels file. Input will be a levels tape containing blocked records 26 characters long (5 records to a block) in the following format: Assume that one tape will contain all the data to be processed and

LEVELS-IN-TAPE

IDENTIFICATION NO. (10 DIGITS)	LEVEL A (4 DIGITS)	LEVEL B (4 DIGITS)	LEVEL C (4 DIGITS)	QUANTITY ON HAND (4 DIGITS)

that the quantity on hand is current. The tape is labeled Levels-Input.

Fields A, B, and C represent stock levels. They are never equal. Find the field with the largest level, and compare it with the quantity on hand. If the level is equal to, or less than, the quantity on hand, all is well and the record is bypassed. If the level is greater than the quantity on hand, the material must be reordered. A record is written on an Output-Reorder tape (containing blocked records, 5 records to a block, each record containing 81 characters). The output tape will be in the following format:

REORDER-TAPE

IDENTIFICATION NO. (10 DIGITS)	QUANTITY ON HAND (4 DIGITS)	BLANKS (3 DIGITS)	APPLICABLE LEVEL (4 DIGITS)	BLANKS (60 DIGITS)

The job is finished when the end-of-file is reached.

The system chart for this problem would be quite simple, as shown below.

LEVELS-IN TAPE	X COMPUTER	REORDER TAPE
INPUT	PROCESS	OUTPUT

DECISION SYMBOLS AND TECHNIQUES

The decision block is somewhat unique in that a great deal of symbology is associated with it. This is the block that causes the program to make a choice between two or more paths to follow, depending on the condition being tested.

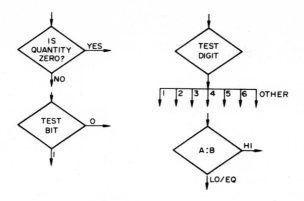

Fig. 8-6. Decision symbols.

A few of the possible conditions and some of the associated symbology are shown in the list below and in Fig. 8-6.

Statement	*Symbol*
Compare A with B (where B is the constant value)	A : B
A is greater than B	A > B
A is less than B	A < B
A is equal to B	A = B
A is not equal to B	A ≠ B
A is less than, or equal to, B (not greater)	A ≤ B
A is greater than, or equal to, B (not less)	A ≥ B
Compare indicator settings	HI LO EQ
Check indicator settings	ON OFF

REVIEW QUESTIONS

9. What is the meaning of the following symbols?
   a. $>$
   b. $:$
   c. $\leq$
   d. $\neq$

10. Draw a three-block flow chart to cover the following tiny problem: Compare quantities A and B. If A is greater, go to subroutine 1. If it is equal to, or less than, B, go to subroutine 2.

11. Now for a more difficult problem—the entire problem can be flow charted with seven blocks, using three decision blocks: Given three fields titled A, B, and C which are of *different* sizes. Determine which field is the largest. When that is determined, the other two fields are added together and the program continues with subroutine 1.

USE OF A COUNTER

All computers contain some form of counter which can be used by the programmer for a variety of tasks. If a counter is to be used in a program, it is usually cleared of any earlier data at the beginning (as part of the program called *housekeeping*) and set to zero if counting upward is desired. It may be set to a predetermined number and programmed to count down until zero is reached, or it may be set to a number which will not vary but which can be programmed to be added to (or subtracted from) other keyed numbers as required by the particular problem.

EXAMPLES:

1. Set to 0; increase by 1 (or any other predetermined number) until a preset point is reached.

2. Set to a predetermined number; decrease by 1 (or any other predetermined number) until zero is reached.

3. Set to a predetermined number; increase or decrease keyed items by that number.

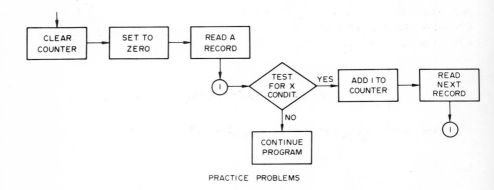

PRACTICE PROBLEMS

REVIEW QUESTIONS

12. Problem statement: We wish to check through a tape file containing both positive and negative numbers so that we can get a total of all the negative numbers (how many there are, not the sum of the numbers). When the last record is completed, we shall add the total obtained and halt.

13. Problem statement: Given variables $a = 3$ and $b = 4$, calculate the value of c if $c = \sqrt{a^2 + b^2}$. A subroutine called *SQRT* is available for determining the square root of a variable x.

Draw a flow chart for solving this problem. Input and output are not to be shown since they are not specified in the problem statement.

14. Problem statement: This problem will contain two input tapes (a backorder tape and a receipt tape). Formats are as follows:

BACKORDER TAPE RECORD   RECEIPT TAPE RECORD

ITEM NO. (10 CHARACTERS)	AMOUNT ON BACKORDER (5 DIGITS)

ITEM NO. (10 CHARACTERS)	AMOUNT OF RECEIPT (5 DIGITS)

Each file is contained on one tape reel, and both tapes are in sequence by item number; but all items on backorder will not be received, and some items will be received that are not on backorder.

Each item from the receipt tape will be written on output processed-receipt tape (format as above). Each item from the backorder tape that is not matched in the receipt tape will be written out on an updated-backorder tape.

As receipts are processed, they are checked against the backorder file. If they match in item number, the amount on backorder must be subtracted from the amount of the receipt and the difference is placed in the processed-receipts file. If they do not match in item number or when the backorder tape is exhausted, the receipt is simply copied on the processed-receipt tape.

If a receipt and backorder match in item number, this means that the material backordered may now be shipped. Therefore, the amount on backorder must be placed on a shipping-order tape from which cards will be produced off line. The format is as follows:

SHIPPING ORDER TAPE RECORD

ITEM NO. (10 CHARACTERS)	BLANKS (65)	SHIPPING ORDER AMOUNT (5 DIGITS)

First, make a system chart of the process, then a detailed flow chart. When tapes are used, a check must be made for end-of-tape. Assume that there is an end-of-tape routine which can be used as needed.

9 ELEMENTARY PROGRAMMING

NECESSARY BASICS

Bits, Words, Characters, and Bytes

To review, the word *bit* is an abbreviation of *bi*nary digi*t*, one of the base-two system components in either the "on" or "off" condition. A specified number of bits comprise a computer word, which is treated by the circuitry as a unit and transferred as such.

To follow bits through to words, two different approaches must be taken, depending on the characteristics of the specific computer under discussion. A computer may accept either *variable*-length words or *fixed*-length words.

Let us first examine the makeup of a word in a computer that accepts *variable*-length words. For this type of computer to have the ability to retrieve data from core storage, each storage position must be classified by the sequential assignment of numbers.

EXAMPLES:

If storage contains 4,096 positions, they are numbered sequentially from 0 through 4,095.

If storage contains 16,000 positions, they are numbered sequentially from 0 through 15,999.

If an item is stored in location 765, the instruction to the computer can simply reference this storage location when the item is required for computation or for any other reason. In other words, the number representing a storage location permits the programmer to *address* any specific *storage location* he chooses.

160

Now, what can be placed in a single storage location? One *character,* alphabetic, numeric, or special, can be contained in one storage location. The character is made up of a number of bits that represent the particular character. The code used to make up the sequence of bits may vary with different machines, but the bits are the ones and the zeros of the binary system. Assuming (for example) that six bits represent one character, the various combinations of these bits in the "on" or "off" condition, tells the computer which character is stored at that position.

EXAMPLE:

We wish to place the number 274 in storage at sequential locations 120 through 122. Assume that each location may be represented as a little box large enough to hold one character, and there are as many boxes as there are storage locations. After the correct instruction has been given to, and executed by, the computer, the result may be represented as follows:

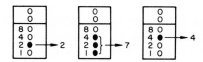

The bit representation within each box could be symbolically shown:

Consider the darkened bits to be "on" and the open ones to be "off"

Therefore, we can say that *bits* make up *characters,* which make up *words* in this type of computer. A computer word may refer to a single character or to a group of characters that represent a unit of information. A word, in a variable-word-length computer is not limited to a specific number of storage locations. It may be as long or as short as actually needed to contain the information in consecutive storage locations.

EXAMPLES:

Show the following words symbolically:
1. *Computer,* in locations 725 through 732   a.

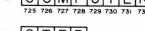

2. *Step,* starting at location 1,260

b.

To summarize, a *variable-word-length* computer contains core storage which may be described by the number of actual storage locations contained in its memory unit. Each such location can contain one character (i.e., a letter, a number, or a symbol), which is made up of six or more bits, and any sequential number of these characters can make up one word.

A word in a *fixed-word-length* machine has a somewhat different makeup. It is still made up of bits, and characters can be represented in the words, but every word is exactly as long as every other word in this type of machine. The size of the word varies with different machines, but the basic principle is the same. A unit of information is represented by a fixed-length word. A word may be 18 bits long, 30 bits, 48 bits, or any other arbitrary number established by the designers.

EXAMPLE:

An 18-bit word in a fixed-word-length machine would look (symbolically) something like this:

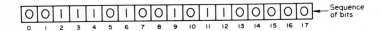

If it takes six bits to represent a digit, three digits would fit into this word.

If it takes 6 bits to make up 1 character, then a 36-bit word would contain 6 characters to a word and a 48-bit word would contain 8 characters to a word.

Because of the differences between fixed-word and variable-word machines, core storage is described differently by the manufacturers. For a variable-word-length machine, they will say that the size of its storage is, e.g., 40,000 *characters*. This means that 40,000 alpha-numeric characters (each made up of 6 bits) can be stored in its memory. For a fixed-word-length machine, they will specify, e.g., 40,000 *words* of storage. This means that, if a word is a fixed 18 bits long, it can store 40,000 times 18 bits in memory, instead of 40,000 times 6 bits as in the variable-word-length example above. Therefore, 40,000-word storage is much larger than 40,000-character storage.

Byte is a term used for an arbitrary number of bits. It is used primarily for data transmission purposes and is essentially part of the internal function of the computer in its interaction with its peripheral (I-O) equipment. For example, data may be transmitted from an input device to computer storage in a specified number of bytes rather than by individual bits, one at a time. This allows larger blocks of information to enter the computer more quickly.

EXAMPLE:

Assume a byte to be 6 bits and the fixed-length word to be 36 bits. The transmission rate from peripheral equipment will be in increments of six bytes per word.

REVIEW QUESTIONS

1. Define the term *word* in both of its contexts as it applies to size.

2. If the size of storage is listed as 36,000, what two meanings may be involved?

3. If the storage of a computer is numbered from 0 through 19,999, what two facts are evident?

4. If the storage of a computer is said to contain 20,000, 36-bit words, what two facts are evident?

5. a. Which storage is larger, the one described in Question 3 or the one described in Question 4?
   b. What is the size differential in bits, assuming six-bit characters?

6. Assuming a variable-word-length machine, show the following words symbolically:
   a. 1264J3, in locations 112 through 117
   b. July, starting in location 118

7. Show the character in location 114 in Question 6 as a symbolic-bit representation of a single character.

Computer Functional Units

There are a number of functional units within the computer which are utilized by the programmer in his work. The most important of these are registers, counters, and adders.

Registers

Registers are devices which are capable of holding information and of shifting or transferring it upon demand by the program. Registers are usually named for the function they perform. For example, a multiplier-quotient register (MQ) would hold either the multiplier or quotient of a problem, an accumulator (AC) would accumulate results, an address register would hold the address of the instruction to be processed, and a storage register would store partial or complete results prior to interacting with core storage.

Registers are usually of fixed size and quantity, often being simply referred to as Register A, B, C, etc. They are used as tools by the programmer in the solution of his problems. Other registers are internal to the operation of the computer and work automatically in the control of the program. An example is shown below.

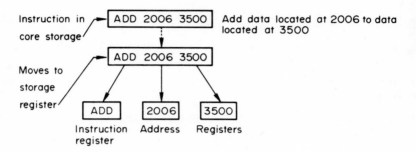

The most important registers are shown on the operator console by small lights which turn on for 1 bits and off for 0 bits, so that the actual binary contents of the registers may be examined at any time by the operator or programmer.

Counters

Counters are closely related to registers. They have the capability of being incremented or decremented by some predetermined number. For example, a counter may be set to zero and keyed to signal a particular operation when it had counted up to 20. Each operation would increase the counter by 1 (or any other predetermined number) until the desired number (20, in this case) is reached.

Adders

The adder receives data from two or more registers, performs the required addition, and transfers the result to a receiving register. The adders are usually not subject to programmer manipulation.

Computer Instructions

Computer instructions are the building blocks of a computer program. They fall into the following three broad classifications:

1. *Transfer* of information from one storage location or medium to another

2. *Arithmetic* manipulation

3. *Decisions* on which path to follow, based upon comparisons, magnitude of numbers, specific keys, etc.

To develop a computer program, the three types of operations listed above are combined in various ways to solve a particular problem. *Coding* is the term used for translating the program into the instructions of a specific computer. It is rather unfortunate that nearly every computer has its own language which is different from the language of every other computer. Except for a saving feature (which we shall discuss a little later under "Symbolic Programming"), each time a programmer changes from one computer to another, he must learn a new programming language.

REVIEW QUESTIONS

8. Name four types of registers, and indicate next to each one whether it can be programmer manipulated.

9. Name the three broad classifications of instructions.

10. What is the function of a counter?

11. Define the term *coding*.

Execution Sequence

Instructions are carried out by the computer in the sequence of core-storage addresses in which they are located. The control unit has an instruction counter which keeps track of the location of the instruction being executed and the one that will follow. If an instruction specifically calls for a change in the sequence, this change will be followed, either to jump ahead or to jump back to a previous part of the program. Otherwise the instructions will be executed one after the other until the end of the program is reached.

Looping Sequence

Instructions that cause automatic repetition are called *looping* instructions. All computer programs contain some variety of this technique. If a program were to be written that would only be used once and contained no loops, it would be more economical to solve the problem on a desk calculator. There are various methods of looping, but to demonstrate its application, one method will be shown.

The loop consists of three definite features: the entry into the loop, the process through the operation to be performed, and the exit from the loop.

The basic method of looping is simply a return to an earlier part of the program. A special instruction is used that tests for a certain condition, then causes the program either to continue sequentially or to jump to a designated program step.

For example, a card is processed through the computer, and, when the processing is done, it must be determined whether this is the last card to be processed or there are other cards to process.

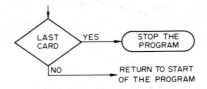

The actual test itself can be very simple. For example, all cards may have a digit 5 punched in column 1, except the last card which will be punched with the letter A. When the test is made for the last card, the computer searches for the digit 5 in column 1. If it is there, the program returns to the beginning to process the next card. If it is not there, the program halts.

More complicated looping techniques use index registers to modify the addresses of the entry and exit instructions for the looping sequence. In this way, the program can go through the desired sequence, do other jobs, then, when needed again, the modified entry instruction routes the program through the desired loop.

MACHINE-LANGUAGE PROGRAMMING

Let us understand at the beginning that machine-language programming is rarely (if ever) used. Today, symbolic (English-like or mathematically oriented) languages are used to streamline and simplify the programming effort. On the other hand, it is imperative for the understanding of programming concepts to delve briefly into the mechanics of machine-language programming. No matter what substitute is used, the computer still works in binary and in machine language.

For this demonstration, we shall assume that the actual data are already stored in memory. We have to write a program to solve the following problem:

$$X = (a \times b) + (c \times d)$$

The flow chart for a single operation (not including the loop to return and do it over) would be

The format of the machine instructions for our example will be 10 digits, 2 for the operation code and 4 each for the memory locations (called addresses) of two sets of data.

We shall need several instructions, and they are as follows:

Operation Code	Meaning of the Instruction
16	Transfer from storage to AC (accumulator), and multiply.
17	Transfer from storage to AC, and add.
18	Transfer from AC to storage.
	(All arithmetic operations occur in the AC)
19	Transfer from storage, and print.
20	Stop the program.

We know that: a is at storage location 2001

b is at storage location 2002

c is at storage location 2003

d is at storage location 2004

accumulator is in location 9999

One final decision will be made: The program we shall write will go into storage starting with location 4001. Now we can write the program.

Storage Loc. of Instruc.	Op. Code	A Address	B Address	Remarks
4,001	16	2,001	2,002	Move data in a and b into AC and multiply.
4,002	18	9,999	2,005	Move contents of AC (result of $a \times b$) into an empty storage location.
4,003	16	2,003	2,004	Multiply $c \times d$.
4,004	18	9,999	2,006	Move result of $c \times d$ into storage.
4,005	17	2,005	2,006	Add the products.
4,006	18	9,999	2,007	Move final result back into storage.
4,007	19	2,007	0000	Transfer from storage and print.
4,008	20	0000	0000	Halt, end of job.

REVIEW QUESTION

12. Given $X = (a + b + c) \times d$, with the addition of two more instructions, we can program the above problem, this time including a method of input and the loop to continue the program until the job is completed. Assume that a, b, c, and d are in the same locations as before. Start the program in location 5,001.

Additional instructions:

Op. Code	*Meaning of the Instruction*
14	Read the contents of a card into storage. (Only the A address will be needed to indicate where the data will go. The B address will be all zeros.)
15	Test and transfer to address in A field. (B address will be zeros.) If the test is satisfied, the next instruction will be taken from the A address. If it is not satisfied, the next sequential instruction will be taken.

Note: The last card will be specially keyed. This instruction checks each card as it is processed and determines when the last card has been reached. Since the last card is different from the others, it will not pass the test.

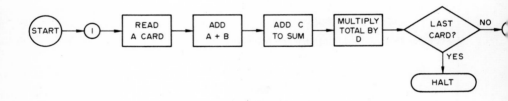

SYMBOLIC PROGRAMMING

Assembly-Language Programs

In the section on machine-language programming, we have shown that the computer follows a set of numeric operation codes; other numerics are used to express memory addresses; still other codes denote plus or minus signs. Such codes are hard to remember and often lead to mistakes. Therefore, a system of symbolic coding was developed which permits the programmer to write his program with symbolic abbreviations in place of codes. The symbolic abbreviations, called *mnemonics,* are then converted to machine operation codes by a special program.

Although the process takes more time, the mnemonics are easier to work with than machine operation codes. Also, it no longer becomes necessary to keep track of actual storage addresses. Labels, made up by the programmer, can be substituted for addresses and actual storage addresses will be automatically assigned by the special program mentioned above.

This special program converts the program (written in symbolic form) to machine language. It is called an *assembly program*. The program originally written by the programmer is called the *source program* and the resultant machine-language program is called the *object program*.

The process may be shown symbolically as in Fig. 9-1.

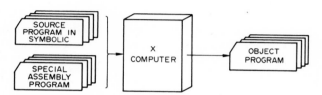

Fig. 9-1. Source program to object program.

The *object program* is the program containing actual machine-language instructions required to do the task of processing data.

Programs written in assembly languages are easier to write and are less prone to clerical errors. They are also much easier to learn. For example, a computer may have from fifty to several hundred instructions, and it is obviously much easier to remember an instruction called ADD than the digits 17, which the computer recognizes as the "add" instruction.

Assembly-language programs are written on the basis of a one-for-one conversion from machine-language instructions. The convenience of writing something a little more understandable than a long series of numbers is the greatest asset of these languages.

As an example of assembly-language programming, let us take Question 12 on page 168 and rewrite it in symbolic form, using mnemonic operation codes and labels for addresses.

When writing a program in "symbolic," every symbol used must be defined by the programmer. The symbol itself may be anything the programmer desires (within certain size limitations prescribed by each language).

EXAMPLE:

The program for Question 12 written in symbolic code would be:

Loc.	Op.	Address	Remarks
START	RD		Read a card into storage.
	CLA	A	Clear out AC and move in A.
	ADD	B	Add B to A.
	ADD	C	Add C to sum of A + B.
	MULT	D	Multiply final sum by D.
	TRNS	START	Test and transfer back to START if not the last card.
END	HLT	END	Halt, end of job. (Placing the same symbol (END) in both location and address permanently halts the program.)
A	ALLOC	1	Allocates one word of storage to A.
B	ALLOC	1	Allocates one word of storage to B.
C	ALLOC	1	Allocates one word of storage to C.
D	ALLOC	1	Allocates one word of storage to D.

Note that the mnemonics used for operation codes are practically self explanatory. A, B, C, and D are defined as one computer word each and the assembly program decides on the memory location assignment. Any time they are needed in the program, they are simply used in the address field, but they *must* be defined either at the beginning or at the end of the program so that the assembler will know what to do with them. Any symbol found in the address field must also be found in the location field.

Assembly languages, although better than machine-language programming (coding), are not as practical as the higher-level languages which will be discussed on the following pages.

EXAMPLE:

Problem statement: Store in symbolic location X, the sum of the contents of locations A and B. If the sum is zero, do not store the sum into X. Instead, store the contents of symbolic location HOLD in X.

Three new instructions are needed:

TRA - Unconditional transfer from accumulator to storage

TZE - Transfer on zero (if not zero, take next sequential instruction)

STO - Store in specified memory location

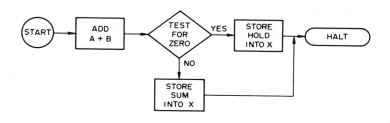

Loc.	Op.	Address	Remarks
	CLA	A	Move A into accumulator.
	ADD	B	Add B to A.
	TZE	JUMP	If sum is zero, go to JUMP for next instruction.
STORE	STO	X	If not zero, store sum in X.
END	HLT	END	Halt, end of job.
JUMP	CLA	HOLD	Move HOLD into accumulator.
	TRA	STORE	Transfer back to STORE, which will now move HOLD (which is in the AC) into X.
A	ALLOC	1	⎫
B	ALLOC	1	⎬ Assign storage locations to A, B, and HOLD.
HOLD	ALLOC	1	⎭

REVIEW QUESTION

13. Problem statement: Input cards contain four integers (whole numbers). The first two integers are to be added together. The fourth integer is to be subtracted from the third integer. Store the sum in symbolic location HOLD, and print the difference.

First, make a flow chart of the problem, then write the program in symbolic, using the instructions already given. The operation code for subtract is SUB, and for print, PRT.

Compiler-Language Programs

We have discussed machine-language programming and assembly-language programming. Now we shall consider languages which are generally referred to as *higher-level* languages because they are more English-like or mathematically oriented than either of the two previously described systems.

The program that changes the higher-level language into machine language is called a *compiler*. A single statement in such a language may cause the *compilation* of a whole subroutine of instructions, and this is where it differs from assembly languages, in which one symbolic instruction caused the generation of one machine-language instruction.

The most popular scientific language is called FORTRAN (*FOR*mula *TRAN*slation) and the most popular business language is COBOL (*CO*mmon *Business Oriented Language*). There are quite a number of other higher-level languages, some of which are in fairly common use (ALGOL, NELIAC, JOVIAL, and SIMSCRIPT to name just a few), but FORTRAN and COBOL are by far the most commonly used. Another new language that is moving into some prominence is PL1 (*Programming Language 1*) developed by the IBM Corporation. It is of special interest because it attempts to override the differences between scientific and business languages, and it can be used for both types of programming.

Each computer has its own unique machine language. By this we mean *type* of computer, not each individual computer. Therefore, for a higher-level language to be operable on any particular type of computer, a compiler must be written for it.

Let us examine what this means a little more closely. If an installation has an IBM 1620 computer and the programmers wished to write FORTRAN programs to be run on this computer, it would be necessary to obtain a FORTRAN compiler for the IBM 1620 computer. If another installation had a UNIVAC 1107 computer and they wanted to write FORTRAN programs, a FORTRAN compiler would be required for the UNIVAC 1107. This is because the machine language of the 1107 is entirely different from the machine language of the 1620. Each compiler must translate the original FORTRAN program (source program) into the language of the computer which will run the translated (object) program.

Although each different type of computer must have its own compiler, the source program written in FORTRAN (or one of the other higher-level languages) does not have to be rewritten to run on different computers. Usually only minor modifications are required plus a recompilation of the source program to the object language of the other computer.

This has a very important advantage. It takes a great deal of programming effort to produce operational runs that accomplish the data-processing requirements of an installation. If the programs are written in a higher-level language and the computer equipment is changed, the programs are still useful on the new equipment after recompilation. Otherwise years of effort and many thousands of dollars would be wasted, and all new programs would have to be written for the new equipment.

Special programs, such as compilers, are generally termed *software,* as opposed to *hardware,* which refers to actual computer equipment. In the past few years, software has become almost more important than hardware, and manufacturers vie with each other to produce more and more sophisticated software packages to help sell their hardware.

REVIEW QUESTIONS

14. What are the three features of a loop?

15. Explain the terms:
   a. Source program
   b. Object program

16. What is the function of an assembler?

17. What are the two most commonly used higher-level languages?

18. What is the function of a compiler?

The COBOL Language

The programs developed on the previous pages consisted of instructions that were made up for demonstration purposes but were similar to real machine-language and assembly-language instructions. The material to be covered in this and the following section is actually the way the languages are used.

COBOL programs are written in four separate and distinct parts, called *divisions*.

1. *Identification Division*. This division is used to identify the name of the programmer, title of the program, current date, and any pertinent information about the process. It has a very specific format but is quite simple and needs no further explanation.

2. *Environment Division*. Since COBOL is written in the same manner for any computer, basic information about the machine configuration is described here. Each computer that has a COBOL compiler comes equipped with a special publication which spells out how the equipment is to be referenced in the program. This is also quite straightforward and needs no further amplification.

3. *Data Division*. Each kind of data used in the program is described in this division. All of the input and output files used in the program must also be defined in this division. The division is separated into two parts, WORKING STORAGE and CONSTANT sections. This is usually the first division to be written in the program, and there are quite a number of special rules that must be followed. Although it is fairly detailed, it is not too difficult to assimilate the rules necessary to write the data division of a program.

4. Procedure Division. This division is the heart of the system. It describes the operations to be performed, and it is not oriented to any machine. It details what the program is expected to accomplish.

Usually, a special program writing form is used. It is divided into 80 little blocks so that a keypunch operator can easily punch up cards from the work sheets used by the programmer. Figure 9-2 is a sample COBOL work sheet. Note the 80 columns of information which corresponds to the 80 columns of a card.

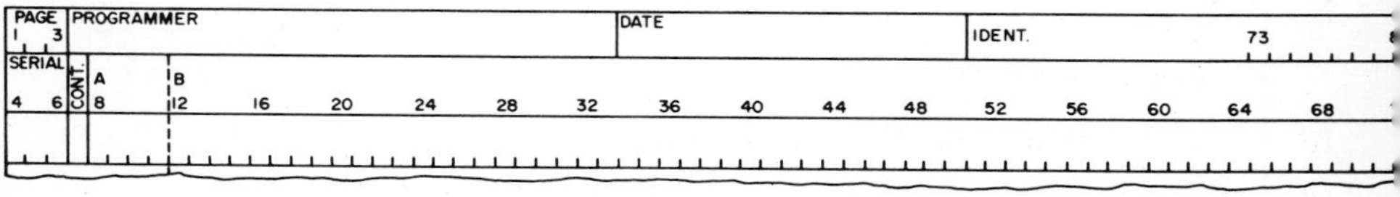

Fig. 9-2. COBOL worksheet.

The programmer always prints (in capital letters) on the form to make it easier to read and because it is practically impossible to write one character to a block in long hand.

Certain letters of the alphabet resemble numerics very closely. It is essential that the keypunch operator know, without doubt, exactly what the programmer desires. For this reason, a standardized method of printing has been adopted by most programmers. The letters I, O, S, and Z resemble very closely the numbers 1, 0, 5, and 2. Also, U and V are sometimes hard to tell apart. Therefore, the following method of printing these letters is suggested:

I   O   S   Ƶ   U   Ʋ

To identify the numeric zero from the letter O, some installations insist on a slash through the zero (∅), others prefer the slash through the letter (∅).

Punctuation is extremely vital in COBOL. The omission of a period could cause the program not to run. Also, when names are used in several places in the program, the spelling must be very carefully observed since once a name is defined in the data division, no variation is permitted.

To demonstrate a COBOL program, the following flow chart will be used. Only the procedure division will be shown. Notice how easy it is to read the program. With a little more careful examination, the program segments can be related to the individual blocks of the flow chart.

4	6	7	8 A	B	REMARKS
0 1 0			PROCEDURE DIVISION.	
0 2 0			START. OPEN INPUT MAIN-INV-BAL-FILE	To open all input
0 3 0			TRANSAC-FILE BACK-ORD-FILE OUTPUT	and output files.
0 4 0			UP-INV-BAL-FILE UP-BACK-ORD-FILE	
0 5 0			SHIP-ORD-FILE.	Block 1
0 6 0			PROCESS. READ TRANSAC RECORD AT END GO	
0 7 0			TO END-OF-JOB.	Block 2
0 8 0			READ-BACK-ORD. READ B-O RECORD AT END	Block 3
0 9 0			GO TO END-OF-JOB.	Block 4
1 0 0			COMPARE. IF STK-NO OF TRANSAC IS EQUAL TO	
1 1 0			STK-NO OF B-O NEXT SENTENCE ELSE	Block 5 (= leg)
1 2 0			GO TO NOT-EQUAL.	
1 3 0			IF QUANTITY OF B-O IS LESS THAN QUANTITY	Block 6 (no leg)
1 4 0			OF TRANSAC NEXT SENTENCE ELSE	
1 5 0			GO TO PROCESS.	Block 6 (yes leg)
1 6 0			MOVE CORRESPONDING TRANSAC TO SHIP-ORD.	Block 7
1 7 0			SUBTRACT QUANTITY IN SHIP-ORD FROM	Block 8
1 8 0			QUANTITY IN B-O THEN GO TO PROCESS.	
1 9 0			NOT-EQUAL. IF STK-NO OF TRANSAC IS LESS THAN	
2 0 0			STK-NO OF B-O NEXT SENTENCE ELSE GO	Block 5 (> leg)
2 1 0			TO READ-BACK-ORD.	
2 2 0			READ TRANSAC-FILE THEN GO TO COMPARE.	Block 5 (< leg)
2 3 0			END-OF-JOB. CLOSE MAIN-INV-BAL-FILE TRAN	
2 4 0			SAC-FILE BACK-ORD-FILE UP-INV-BAL-FILE	Blocks 10 and 11
2 5 0			UP-BACK-ORD-FILE SHIP-ORD-FILE. STOP	
2 6 0			'END OF JOB'. STOP RUN.	

This program is courtesy of J. A. Saxon, *COBOL: A Self-Instructional Manual*, Prentice-Hall, Inc., Englewood Cliffs, N.J., 1963.

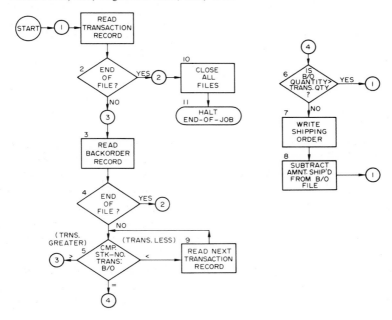

The sentences in the COMPARE and NOT-EQUAL paragraphs were separated to simplify the association of sentences with flow-chart blocks. Normally, no large blank spaces would be left.

The literal END OF JOB on line 260 will print the words END OF JOB on the display unit.

The FORTRAN Language

FORTRAN programming is used for the solution of scientific and mathematical problems. This language attempts to stay with normal mathematical notation as much as possible, but certain special rules must be observed.

For example, in normal algebraic notation AB means A times B (the times sign is implied). In FORTRAN, all arithmetic symbols (called *operators*) must be specifically shown.

Add	+
Subtract	−
Multiply	*
Divide	/
Exponent	**

A times B would have to be written A * B.

Another important point is the order of execution. If you were to write A + B * C / D, you might mean Add A + B, multiply the sum by C, and divide the product by D. But the computer works on a specific order of preference, and all formulas must be written with this order in mind.

1. Expressions enclosed in parentheses
2. Exponentiation
3. Multiply and divide
4. Add and subtract

All other things being equal, execution will be from left to right. To get the desired result for the formula above, it would have been written

$$(A + B) * C / D.$$

FORTRAN has the ability to operate in either fixed-point or floating-point mode. Floating point is advantageous because the computer automatically places the decimal point. If there is a decimal point in your number, it is considered by the compiler to be a floating point; and, if there is no decimal point, it is a fixed-point number.

As in COBOL, or any other language, there are a number of rules that must be learned. There is no shortcut method that can be used. You must know the rules to use the language. For example, the equal sign has a special meaning in FORTRAN:

$$A = B + C$$

Replace the contents of *operand* A with the result of the calculation B + C. Equal, then means *is replaced by* rather than *is equivalent to*.

The constants and variables used in a FORTRAN program are called *operands*. They are separated by the *operators* (+, −, *, etc.) mentioned above.

Even as in COBOL, the writing of FORTRAN programs is accomplished on a special work sheet divided into 80 sections. This is used for ease in keypunching the FORTRAN programs. Figure 9-3 shows a sample of such a worksheet.

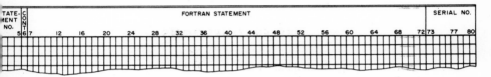

Fig. 9-3. FORTRAN worksheet.

A brief FORTRAN program will be demonstrated based on the following formula:

$$X = A + (B * C) ** D / (E + 16.0)$$

Assume that the data are on cards and the program will halt when the last card has been processed; also, that there is a special punch on the last card to identify it from the other cards. The figure below shows the flow chart, and the program solution.

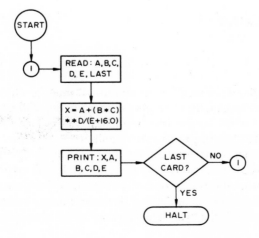

Program Solve	*Remarks*
10 READ 20, A, B, C, D, E, LAST	Read cards with format at 20.
20 FORMAT (5 F 10.2, I 10)	Five fields, flt.pt, 10 place fields, two places to right of decimal; one field integer 10 places.
X = A + (B * C) ** D / (E + 16. 0)	Formula.
PRINT 30, X, A, B, C, D, E	Print, format at 30.
30 FORMAT (6 F 10.2)	Output format, 6 fields, flt.pt., 10 place fields, 2 decimal places.
IF (LAST) 40, 10, 40	Test for last card.
40 CONTINUE	Continue to end if last card.
END	

REVIEW QUESTIONS

19. a. How many divisions are there in COBOL?
   b. Name the two most important divisions.

20. Print the six letters of the alphabet that require special handling.

21. What is an operator?

22. Show the FORTRAN symbols for five different operators, and name each one.

23. What is the meaning of the equal sign in FORTRAN?

24. What is an operand?

25. List the order of execution of FORTRAN formulas.

SYSTEM CHECKING

Desk Checking

Before a program is ready for general use, it must be checked and tested to be sure that it does exactly what it is supposed to do. There are two types of errors that occur with the greatest frequency, errors in coding (the actual instructions written by the programmer) and errors in logic.

When the program is written, the first step is to go over the entire sequence of instructions at your desk to look for clerical errors and to check the logic of the program. It is important to note that there are no open-ended legs of the program. For example, at a decision block, where there is a two-way branch, have both the "yes" and the "no" sides been completely coded?

When you are certain that the coding is accurate, the work sheets are turned over to the keypunching section to produce a deck of cards and a listing (print-out). The print-out must then be checked against the original work sheets to make sure that no keypunch errors have crept into the program. In spite of the fact that keypunching is verified, there is still the possibility of error. If the original coding has been accomplished in a symbolic or higher-level language, the chance of clerical errors is somewhat diminished, but is still ever present.

Now the source-program card deck is ready for compilation (assuming that a higher-level language has been used). The source program is submitted to the machine operations staff for compilation. If any of the rules of the language have been violated, the compilation will not be successful, but a diagnostic print-out will be returned to the programmer along with his source program card deck. After making the designated corrections, it can be resubmitted for compilation and, if successful, the programmer will have the object program in hand, ready to run live data.

The trouble is that even if the program compiles, there may still be undetected errors in it. Logic errors may not have been noticed or legal instructions may have been used out of context. For example, a programmer may intend to write TRO (transfer on overflow) and inadvertently write TRZ (transfer on zero). Since both instructions are acceptable to the compiler, it will not detect an error, but when the program begins to operate, it will certainly generate unwanted material, called garbage in computer jargon.

Therefore, after all possible desk checking has been accomplished, it is necessary to develop test data to give the program a final checkout before it can be placed into operational status.

Test Data Development

The purpose of developing test data is to check out every facet of the program before it is used on live data. Data must be generated that simulates the type of data to be processed when the program is operational, and it is important to develop enough different types of data to test out every leg of the program.

For example, if the program makes a check for plus or minus, plus data must be generated to test the plus leg and minus data must be generated to test the minus leg of the program. If the computer reads input data correctly, performs the required processing and calculations correctly, and produces correct results, it can be assumed to be correct and ready for operational use.

When the test data have been developed and punched into cards, the program is *loaded* (read into the memory) into the computer, followed by input of the test deck. If it runs well, then the printed results of the test run are compared with the hand calculated results of the test data to assure the accuracy of the processing.

Even after all of these tests and checks have been accomplished, it is still more than possible that other "bugs" will show up under operational conditions. All of this program cleanup is called *debugging* (getting rid of the "bugs") and is absolutely necessary as part of the programming process.

Use of Subroutines

One method of simplifying the debugging process is to write the program as a series of subroutines. If this is done, then each subroutine can be checked out and cleaned up individually, and it is much easier to spot errors in a short routine than in a very long and complex program.

Restart Procedure

If the program runs on the computer for any considerable period of time, it is wise to program restart capability. For example, assume that it takes an hour to run a particular program. If there is no restart capability and an error-halt occurs after 45 minutes of the program has been executed, the entire time has been lost and the program must be run over after it has been corrected. There are some applications where this technique is not feasible, but it should used wherever it is possible to do so.

One method of programming restart capability is to cause the data being developed by the program to be dumped onto tape at specified intervals. Then, if an error occurs, the program can be restarted from the last of these dump points.

10 COMPUTER APPLICATIONS

GENERAL

The computer is causing one of the greatest changes in the history of man. Every facet of life and every person in the civilized world is touched by it one way or another. Our electric bills and paychecks (to name but two) are direct outputs of computer processes. Our space program would come to a complete halt without the services of computers, and it is obvious to most people that society is undergoing far-reaching changes as a result of this new technology.

The list of computer applications is endless, and the efforts of thousands of brilliant men and women are concentrated on further developments in all phases of data processing from equipment design to student instruction. A few applications that may be of interest will be discussed in this chapter.

EQUIPMENT DEVELOPMENT

Improvements in computer equipment have been phenomenal in the past 20 years. The Mark I, developed in 1944 by Dr. Howard Aiken of Harvard University, operated at a rate set by a shaft which turned at 200 revolutions per minute. Vacuum-tube equipment was capable of performing operations at the rate of 40,000 per minute. Vacuum-tube computers were known as the first generation computers and really had their beginnings in 1954 with the introduction of the first UNIVAC.

The advent of transistorized computers (second generation, starting in 1958) increased processing speeds to microseconds (millionth of a second), and the present-day solid-state, printed-circuit computers (third generation, starting approximately in 1963) are operating in nanoseconds (billionth of a second).

At the same time that computer speeds have been increasing, developments in storage devices and I-O devices have been attempting to keep pace. Larger and less expensive memories have been developed. Mass storage media, such as disks and drums, have been perfected, and mass production methods have brought down the prices of both computers and peripheral equipment. The speed and reliability of I-O equipment have been increased in an attempt to keep pace with the speed of the computers. Input and output will always be slower than computer processing, and for this reason much of the on-line input and output is carried on with magnetic tape and with various buffering techniques and devices.

MULTIPROCESSING AND TIME SHARING

One of the newer innovations of computer usage is in the area of multiprocessing and time sharing. The myriad possibilities of these systems have not yet been explored too deeply because of the newness of the systems, but more and more computer users are leaning in this direction because of the many advantages it offers.

Some of the features of these systems are:

1. Many users share the computer (or computers) according to a built-in scheduling algorithm which includes priority processing.

2. Input and output requests from a job being executed produces transfer of execution control to another job that does not demand the use of I-O devices and that is next in priority sequence.

3. Once a job has been interrupted, resumption of execution depends on the allotted time slice, the priority of incoming jobs, and the nature of the interrupt.

4. Time sharing with this type of system includes the use of remote consoles. It permits direct man-machine interaction in the solving of problems.

The really wonderful feature of such a system is that 1 to 300 people can be interacting with the machine, and each one has the feeling that he alone is using the computer. At the same time, the system is multiprocessing batch jobs such as payroll or inventory-control processes. The systems are complex and in the early stages of development, but they do work and work well. A highly complex monitor-executive program, stored in memory, schedules all jobs, performs all input and output scheduling, manages the priority features, and provides job protection and data protection at the same time that it allows the use of common data among programs. It interrupts and restores jobs, logs real-time data, performs job accounting, and employs security measures where required.

A few additional duties of the monitor-executive program are to provide linkage between programs, to control all processors and peripheral equipment in the system, and to detect and diagnose computer errors.

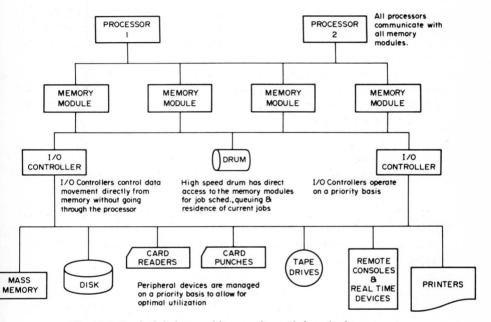

Fig. 10-1. Logical design; multi-processing and time-sharing system.

The diagram in Fig. 10-1 may give a more graphic picture of how a large-scale multiprocessing and time-sharing system operates. It should be obvious that the heart of the system is the monitor-executive program, without which the system could not operate.

REAL-TIME PROCESSING

Real-time processing refers to the immediate interaction of man and machine or of machine and machine (such as radar or telemetry equipment interacting directly with a computer). The man-machine aspects were touched upon very lightly in the previous discussion of time sharing.

The following is a rather generalized definition of real-time processing, but it may help to clarify this somewhat ambiguous terminology:

> Real-time processing is the processing of information in a sufficiently rapid manner so that the results are available in time to influence the process being monitored or controlled.[1]

New multiprocessing computers, connected to hardware explicitly designed for time sharing, make it feasible for many different users to share the same computer. The user can be in either the scientific or business field and may be close to, or a great distance from, the location of the computer. Response to users is immediate, with a maximum waiting period of about one or two minutes.

A very important aspect of real-time processing is the terminal equipment to be used. The system requirements will be as restrictive as the available terminal equipment. The following are among the most commonly used terminal equipment:

Teletypewriter	CRT video display
Paper tape	Remote printer
Punched card	Special-purpose equipment (plotters, microfilm, etc.)

Real-time systems have definite advantages over the older, more conventional methods of processing data. Such a system is equipped to accept inputs from remote devices and to respond in either a static or dynamic fashion.

It (the system) can accept inquiries, examine the stored files and respond directly to the inquirer. It can provide the facility of making scheduled search of the files and report critical conditions even without being keyed by a request. This would result in printed messages, orders, or messages of advice. It can accept and verify orders received from remote points, update inventories, verify stock and carry on a variety of basic clerical functions. It has the ability to conduct message switching services; to accept messages, store them and forward to the recipient as required.

At this point in time, there are not too many real-time systems in operation. Many are in the process of development, and others are in the planning stage. One outstanding operational system is American Airlines' ticket and scheduling system called SABRE. Another large-scale time-

---

[1]Glossary, Automatic Data Processing, *Bureau of the Budget,* Washington, D.C., 1962.

sharing system is the Massachusetts Institute of Technology's project MAC (Machine Aided Cognition) which solves problems on an experimental basis for approximately 400 users scattered across the nation and tied to the computer by teletype hookup.

In a real-time data-processing atmosphere, where many people have the opportunity of interacting directly with the computer, it becomes necessary to simplify the language used as the interacting agent. Special languages are being developed so that nonprogramming personnel can "talk" to the computer in what is sometimes called a "conversational mode." Some of the presently existing programming languages (FORTRAN, for example) are being modified to provide the capability of accepting conversational-mode input.

Also, more and more problem-oriented languages (POL) are being developed for special-purpose applications. A language is problem oriented if it relieves the programmer from the necessity of specifying all the details which the associated processor can automatically provide. Some of the features of such a language are:

The source program is meaningful to the user.

The POL contains provisions for exercising judgment.

Output provides meaningful responses based on previous decisions.

No constraints are placed on input format, problem size, or complexity.

It permits ease of change or modification.

It provides for ease of expansion of vocabulary and scope.

POL makes the role of the scientist more challenging and creative. Rather than being burdened with lengthy calculations and routine decisions, he can concentrate on the problem with all the facilities of the computer as his technical assistant, providing him with relevant procedures and data.

The remote station will be the tool of the real-time application user. He need never see a computer or understand the operations involved. He will have to learn to use the remote station, the associated keys and buttons, and what he can and cannot do or expect the computer to do for him.

The following are a few of the activities that a remote station provides the user:

Provides conversational mode of communication to compilers, the operating system, one's own program in memory, the library, and other user programs.

Allows modification of programs and data easily and quickly.

Allows monitoring of problems during execution.

Provides interaction of CRT and light pen for system design (e.g., circuit design, structural design, logical networks, etc.)

Displays information by CRT, hard copy, or film.

BUSINESS APPLICATIONS

A few applications, selected at random, will be given to demonstrate the scope of the computer in industry. It would not be possible to attempt to mention all types of applications since they now cover the entire spectrum of human endeavor.

Government

In the business area, the government is the largest user of computers. The complexity of military weapons systems has increased the need for electronic (and other) components from a few hundred per system to hundreds of thousands per system. This poses a challenge in logistics to store, supply, and maintain parts to preserve operational capability and availability. Without computerized inventory control and file maintenance systems, this just could not be accomplished.

Many other routine clerical functions have also been absorbed by computers, both in industry and in the government services. Such activities as payroll, personnel services, and supply have been greatly expanded and speeded up through computerized systems. In 1966, for the first time, all business income tax returns and a third of the individual tax returns are being checked by government computers.

Power and Light

Electric power and light companies have been able to give better and faster service to their customers and at the same time lower the cost of operation, which has been passed on to the customer in lowered rates. All of this was possible at the same time that the rising demand of a growing population has increased the kilowatt output requirements of the companies. This could not have been accomplished without the use of computers and automation.

Transportation

During the past 10 years there has been an increase of nearly 50 per cent in the people who drive and own automobiles. Freeways designed to handle large volumes of traffic are subjected to many times the traffic expected, immediately upon completion. Large-city traffic problems are out of hand, and the only feasible solution is computerized traffic control systems. Toronto, Ontario, already has such a traffic control system in operation, and other large cities are following the trend.

The trucking business has also benefitted from the use of computers.

Constant and immediate knowledge of the whereabouts of trucks and shipments and computerized cost analyses are of great help in this highly competitive business. In addition, such things as maintenance history and a complete check of all vehicle parts and garage parts help in keeping the trucks rolling.

Air traffic is becoming nearly as jammed as ground traffic. Without computerized control, traffic in the air will get as badly snarled as it presently is on the ground. Proper use of computers can eventually alleviate these traffic problems, both on the ground and in the air.

Our railroad system presently utilizes over 100 computers to do the routine record keeping, to instantly locate cars (which used to take a half day's work) and to perform many other tasks such as traffic statistics and control of bills of lading.

Warehousing and Inventory Control

Nearly every manufacturer must maintain a supply of raw material from which his product is made, and he must store the finished product until it is sold and shipped. This implies large warehousing and inventory control problems.

Mechanization of the warehousing operation has been supplemented by computerized control, accounting, and management of the inventory. Stock levels are automatically checked, and reorders are generated just as automatically. The entire management of stock and the flow of materials is controlled, and management decisions can be made based upon up-to-the-minute facts instead of intuition or guesswork.

The extent of automation in warehousing is somewhat varied, ranging from no automation to fully automated businesses. A prime example of the fully automated production and warehousing approach is the factory of Sara Lee, bakers of cakes which are available on the freezer shelves of nearly every grocery store in the country. This factory is so fully computerized that the mixing of all ingredients, blending according to recipes, time cycles, oven temperatures, and all other baking processes are computer controlled. The finished products are automatically moved from the ovens to the warehouse, and the computer maintains full control of each pallet load of cakes until the final loading and preparation for shipping has been accomplished. This is done to be sure that the first processed is the first shipped. The bookkeeping and billing operation is also computerized, of course.

Graphics

Graphic design and plotting equipment connected to computers is one of the newer outgrowths of the data-processing explosion. Some of the areas in which plotters are used are in the preparation of maps, analysis of brain patterns, studies of traffic, and satellite flight tracking.

One of the most fascinating aspects of this new computerized tool is the ability it gives the architect, civil engineer, or electronic design engineer to interact directly with the computer in the basic design work. For example, an electronic circuit can be drawn directly on the grid of a CRT with a light pen. The circuit is checked by the computer, hard copies and microfilm copies are automatically made, and many hours and days of drafting and printing work are thus saved.

The completed drawing can be placed in an automatic production sequence, and the final product is generated, completely bypassing the usual many-step process involved in similar manual operations. Corrections to the original design (and ultimately, to the process) can be made equally simply by the use of controlling keys and the light pen.

It is difficult for people not close to the computer industry to realize that, if all of our computers were to stop working today, the country would be practically paralyzed; plants would have to shut down, telephones would quit operating, the finances of the country would be in a condition of havoc, and we should have virtually no defense against enemy attack. We may be right in assuming that computers are here to stay.

SCIENTIFIC APPLICATIONS

Government

The largest single user of computers is the United States government. It ranges in its use from purely military applications, such as fire control systems on our fighting ships, to miniaturized computers hurled into space inside our various space capsules. Space flights would not have been possible without the aid of computers, and, now that they are possible, the reduction into usable form of fantastic amounts of data coming to us from our space vehicles could not be accomplished without the use of computers. Space-tracking stations are located at strategic spots around the world, and each station is busily collecting engineering and other scientific data at the same time that it is issuing commands to the space vehicle. All of these incoming data are gathered on magnetic tapes and sent to a central location for data reduction and study.

The computer is used extensively in every area of military research from huge worldwide command and control systems (known to the initiated by various letter sequences such as NTDS, FFDS, etc.) to individual specialized research such as the study of hydroelasticity in submarines. This research is concerned with methods of predicting flutter in submarine hulls and hull-foil systems. Both digital and analog methods have been devised to aid in this research.

Medicine

A wide-open field of inquiry for scientists is in the area of medical diagnosis aided by computers. Much can and will be accomplished in this area in the not too distant future, but for the present the medical profession has lagged somewhat behind the other sciences in the utilization of computers.

It is true that a few hospitals are being computerized to eliminate much of the clerical work presently accomplished by doctors and nurses, but this type of application falls more correctly into the business area. On the other hand, when medical use of computers is accomplished, it will allow doctors more time for doctoring and nurses more time for nursing.

Many areas of biological and biomedical research utilize a computing facility as an experimental aid in the study of subjects. The computer becomes a powerful assistant because it permits a free flow of information between the experimenter, the experiment, and the computer.

Mathematics

Many complex mathematical computations are accomplished by computers. Problems that would take years to solve and a great number of mathematicians are accomplished by computers in relatively short periods of time. This is certainly a fruitful area for computers, but the teamwork of mathematics and computers has produced many other interesting applications.

One of the more important uses of mathematics in automatic computation is in *simulation*. Simulation is the process of operating a model to determine how the real-life situation may turn out. If a problem contains a great number of variables or if it would be very expensive or dangerous to try out the processes actually, a mathematical model is created and computerized and then data are fed to the model to try out all the possibilities and find the best possible choice of action. For example, without mathematical models and the art of simulation, we should undoubtedly have lost many lives in the space-probe attempts. Careful research and the teamwork of mathematics and computers have helped to reduce the risk of these dangerous missions.

A mathematical model can be devised for any process that can be expressed in mathematical terms, and it is surprising how many nonmathematical areas of activity can be reduced to mathematical terms. Simulation is the practical method of exploring difficult and costly processes because the probabilities of success or failure can be explored and charted without any risk and without the use of costly trial-and-error methods.

Oceanography

Oceanographers have used computers as active aids to their research for some time, but more and more computers are being utilized on board oceanographic vessels to store, collate, reduce, compute, display, and permanently record data as they are generated. Use of the computers helps to eliminate the tedious hand calculations and therefore allows the researcher to attempt more complex research problems.

With on-board computers, data can be analyzed on the spot and creative variations can be attempted quickly and easily. Instrument failures can be spotted immediately, and corrections can be made without loss of valuable time or data.

To mention just one specific use, oceanographic bathythermographs are used to record temperatures of ocean waters at various depths. These data are usually recorded by lines drawn across a grid coordinate system. Reading and deciphering these line drawings is an extremely tiring and tedious job. With the use of a computer, the tedium disappears because the data can be rapidly read and digitized. Summary information is quickly available to the researcher, eliminating much of the unpleasant aspects of his work.

Although only a few areas of scientific research have been mentioned here, every aspect of science and technology has been touched, and improved, by the advent of computers.

EXAMPLE OF A BUSINESS APPLICATION

To demonstrate the complexity of the job of preparing an application for computer solution, a fairly simple but practical inventory job will be discussed here and taken to the point of actual programming. Detailed programming of such a job is beyond the scope of this text but is well within the scope of a first semester course in computer programming.

Assume an imaginary company which has a central warehouse and 15 branch stores, each ordering its wholesale stocks from the central warehouse. Orders for stock are telephoned in to the inventory-control section located at the warehouse. These orders are written on slips, one slip for each type of item. The slips are checked against a ledger showing stocks in the warehouse. If stock is available, a "picking ticket" is made showing the name and address of the branch, item stock number (a different number for each type of item), warehouse location, quantity ordered, and total weight. The quantity on the picking ticket is deducted from the ledger sheet, and a new balance is written in.

When the ledger record shows no stock on hand for an item, a backorder slip is written and placed where it can be checked in the next day's processing before new orders are processed. If partial stocks are available, the partial picking ticket is created and the remainder is backordered.

When a new shipment of stock is received by the warehouse, the warehouse manager sends a slip called a *notice of receipt,* showing the quantity received. This amount is added to the ledger record.

When the orders are filled by the warehouse, they are all sent to the shipping department, which sorts the items according to branch destination and packages and ships the items. A slip is sent from the shipping department to the accounting department to show items shipped, branch number, price of each, and total price.

A programmer analyst is asked to design a computer system to perform the work of the inventory-control office. After viewing the whole operation, he decides the following records are necessary:

1. *Inventory Ledger File*: This file will contain one record for each type of item. The records will be sequenced by stock number. The record will keep track of total quantities of each type of item ordered by each branch for a report to be prepared in the future. The following record will be required:

Data Field	No. of Digits
Stock number	10
Item name	20
Price	6
Shipping weight (each item)	4
Warehouse location	2
Quantity in stock	8
Quantity on back/order	8
one for each branch { Branch number, 4 digits / Total ordered, 6 digits	150

2. *Order Card*: When a sales order is received, a card will be punched for each type of item ordered.

Data Field	Card Columns
Branch number	1 – 4
Stock number	5 – 14
Card code 3	15
Item name	16 – 35
Quantity	36 – 41

---

[1]This example is courtesy of J. A. Saxon and W. S. Plette, *Programming the IBM 1401,* Prentice-Hall, Inc., Englewood Cliffs, N. J., 1962.

3. *Receipt Card*: When new stock is received at the warehouse, a card will be punched for each type of item.

Data Field	Card Columns
Stock number	5 – 14
Card code 1	15
Item name	16 – 34
Quantity received	35 – 40

(Column 40 will be punched with an 11 punch)

4. *Backorder Card*: When stock is not available, a card is punched exactly like the order card except that this card will contain a "2" in column 15. The quantity is the amount *not* shipped.

5. *Picking Ticket*: A printed slip will be prepared for each order to be shipped. The slip will be used to select the stock. It will be attached to the container when it is sent to the shipping department.

Line 5, Positions 10–13	Branch number
Line 5, Positions 20–39	Branch name
Line 6, Positions 20–39	Branch street number
Line 7, Positions 20–39	Branch city
Line 12, Positions 4–13	Stock number
Line 12, Positions 16–35	Item name
Line 12, Positions 42–43	Warehouse location
Line 12, Positions 50–56	Quantity (XXX, XXX)
Line 12, Positions 60–64	Total weight (X,XXX)

Picking Ticket

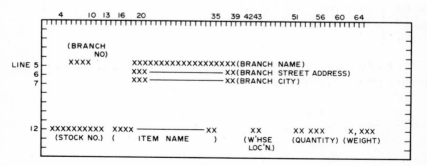

6. *Order Record Card*: Each time a picking ticket is printed, a card is punched for use by the shipping department to check out shipments after which it is sent to the accounting department.

SYSTEM FLOW CHART

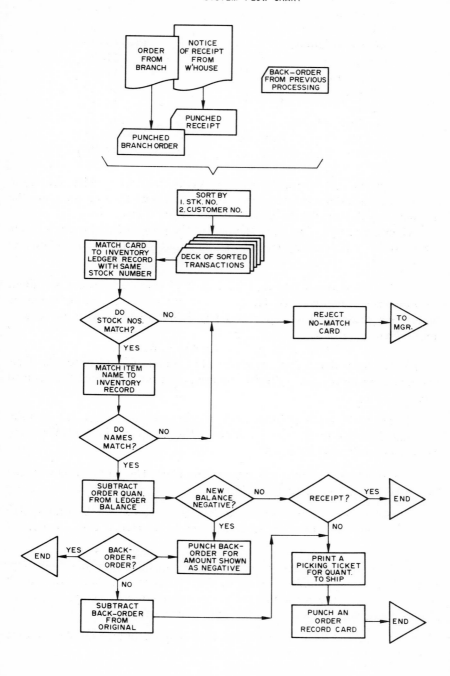

Data Field	Card Columns
Customer number	1–4
Stock number	5–14
Quantity shipped	15–20
Price each	21–26
Total price	27–35
Blanks	36–39
Date	40–46
Day (01–31)	(40–41)
Month (Jan., Feb., etc.)	(42–44)
Year ('64, '65, '66, etc.)	(45–46)

The system analyst usually draws a system flow chart which shows the order in which actions will take place. Each point at which a decision must be made is shown. How the decision is to be handled is also shown.

When the analysis has been completed, the programming aspects of the job must be considered by the analyst. The following important points are noted:

1. The inventory ledger records have 208 characters. There are about 5,000 items in the inventory. He decides to put the ledger file on magnetic tape. Each record will use approximately 1 inch of tape, with an IRG of approximately ½ inch.

$$5,000 \times 1\frac{1}{2} = 7,500 \text{ inches} = 625 \text{ feet}$$

He concludes that a single tape reel will hold all the ledger records. Thus two tape units are needed—one for input and one for outputting the updated file.

2. The three types of input cards (order, receipt, backorder) all have the same data fields in the same columns. (The receipt card has blanks in the branch number columns.)

3. The file will be in stock-number sequence. The input cards will also be sorted on card code (column 15).

4. Both *order-record cards and backorder cards* will be output. He decides to put backorders in Stacker 4 and order-record cards in normal stacker.

5. The order and backorder cards have plus quantities, but the receipt card has a minus quantity (owing to the 11 punch in column 40). If all transaction quantities are subtracted, the minus quantity (receipt) will be *added* to the balance—the others are actually subtracted.

6. The order and backorder cards have only the branch number, not the

name and address as required for the picking ticket. The analyst decides to place a table in memory, in branch-number sequence, cross-referencing the number to the name, street address, and city.

Starting at memory address 8000 to 8959, he will read in a table of addresses for 15 branches, each entry 64 characters long. These must be punched in 15 cards (columns 1 to 63) and read in before the data cards are read.

7. The *date* will be required for the tape label and for the order-record card. A card must be punched before each run and read into memory *after* the program deck, but *before* the table of addresses.

Data Field	Card Columns
Day of month	1–2
Month (3 char. abbrev.)	3–5
Year (last 2 digits)	6–7

8. The code in column 15 of the cards will make the receipts sort first, followed by backorders, and then orders.

9. A tape label will be required, and he chooses a simple form of header label:

Reel No.   Date
INVENTORY—LEDGER—XXX————D D M M M Y Y

These 28 characters are entered as a constant. The date is inserted after the date card is read. The input label will be read from tape, and the first 16 characters will be compared with the constant to ensure the correct tape is used. The whole label will be written on the output tape.

The programmer prepares a *detailed flow chart* showing each step of computer processing. Practicing programmers differ on the amount of detail to be included, but beginners should probably show each distinct computer operation.

The programmer's detailed flow chart is shown on the following pages. Depending on the computer and the language being used, memory areas may or may not have to be allocated for particular functional uses. The routine required for errors is omitted. Error halts are used to make it a bit more simple.

The words on the outside of the flow chart boxes are the tags and program entry points as used in the computer program that was developed from the flow charts. This particular program was written for the RCA 301 computer, which requires some checks (EF/ED, ETW) which are not required on other computers. Some small changes would have to be made if this problem were to be programmed on a different computer.

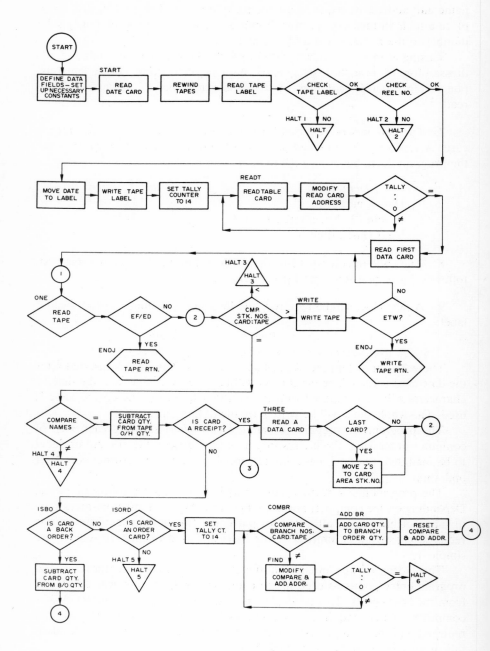

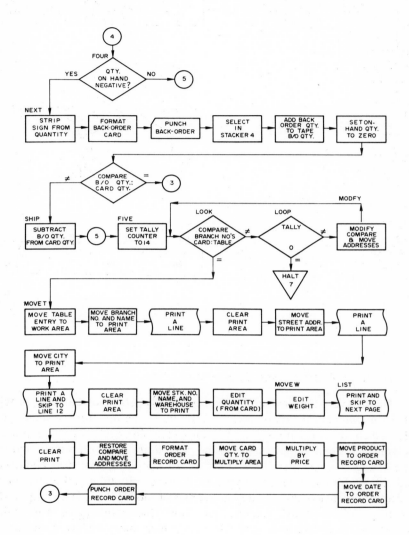

Read tape routine

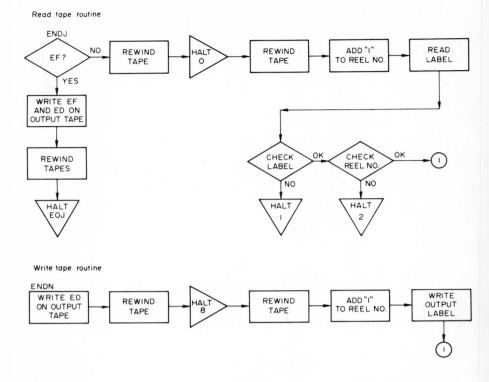

Write tape routine

A FILE MAINTENANCE EXAMPLE

Nearly every business application eventually gets involved in the problem of file maintenance. File maintenance refers to the updating of master tape files which are continuously used in the processing cycle. For example, in a personnel system, all personnel on the payroll are listed on a tape, and with this listing is a complete breakdown of all known information about each individual. Similarly, in a supply or logistics situation, all items in the inventory are listed and detailed in the master file. This file is kept up to date by a periodic (daily, weekly, monthly) file-maintenance run, which processes all transactions and changes which have occurred during the specified period of time. The run finishes up with a new, updated master file.

The detailed system-analysis portion of a small segment of such a file-maintenance run is shown on the following pages. Some of the detail will be difficult to understand since this is a small portion of a huge logistics system containing over 100 interlocking runs, but the system documentation and the method of file maintenance is well worth studying.

Table of Contents

Explanatory Remarks

The following information is inserted to provide the student with an overview of the total system and some of the details of this fragment of the system.

This is a huge logistics system to maintain the inventory (over 100,000 different items) for a particular missile. It is necessary to control the inventory at the Weapon System Storage Site (WSSS), the actual warehouses. It is also necessary to maintain and update the inventory at the operational sites for the squadrons concerned with launching the missiles.

This segment of the system, called *Run I-25,* has the function of sorting sequencing, and updating items that are found to be out of sequence in the inventory master file and of reconciling any items that indicate some error in the levels computational run (by *levels* is meant levels of stock on hand).

The output from this process will be four tape files: (1) the "Active Items Balance File" (AB), containing the updated items that can now be merged with the "Master Inventory File;" (2) all assets for selected items for which computation has been requested by the item managers; (3) prepunched cards (PPC) showing all changes in the inventory and all new levels that have been established for particular items; and (4) "Resupply Alert" data on new items or new families of items. These require the establishment of new levels.

Each of these four output tapes are then routed to other segments of the system. The entire system is integrated, since the output of one segment becomes the input to another segment. In this case, the output of Run I-25 becomes the input to a number of other runs (as shown in the illustration of the "File Description Chart").

The concept of families of items should also be understood prior to studying the details of the system. Families of similar or interchangeable items are grouped by applications. An item may be a *bachelor* (no other item can be substituted) or it may belong in a family. Families are broken into still smaller groupings by subfamilies. The items are identified by "Application Group Numbers" (AGN), and all transactions are processed by this basic identifying number. The particular transactions processed by this run are listed and detailed in the section "Processing Methodology." Each item is identified by its stock number (S/N), which is part of the total AGN.

It must be further understood that the flow charts on the following pages are system flow charts. These are not used for detailed coding. They are used to show how the various segments are tied together to do the job required of this run. From these charts, the programmer constructs much more detailed flow charts which are used for the actual programming of the problem.

This is the type of work that analysts and programmers do in real life situations. The scope is much broader than the usual textbook problem, but it shows the real challenge that such problems pose for the person who works in data processing.

GENERAL NARRATIVE

Functions

The basic functions of this run are to sort the incoming transactions, rebuild items and families of items and recompute levels.

Secondary functions include generation of prepunched master cards to Squadrons and Storage Sites, generation of transactions for Main Posting and processing of "Selected Items for Computation" transactions.

Inputs

File Description

1. Out-of-Sequence Inventory Balance Record File (I1506). Input from Run I-15 containing all records that could not be processed in I-15 because of transactions causing out-of-sequence conditions (i.e., Consolidation, AGN change). After processing, this file becomes the new Active Balance File which is used by Main Posting (Run I-05) during the following week to post all daily transactions.

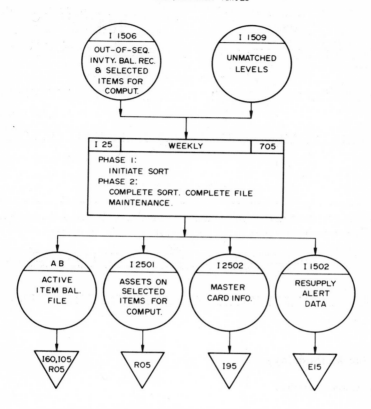

File description chart – run I 25

Output to various other runs in the system

2. Unmatched-Levels File (11509). Input from Run I-15 containing any levels that do not match in I-15 due to error and all transaction-903 cards (new items).

FILE FORMATS:

1. The format for the Out-of-Sequence File may be found on the following page. [See accompanying illustration.]

2. The format for the Unmatched Levels Tape is identical to the Run I-15 input tape F2002, Major Transactions (R card format only). It may be found on the following page. [See accompanying illustration.]

Out-of-Sequence File Format

Unmatched Levels Tape Format

Processing Methodology

Transaction Narratives

Trans. Code	Element	Instruction and Remarks
001 (991)	AGN chg. due to new highest stock no.	Rebuild family. Bring in levels from tape I1509. Generate prepunched cards. Transac. to Main Posting.
003 (903)	New item(s), bachelor or or family	Build up the bachelor or family. Bring in levels from tape I1509. Generate prepunched cards. Transaction to Main Posting.
(803)	"R" cards only	Bring in from tape I1509 and process as 903 R cards; rejecting the 803's against type 2's and processing the 803's with the subfamily suffix only.
005	New S/N to replace existing S/N	Put in proper AGN sequence if bachelor. If family item, will be processed in I-15 unless the chg. is to highest S/N in family. In this case, the AGN will change.
006	Chg. erroneous S/N	Same as for transaction 005 above.

007 (807)	Chg. AGN or family group number	Build new type 1 from bb7 transaction. Build up type 2's. After record rebuilt, recompute levels and put "F" in levels code field. Generate pre-punched cards for all S/N's to all locs. Details of this transaction (also 001 and 003) may be found in Chap. III of Work Specifications for Run I-15.
009 (809)	Consolidate	This transaction will consolidate all bals. for an existing AGN with the corresponding bals. for another AGN. The losing AGN will be deleted. Type 1 record—same as 007. Type 2 chg. the AGN. If consolidation within a subfam: No. of S/N's in subfam. will chg. Other consolidations: Length of rec., total no. of subfam's., no. of WSSS, no. of sqds. and bals. by subfam. may chg. Generate pre-punched cards.
050	Section Mgmt. Code	This transaction comes to File Maint. as an 807 and will be processed in the same manner as any other 807 transaction.
999	Selected Item Requirements Computation	Print out all asset data for the requested AGN on a special tape. Also output to AB tape.

Additional Detail Information

1. Method of recomputing levels.

a. The following transactions will cause an item or family to be put on the Out-of-Sequence tape in Run I-15.

001, 003, 005, 006, 007, 009, 050.

b. Those actions that cause AGN change, will also cause all levels to be set to zero. Levels are recomputed with the following formulae:

(1) Weapon System Storage Sites (WSSS)
   (a) Stockage Objective—Serv. O/H assets.
   (b) Warning Point—Serv. O/H assets.
   (c) Allocation—Serv. O/H assets.
   (d) Minimum—Zeros.
(2) Squadron
   (a) Maximum—Serv. assets × $1\frac{1}{2}$
   (b) Stock. Obj.—Serv. assets × $1\frac{1}{2}$
   (c) Resupply—Serv. assets × .6.
   (d) Self Suffic.—Zeros.

c. An "F" will be placed in the levels code field for all recomputed levels. During the monthly I-15 processing, when the Stock Levels tape is processed, if the "F" is still in the file, levels will be set to zero and a print-out will be generated for the item manager.

SYSTEM LOGICAL FLOWCHARTS

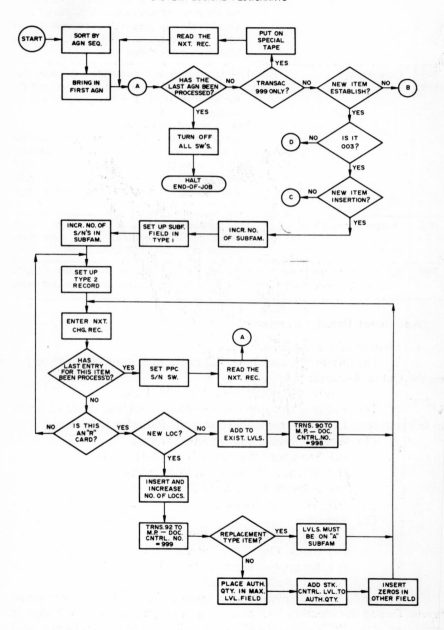

New Item Establishment

Job Logical Flow Chart
Job No.:I25 Pg. 2 of 4 pgs.
Title: Inventory File Maintenance
Analyst: J. Saxon
Programmer: A. Olsen

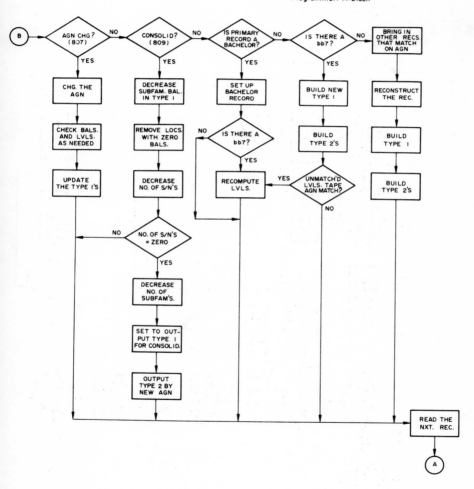

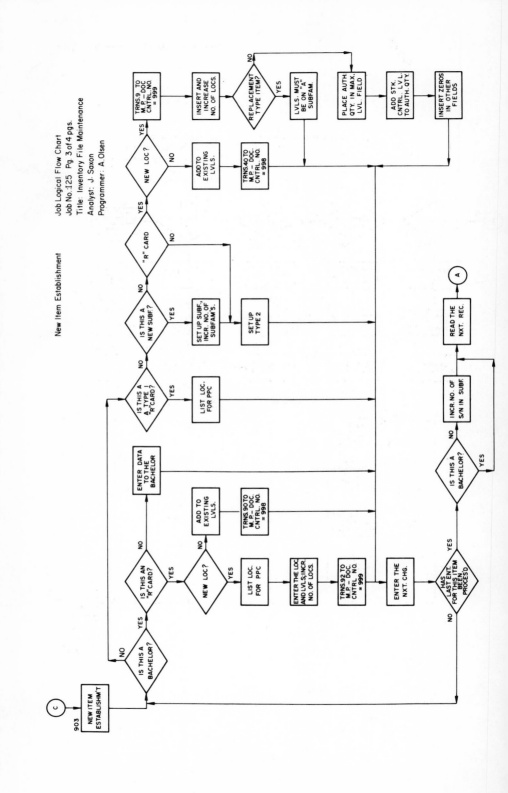

Job Logical Flow Chart
Job No.: 125   Pg 3 of 4 pgs.
Title: Inventory File Maintenance
Analyst: J. Saxon
Programmer: A. Olsen

New Item Establishment

New Item Establishment

Job Logical Flow Chart
Job No. 125 Pg 4 of 4 pgs.
Title: Inventory File Maintenance
Analyst J. Saxon
Programmer: A. Olsen

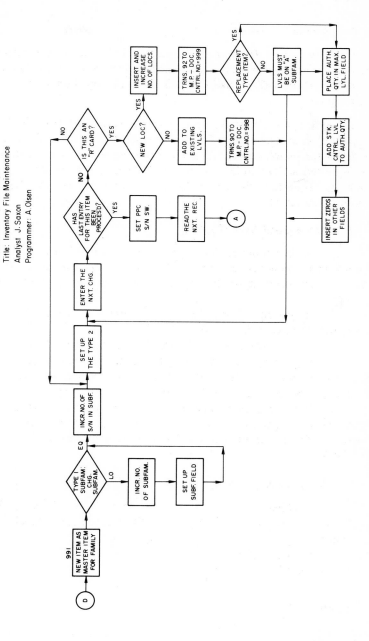

Outputs

Description

1. Active-Item Balance File: (AB). This file will contain all the updated records that were not processed in I-15 to the Main Balance File. It is used by Runs I-60 and R-05, but primarily by Run I-05 to post daily transactions.

2. Assets on Selected Items for Comput. (I2501). A 999 transaction will cause Inventory File Maintenance to extract all asset data for the AGN for which computation has been requested. The entire record for the requested AGN will be put on the I2501 tape (If one stock number in a family is requested, the entire family will be put on the Requirements Computation tape).

3. Master Card Info. (I2502)

    a. A prepunched card will be generated by Inventory File Maintenance whenever an element of data contained in the master deck of cards changes and upon the establishment of initial levels for specific location.

    b. Any one of the following transaction codes will cause the generation of prepunched cards to the field.

          001, 003, 005, 006, 007, 009, 050

    c. If a change effects any part of a family, prepunched cards will be generated for all stock numbers within the family and sent to all locations affected (both old and initial locations).

    d. The prepunched cards will be produced in Run I-95. The information for producing these cards will be accumulated on the tape mentioned above, but the final sort and punching operation will be handled in Run I-95.

4. Resupply Alert Data (I1502)

    a. Detailed description of this file may be found in the Work Specifications for Run I-15. Only 90 or 92 transactions will be generated by this Run.

    b. Only transactions 001 and 003 may cause Resupply Alert Data to be generated in Run I-25.

Formats

1. The format for the active-items balance file will be the same as the main balance file (see Work Specifications for main posting, Run I-05).

2. The format for Selected Items for Computation File will also be the same as the Main Balance File.

3. The format for the Master Card Information File is identical to the file bearing the same name in Run I-15 (tape I1508).

4. The format for the Resupply Alert Data File is identical to the file bearing the same name in Run I-15. (The two file formats mentioned in (b) 3 and (b) 4 may be found in the Work Specifications for Run I-15.)

EXAMPLES OF MATHEMATICAL APPLICATIONS:

The following mathematical applications are meant to illustrate the type of handling required prior to detailed programming of a job. These are typical applications and are certainly not meant to be taken as ultimate solutions to the problems.

1. To find the natural logarithm of a positive floating-point argument

$$X \quad Y = \log_e (X)$$

where
$$t = \frac{\sqrt{2m} - 1}{\sqrt{2m} + 1}$$

$$Y = (I - \tfrac{1}{2}) \log_e (2) + t\left[a + t^2 \left(b + \frac{c}{t^2 + d}\right)\right]$$

where I = characteristic of the argument
m = mantissa of the argument

Given
$$a = 1.9999999994913$$
$$b = .109078890503$$
$$c = - .77731400100549$$
$$d = -1.3940651451761$$
$$\ln 2 = .69314718055995$$

The flow chart for this problem is shown in the accompanying illustration.

2. A simulation program received smooth missile-flight-position data in intervals of 1 second. These data were then linearly interpolated in $\frac{1}{10}$-second intervals. In an effort to reduce round-off effects and add noise, a random-number-generating subroutine was developed to perturbate the simulated data. The noise data were generated by a subroutine titled RANNUM as a fraction generator and then scaled to the magnitude of in-flight data by the main program.

A flow chart of the subroutine is shown here utilizing two registers (A and Q) for the generation of random numbers and an index register (XR4).

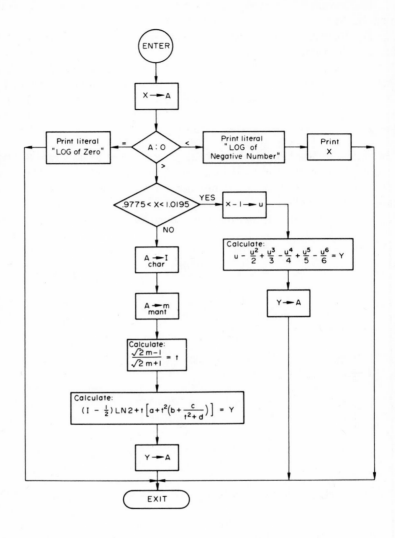

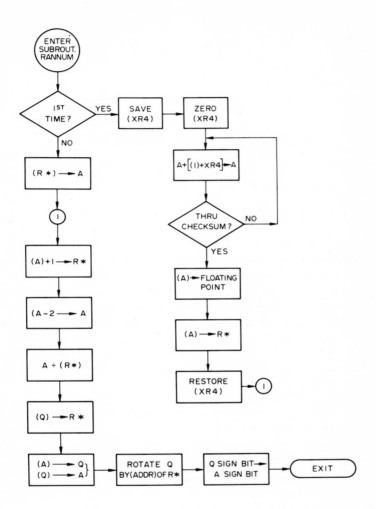

11   FUTURE DEVELOPMENTS

Statements made with reference to future developments in data processing must be made with a great deal of humility. It can be said, with justification, that the computer may prove to be the most significant development in the history of man. It is within reason to estimate that man will double his store of knowledge in the next ten years. In other words, man will learn as much more about himself and his environment in one decade as he has learned in the millions of years which have elapsed until now. One must be awed by such observations, and questions must be asked so answers might be sought.

Can man cope with the information explosion? What demands will be placed on society and on the individual? Will man's values change? What use is to be made of leisure time? Who will be privileged to work? How should our productivity be distributed? Most of these questions are not within the scope of this textbook for extended discussion, but the reader may be led to think on and investigate these basic philosophical and sociological problems. For one thing is sure, cybernetics, the science of computers, will certainly be the root of the greatest change in the history of man. The generation at hand is the *"cybernated" generation*.

THE EFFECTS OF CYBERNATION

Effects on Economy

The basic effect of the computer on the economy comes from its role in the automation process. Human labor has always been a major factor in the economics of production, but automation will all but eliminate the need for labor in our manufacturing, processing, and fabricating plants. Machines can and are producing goods for man at an ever increasing rate. Machines, however, are not consumers of goods and herein lies the problem.

The problem is not which is the more efficient method of production. Clearly, machines are more productive than man. The problem is how the goods and services are to be distributed. When man was directly responsible for the production of goods, he presumably shared in the fruits of his labor in direct proportion to his contribution to the productive process. His contribution was measured by the wages he received, which, in turn, represented his purchasing power. Now, if the factor of labor is removed, who is to receive the goods produced?

Often automation is disparaged or condemned because it eliminates jobs, but it is not the elimination of work which should be decried. It is, instead, the loss of an established method of sharing in the productivity of the economy which should be recognized as the problem demanding a solution.

Insofar as the material well-being of the population is concerned, the computer should be harnessed to do as much as possible to serve man. It should be developed no less than any other of man's inventions. And as the machines do the work, man must establish fair and equitable methods of sharing in the productivity of an automated economy. There is no reason to believe that the economy will not continue to produce more and better products at smaller per unit cost. *New* products will be developed. Many, probably most, of the products which we shall buy, use, and enjoy even 10 years hence have not as yet entered the idea stage. Production of goods seems not to be a problem. It is reasonable to expect the economy to produce more and more wealth as measured in goods and services.

Effects on Employment

If an economy is to produce wealth in the form of goods and services, there must be consumption of the goods and services. Unlike the individual whose wealth is measured by his store of goods, a nation's wealth is measured by the standard of living or consumption level of the people of that nation. And it is measured by the amount of work which the people must do (or not do) to maintain that level of consumption. The poor nation is the nation where the people must work long and hard for a mere subsistence. A rich nation is one where the population works relatively little and has an abundance of goods.

As the machines gradually take over more and more of the work, what will be the effect on employment? Technological advances invariably cause unemployment. The computer revolution is no exception. However, in all cases of technological unemployment, the unemployment effect has been a temporary one. Society adjusts and man's stride forward is completed. Society must adjust to automation also.

What are some of the adjustments which will be made? With less work to do, man will have more leisure time. Ideally, the leisure time will come through reduction in the work week, more holidays, longer vacations, earlier retirement, etc. On the undesirable side, leisure time might take the form of unsolicited and unwanted unemployment. The 20-hour work week may be the standard in the lifetime of those just now preparing for their life's work. The responsibility is to provide 20 hours for everyone rather than 40 hours for some and none for others.

In an economy of abundance, it is natural that the people will be able to afford and demand more services as well as more goods. Enterprises of the service type will increase in scope and number to satisfy the demand. Businesses directed at the leisure-time activities of the newly liberated work force is an example already evident. There are many business enterprises based on our recreational activities which could not have existed a few years ago because there would not have been a demand for the services being provided. Longer vacations and shorter work weeks will allow more travel, more recreational time, and more of all kinds of activity which create a demand for services. These demands for services, in turn, provide many opportunities to share in the automated productivity. Jobs are created because the machines have released man from his assembly-line prison. He is now free to enjoy the fruits of the economy. It is still for man to determine, however, whether he will use his leisure and affluence for his betterment or his detriment.

So then, the opportunities for sharing in the productivity (jobs) can be spread by decreasing the time that any one man works and thus creating an opportunity (job) for another. Additional opportunity can be created by additional demands for services. Probably, like an iceberg, the greatest opportunities lie beneath the surface. These are the opportunities created by the unknown products which will be invented and developed. Today, we have prime examples of such products, which bring with them a whole new array of direct and indirect commercial activity. Just start to make a list of all the business activity which is based on the automobile. The list is nearly endless. There are other examples only somewhat less phenomenal. Television, the airplane, the computer, as well as the automobile, all brought with them a chain reaction of related economic activity previously not necessary or not possible, all the way from the drive-in restaurant to the space program. New jobs are created with each new product or idea. The ideas which will be the job producers of the future have probably not as yet reached the drawing board.

There is, however, another aspect to the employment picture as it relates to automation, the computer, and data processing. There is the short-range transitional picture, and it is important. When a machine displaces a person, the person displaced is not concerned with the ultimate benefit. He is concerned with the very real, current and personal situation. This is the problem with which the individual, companies, labor organizations, and government are confronted. Solutions to the problem of technological unemployment take several forms. Retraining workers is a necessity. Skills are easily and quickly obsoleted with the advent of the machine, and new skills must be developed. Through cooperation between and among company, union, government, and worker, retraining can fit the worker for a new job. In some cases companies have lowered the retirement age to make room for the technologically displaced. Also, the process of automating a plant can be done on a gradual basis so as to cause a minimum of worker displacement. In any event the problem of the technologically displaced worker is one which demands a solution. It is unreasonable to expect a few to pay the price of progress for all.

Effects on Society

With the speed of change which our society is undergoing, we can well wonder whether it can withstand the impact. Some long-standing concepts are likely to be tested. Work, not leisure, has been the measure of a good man. But, we are on the threshold of mass leisure. Can men adjust to nonfunctional lives? It would seem that they must. Man and society must strive to build a better place to live, must rise to a higher level of civilization. The challenge to society is apparent. We may rise or we may fall, but we cannot have the *status quo*. The computer and automation can be a blessing or a curse.

The Greeks developed a high level of civilization by constructive use of leisure time. With slaves to do the work, they could devote their time to self-improvement. The modern-day slave is the computer, and modern man has an unprecedented opportunity for individual and collective improvement. What forms can this self-improvement take? Learning is undoubtedly high on the list. Education will be sought, and sought for different purposes. Much of it will be technical so that communication may continue between man and machine. Even more education, however, will be education for leisure. Continuous education might well become a natural way of life. We can hope to use leisure time to build understanding among men and the betterment of human relationships. With leisure, man can appreciate and enjoy the arts, his environment, and life itself.

On the other hand, leisure improperly used could be a nightmare of crime and human degradation. Leisure time is neither good nor bad in itself. It will be the use to which it is put which will determine its value.

REVIEW QUESTIONS

1. What is the basic problem brought about by automation?

2. Contrast the measure of individual wealth with the measure of a nation's wealth.

3. What are some ways possible for solving the unemployment problem?

4. Describe what is meant by the statement, "Leisure time is neither good nor bad in itself."

SCIENTIFIC MANAGEMENT

Role of the Computer In Management

Automation and electronic data processing have brought about a drastic change in business management. A large segment of the business management hierarchy is no longer necessary because the computer has taken over the function formerly performed by this group. The computer with its programmed instructions can make certain routine "decisions" once made by management personnel. Decisions which are automatic when the facts are known can be made by the computer.

A decision to order goods when a minimum stock level is reached and to order from the vendor who quotes the lowest price for the product is a decision which needs no human deliberation. A computer which has been given the guidelines (program) and the information (data) can make the necessary decision automatically. With the elimination of routine decision making by management personnel, the need for the personnel is eliminated.

The role of the business manager has changed. Business management is now a scientific endeavor with decisions made on the basis of fact, not hunch. Management is no longer an art, it is a science. The availability of current and accurate information regarding business operations not only makes it possible but dictates that decisions must be made clearly and promptly. There can be no hedging on a decision under a pretext of insufficient information.

Management by Exception

Because the routine decisions can be programmed by man and made by the computer, the business manager is now faced with the difficult decisions only. He must deal with the exceptional cases. The luxury of making routine decisions is no longer available to the executive. If a situation is predictable, the decision can be predetermined and a computer can be programmed to select an alternative. The computer will turn a problem over to the executive for a decision only if the problem is abnormal or nonroutine. This reporting of abnormal performance to management for action is termed *management by exception.*

The computer is a powerful tool. Millions of calculations can be made in a second. Thousands of characters can be printed in a minute. Where speed and volume are concerned, the computer has far outstripped man. In fact the computer can produce per se more information than man can consume. A computer can easily print a thousand lines per minute, but an executive cannot read one thousand lines a minute. A computer can easily report the inventory balance of tens of thousands of inventory items, but a procurement officer would find it difficult to analyze and act on each item to keep inventory levels above established minimums. In such cases the exception principle needs to be employed so that only abnormal performance is reported to management. Management by exception is really not new. Essentially, the principle is being employed when employees bring only the exceptional problems to the attention of the supervisor. What is new is the immense volume of data which can be processed in a modern data-processing system and the inherent absolute need to employ the exception principle.

Some areas of application are apparent. Customer accounts or mortgage accounts which are being paid on a regular basis need no attention. Overdue accounts are the only ones which need to be reported to management. Bank checking accounts need little or no attention until an overdraft occurs. In the case of student achievement, reporting need not be done for all students at a particular time, but a listing of *exceptional* students might be called for and an honors list and a probationary list prepared. In the area of production control, production is measured against standards and only the incidences of variation from the standard are reported. Product quality is reported only if quality falls beneath a certain standard. Machine and human operations call for management attention only when efficiency fails to meet the established standard. Production schedules and delivery schedules need not concern the manager unless the schedules are *not* being met.

REVIEW QUESTIONS

5. How has the computer changed the role of management?

6. How is the management by exception principle applied when EDP equipment is used to process the data?

DATA-PROCESSING EMPLOYMENT AND EDUCATION

The area of automated data processing and the computer are, in themselves, good examples of the creation of new jobs in occupations which did not exist before the advent of the machine. It is not likely that more jobs have been created by the computer than have been eliminated, but nonetheless many opportunities have grown out of the usage of these improved methods of processing data. People who are knowledgeable in the area of EDP are in demand, and there is every reason to believe that this will be a continuing situation for some time to come. Programmers and systems analysts with training, experience, and proven ability can nearly "write their own ticket" in today's employment market. Other areas of the data-processing field are not in such critical need of personnel but do provide considerable opportunity for employment. Again, training or experience or both are desirable possessions.

There are several levels of employment in data processing. Educational requirements range from graduates of high school to levels equivalent to the most advanced college degrees. Jobs vary from those at the strictly skill level to those requiring the ultimate in imagination and creativity. Data-processing jobs range from the simple to the complex. Special training for some jobs can be completed in a few weeks or a few days. Other positions are open only to those who have had many years of special training or experience.

As is the case in any occupational field, financial remuneration is based, in general, on what the employee has to offer in the way of skills and abilities. The different levels of employment in data processing result in widely divergent salary and wage scales. Most systems analysts easily command five figure annual salaries, while salaries on the other end of the spectrum of training and ability are more modest.

Types of Data-Processing Occupations

Data-processing occupations can be classified into three major fields plus a group of related occupations.

Major areas are:

1. Machine operation
2. Computer programming
3. Systems analysis

Related areas include:

1. Data-processing installation management
2. Data-processing equipment sales

3. Data-processing equipment maintenance
4. Data-processing-related clerical

Machine Operation

The occupational area of machine operation covers three distinctly different ability and skill levels. They are:

1. Card-punch (or other keyboard type of machines) operation
2. EAM equipment operation
3. Computer operation

Each of these machine-operation jobs requires a somewhat different type of ability and training.

The primary skill needed for card-punch operation is a manipulative skill similar to that required for proficiency on the typewriter or 10-key adding machine. A good typist or a good adding-machine operator would ordinarily make a good card-punch operator. Speed and accuracy are the measure of a good card-punch operator. In addition, however, a card-punch operator must be able to analyze the need for program cards and design and prepare them. She (or he) should also be familiar with the use of the various control keys and switches on a card punch and be able to make full use of the available features of the machine. In some cases a card-punch operator is expected to be able to operate some of the basic EAM equipment such as the sorter, interpreter, and reproducing punch.

Requirements for a verifier operator are the same as for a card-punch operator, since verifier operation is nearly identical with card-punch operation.

Salaries paid card-punch operators vary but are generally lower than those paid to other data-processing personnel. Most employers prefer female card-punch operators, but there are examples where men are performing well in this role.

Those who operate the machines in an EAM system are identified by various job titles, e.g., tabulating machine operators (tab operators), electric accounting machine operators (EAM operators), and unit record machine operators. These job titles are used interchangeably and refer to the operation of the IBM and UNIVAC punched-card machines. Requirements include the basic ability to operate the machines, an understanding of their functions, knowledge of machine features, ability to handle cards, and ability to follow written instructions and operating procedures to accomplish mechanized data-processing jobs.

The level of ability required in any one EAM job might vary from another similarly identified job to a considerable degree. A large EAM installation might be able to divide the labor so that one operator would specialize on one or a small group of machines. In such a case an operator might operate only a sorter or only an accounting machine, etc. These operators would represent different levels of ability, with the more experienced or able operators operating the more complex machines or a greater variety of machines. Or, the ranking operators are sometimes given lead operator or senior operator status with additional responsibility. A lead operator in some cases is in charge of a section or a shift, or he might be called upon to supply technical knowledge on machine malfunctions, panelboard wiring, or procedural problems. In smaller installations an EAM operator may, in fact, be performing tasks ordinarily assigned to a systems analyst. He may be required to design and implement new jobs. He may be called upon to wire boards, develop procedures, schedule jobs, and do other related work as well as operate the machines. Therefore, some jobs require no more than basic ability, while others require facility on all the machines, ability to wire control panels, an understanding of accounting and data-processing systems, and the general ability to conduct the activities of the installation.

Tab operators do not ordinarily operate card punches. The skills required in the two jobs are dissimilar. It is uncommon for a card-punch operator to progress to tab operation. A good card-punch operator does not necessarily make a good punched-card machine operator, or vice versa. This is not to say, however, that there have not been exceptions to this generalization. There are undoubtedly some instances in which card-punch operators have advanced to and performed satisfactorily as EAM operators.

Punched-card machine operators are in a good position to become computer operators when an organization makes the transition from EAM to an EDP system. Experience gained as an EAM operator is of considerable value in becoming a console operator. A computer system (especially a card system), will require many of the same abilities of the operator as does an EAM system. The EAM operator's knowledge of the machines, understanding of and ability to follow written job instructions, and familiarity with the particular company's accounting and information processing procedures give him a decided advantage in becoming a good console operator.

Computer operation, or console operation as it is sometimes known, represents another area of machine operation. The operation of a computer generally implies the operation of the entire EDP system including such hardware as tape drives, high-speed printer, disk drives, card reader-punches, etc. As compared with EAM operation, computer operation requires less manipulative skill and more ability and understanding of systems and procedure. Again, the requirements for any particular operator job would vary from any other depending upon the circumstances. In a large installation there can be specialization, whereas in a smaller installation the operator would need to take command of the entire system and perform all or most of the procedures.

Although a console operator can generally perform the ordinary duties of computer operation without any knowledge of computer programming, in most cases it is advantageous to have this knowledge. Facility in programming not only enables the operator to be a better operator but also provides him an avenue for advancement to the programming and systems-analyst ranks.

Programming

Although the instructing of a computer has been greatly simplified since the machines first became operational, the computer is still under the direction of the human being. It still must be given directions in order for it to do the simplest of tasks. The job of providing machine instructions has been made easier, but it has not been eliminated. Assemblers and compilers, programs for the translation of problem-oriented languages to machine-level languages, remove only the tedious job of coding. They do not perform the programmer's job. Programming, therefore, represents an occupational area where the demand will undoubtedly be great for some time to come.

It is safe to say that not everyone can hope to be a programmer nor would everyone want to be a programmer. A good programmer must be a particular kind of person. In fact, particular, might be the best way to describe the kind of person who can be a good programmer. It is no more possible to list all the attributes which account for programming ability than it is to list them for any other occupation, but certain attitudes and aptitudes are usually apparent. A programmer must possess a level of intelligence commensurate with success in other endeavors such as accounting, law, or teaching. Programming calls for a high level of logical ability and attention to detail. Programming is problem solving. One who does not like the challenge of a logic problem will probably not like programming.

Programmers are recruited from all walks of life. As one of the newest 20th-century careers, men and women enter into programming with backgrounds as mathematicians, accountants, musicians, longshoremen, tabulating-machine operators, etc. No one area seems to represent the one best source of programming talent. Programmers may hold degrees in a variety of areas such as philosophy, mathematics, business administration, or engineering or have no college training at all. The present-day trend, though, is for formal programming training in colleges and universities. Programmers are both male and female with no apparent advantage belonging to either. There are probably more men programmers than women programmers simply because there are more career men than career women.

In general, the programmer starts with a system designed by the systems analyst and makes the system operational on the computer. A programmer may be assigned only a segment of a total system which will later be fitted into the work of other programmers to complete the larger systems job. On the other hand, a programmer may be responsible for the entire job which entails a close working relationship with the systems analyst. In either case the programmer supplies the technical knowledge to turn a general plan into a specific accomplishment.

Systems Analysis

At the top of the data-processing job pyramid is the general category of systems analysis. Those who develop procedures and design systems are called systems analysts. System analysis involves analysis and evaluation of existing data-processing methods in a particular business or department, the formulation of improved methods, and the implementation of the new system. The function of the systems analyst is a broad one. His concern is for the total problem of developing the most efficient method of accomplishing the processing job. Drawing an analogy, the systems analyst is the architect and the programmer is the builder. Just as the architect must be knowledgeable in many areas, so must a systems analyst be competent in more than one area. He must have a broad knowledge of machines, their function, and capabilities. He must be competent in the area of systems design, and he needs an understanding of the field for which the systems are being designed. Therefore, if accounting systems are being designed, it is important to know accounting. If designing engineering systems, engineering knowledge is appropriate. In addition, the systems analyst needs to be capable in the area of human relations. He will need to work with many other people as he performs his functions of evaluating and implementing systems, people at all levels from the accounting clerks to the managers.

There are many occupational activities which are related to the data processing field, either directly or indirectly. Directly related positions are represented by management and clerical positions within the data-processing department. Indirectly related jobs include sales and service activities.

Data-Processing Management

Management positions include card-punch supervisors, tabulating department supervisors, computer operation managers, manager of programming, systems manager, data-processing manager, and other similar positions. These supervisory positions are usually filled by those who have gained experience in nonsupervisory positions, but not always is this so. Supervision and management require an ability not needed by operating personnel. Persons occupying these positions must be capable of supervising and managing and must devote their time and energies to this end. Therefore, the manager or supervisor must be willing to delegate the work rather than do it himself. He will be required to guide and direct others to a successful completion of systems projects or successful and orderly fulfilling of processing schedules. The mark of a good manager is the level of attainment reached by those under his direction. A programmer who becomes manager of the programming section and finds that he would rather do programming than direct the activities of the programmers is not likely to succeed as manager regardless of his proficiency as a programmer. On the other hand, a supervisor or manager ought to be fully capable of performing the work that he supervises so that he can evaluate and improve the performance of others.

Data-Processing Clerical Occupations

Clerical positions directly related to data processing include such jobs as control clerk, magnetic-tape librarian, encoder, communication-equipment operator, converter operator, etc. In jobs of this type, extensive technical knowledge is generally not required. However, some basic understanding of data-processing concepts and familiarity with the terminology of the field is desirable from the standpoint of securing the job, job performance, and advancement to a more responsible position.

A variety of job duties are represented in this group. Control clerks, for instance, would prepare adding-machine tapes from source documents and do posting work. Tape librarians would be employed where there is extensive use of magnetic tape and they would be responsible for maintaining orderly control of the tapes in the library. Encoding of magnetic or optical characters on input documents would require manipulative skill on a keyboard similar to that required to operate a typewriter or adding machine. Each piece of peripheral equipment, such as card-to-tape converters and the various data-transmission devices, would have its similar, but individual skill requirement.

Data-Processing Sales and Service

The selling and maintaining of data-processing systems is another area of related job opportunity. The manufacturers of computers and data-processing equipment establish sales offices in most metropolitan areas. These offices are generally staffed with people engaged in sales and systems installation and those who repair and maintain customer machines. Selling of data-processing systems is not like selling a shirt or a hammer. The customer who is buying a shirt or a hammer, or even an automobile, generally knows what he needs and wants. This is not always true of the potential buyer of data-processing equipment. He may not even be aware that he has a need for a system. He is very likely not completely informed of the capabilities, limitations, advantages, and disadvantages of the various systems. Therefore, the selling of data-processing equipment is often an education process. The salesman will be required to analyze the customer's data-processing problem and make a proposal. The proposal would specify the type and extent of equipment that would fulfill the customer's data-processing needs. To "sell" the customer, the proposal should contain documentation showing how the equipment would be used in specific applications. The salesman, in fact, must be a systems analyst if he is to recognize and present a plan to solve the customer's problem. The salesman must know equipment, but more than that he must know systems and procedures so that he can understand and communicate with his client.

The repair of data-processing machines, whether they are mechanical or electronic, requires men who have had special training for the job. Manufacturers of equipment train their own personnel to repair their machines. Generally this training is done in company schools at home or branch offices. This training is very specialized and usually limited to the machines which the employee will encounter. A knowledge of data-processing techniques is not essential for performance as a machine-maintenance man. More important is a good basic understanding of electricity and electronics. Here again, however, maintenance personnel deal directly with data-processing people, and it will be beneficial for all if he can "talk the language." He should know data-processing terminology and techniques. For instance, a person who expects to repair computers should know how to program one.

REVIEW QUESTIONS

7. What is wrong with the question, "How much money do data-processing people make?"

8. Describe the different machine-operation job areas. How do they differ in skill requirements?

9. How does programming differ from systems analysis?

Education for Data Processing

Data-processing education is one of the newest segments of any school's curriculum. The real impact of the computer is just now beginning to be felt. The use of computers has been limited, and education for computers and data processing has likewise been limited. This situation is rapidly changing, however. As the computer and automated data processing have become commonplace, education for their use also is becoming an accepted part of the educational pattern.

Need for Basic Data-Processing Education

How much training is necessary in preparation for employment in the field of data processing? Let us repeat that the *amount* of training varies with the job being sought. The job also dictates the *type* of training needed. All data-processing positions require some sort and degree of special training, however.

Throughout the foregoing discussion of the various data-processing occupations, each required at least a basic understanding of data-processing concepts and a working vocabulary of data-processing terms. Such a minimal background would be sufficient for only the least demanding and the least technical occupations, however. Many high schools and colleges are now including such introductory courses in their curricula.

Need for Specialized Data-Processing Education

Specialized data-processing training is needed for specialized data-processing occupations. If a person expects to be a programmer, he must learn programming. Programming can be learned in classes available in high schools, colleges, universities, company schools, and private schools, or programming can be self-taught. A single class in programming or the reading of one book will not make a programmer, however. It takes extensive training followed by experience or extensive experience to become a proficient programmer.

Most computer operators are trained on the job or in short classes provided by the manufacturer or the user of the computer. Students do not usually train specifically for console operation, but rather console operation provides an entry job and stepping stone to programming and systems analysis. Schools are not generally equipped to teach console operation because it is rare to have more than one computer, and that may not be the one that a student is likely to encounter. Console operator training is a by-product of programming training.

For those who would become tabulating-machine operators, training in EAM operation and board wiring is desirable. Machine manufacturers have generally been the sole providers of this training in the past, but the schools are now making this type of training available. Some high schools, some private schools, and many two-year colleges have classes in machine operation and wiring. Machine operation does not require extensive training.

A few hours of instruction and practice would be sufficient for the simpler machines and a few days training could make a productive machine operator in the tab department. The learning of panelboard wiring, however, takes much longer. Several days of full-time instruction might be needed to learn just one machine. EAM technicians would need the training in board wiring whereas operators generally would not.

Card-punch, or key-punch, training is provided by the manufacturer. IBM conducts classes in the operation of the card punch. Private schools, some high schools, and a few colleges offer this kind of training. Only a few days are necessary to become productive on the card punch if the trainee has a good typing ability as a base.

Need as Supplemental Education

A common misunderstanding among students and prospective students is that technical knowledge of machines and programming is sufficient for entry and success in the data-processing field. The technical knowledge is indispensable but tends to become sterile if allowed to stand alone. Electronic and mechanical devices are tools and supply a means to an end. Their functions are not an end in themselves. Therefore, technical knowledge is only a part of the background needed by the EDP professional. The other segment, and possibly the largest segment, of knowledge and ability needed by the data processor is outside the technical area. Creativity, vision, and perspective (common sense) are vital ingredients. Extensive and comprehensive understanding of the area in which the problem is to be solved is the paramount requirement. It should be recognized that the ability to program a computer can in no way substitute for an understanding of mathematics. The computer is a tool for the mathematician, not a substitute. Likewise, the computer and computer training do not replace the accountant and accounting training, the scientist and scientific training, the engineer and engineering training, etc.

Data processing and computer training supplements, but does not replace the need for training in the basic areas of endeavor.

REVIEW QUESTIONS

10. Where can data-processing education be acquired? Indicate the type of training afforded by each training agency, whether general, specialized, or professional.

11. Why is data-processing training not necessarily an end in itself?

Future Employment Trends

There can be little doubt about the EDP career picture. The demand for capable and well-trained data-processing personnel will be high. The demand will be greater in the higher-level positions, namely, systems analysis and systems management. But nearly as critical will be the demand for operating and programming personnel. These predictions are based on the continuing computer population explosion and the emerging trend toward a much broader usage of electronic data processing. The number of working programmers and analysts will probably double or triple during the next four to five years, based on an expected doubling of the number of computer installations. The future could hardly be brighter, but requirements are rigid. The EDP profession is no place for those lacking in ambition or ability. A career in EDP will require rigorous training and continual up-dating of skills and knowledge.

Certificate in Data Processing

Evidence of the growing stature of the data-processing profession has been the enthusiastic acceptance of the Data Processing Management Association's program for certification of data-processing personnel. The certificate is meant to be a measure of competency in the field of data processing. Through a combination of training, experience, character qualification, and successful completion of the CDP examination, a person can qualify and earn the certificate.

The examination covers a range of subjects deemed essential for performance at the professional level in the field of data processing and systems analysis. The areas from which questions are taken are as follows:

1. Computer concepts and equipment
2. Unit record concepts and equipment
3. Data systems concepts and equipment
4. Accounting
5. Mathematics
6. Statistics

In order to qualify to sit for the examination, the candidate must have completed a prescribed sequence of courses including mathematics, managerial and cost accounting, data-processing systems, English, and statistics plus eight courses selected from a list of electives. In addition, a minimum of three years of direct work experience is required, and the applicant must have satisfactory character references before he can be awarded the CDP certificate.

TRENDS IN COMPUTER DEVELOPMENT

The development of the electronic computer has bordered on the phenomenal. What seems a dream one day is often reality the next. The pocket-sized computer is probably not imminent, but computers are getting smaller and more powerful. Steady improvement in computer hardware is being, and will continue to be, made at a rapid rate. These improvements can be classified in two general areas as follows:

1. Miniaturization of electronic components
2. Better man-machine communication

Miniaturization

Miniaturization of the components of storage devices is a current development. Research laboratories have developed smaller magnetic cores (Fig. 11-1), thin film, and microscopic integrated circuits. Magnetic cores have been developed which have an internal diameter of 7.5 mils, a space

Fig. 11-1. Miniaturized cores.

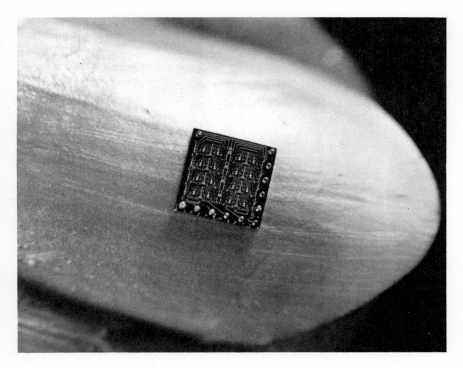

Fig. 11-2. Integrated circuit.

which would crowd three human hairs. Use of cores of this size provides storage capability of 4,000 bits of data in 1 square inch and enables the unit to perform nearly three memory cycles in 1 microsecond.

Thin-film memory is based on the same working principle as core storage. Instead of individual cores strung on wires, however, small metallic spots with connecting "wires" are implanted on the surface of a thin film insulating base. The film might be a plastic or glass substance. These paper-thin wafers are then arranged into planes to form a memory unit. The use of thin film provides a greatly reduced space need for memory areas.

The integrated, or monolithic, circuit represents another approach in the trend toward miniaturization. *Monolithic* means *single* or *single solid block,* and so the *monolithic integrated circuit* is the term applied to a single piece of semiconductor material which is formed by diffusing different materials together (Fig. 11-2). The formation of the block, or "chip," is accomplished in such a way as to produce the desired electronic circuitry (transistors, diodes, resistors, and connections). The material generally used is silicon. Each silicon chip may house as many as 16 complete electronic circuits consisting of as many as 148 components and be as small as $\frac{1}{10}$ inch square. Each circuit stores one bit of information. Thus, up to 16 bits can be stored in one monolithic memory chip.

There are two reasons for the emphasis on making computer memory and logic components smaller:

1. To provide greater processing speeds
2. To provide greater storage capacity

Increased processing speed has its greatest implication for real-time processing. It is of significance in such areas as guidance systems, process control systems, simulation, communication systems, and other applications based on the *feedback* principle.

The reduction in size of components will provide for storage of greater amounts of data in the same space. The implication here relates to information retrieval and mass storage of data. The narrowing of the space-to-data volume ratio opens the way for unlimited use of electronically stored and electronically accessible data libraries.

Man-Machine Communication

The problems of input and output have been apparent since before the current trend to more sophisticated CPUs. Input-output equipment has remained predominately mechanical. Card readers and card punches have been made faster. Magnetic-tape drives have been improved, and the character density of magnetic tape has been increased. Other devices have been improved. But, in these cases improvements were mere modifications of the existing concepts. With faster processing speeds, the need for new methods of imputing and outputing data becomes critical.

The ideal situation in any data-processing system is the elimination of any appreciable time lapse between the creation of data and the evaluation of the effect of those data upon the total operation. In other words, real-time processing. Up to and including the present, data have been, and are, laboriously translated from human language into machine language before being processed. Cards have had to be punched from source documents, for instance. Such a time lag from transaction to processing is becoming intolerable, and the remedy for the situation is more direct input into the information-processing system. The future will include the use of more direct input systems. Today, cash registers print an input paper tape which can be read optically. The next step will be to link the cash register directly to the central processor so that transactions can be processed immediately. Input stations will be located at the data source in classrooms, on hospital floors, on construction sites, etc.

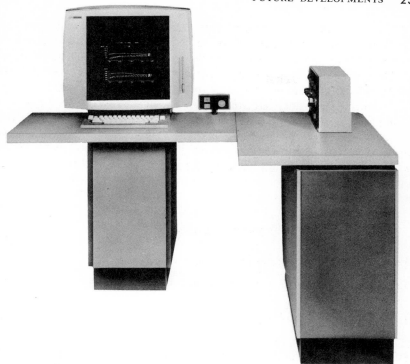

Fig. 11-3. CRT output unit.

Likewise, output will be more readily and immediately accessible. Cathode-ray tube (CRT) output (Fig. 11-3) will become more widely used. Such output will be used extensively by corporate managers, bank tellers, students, and many others. Corporate managers will be able to see the very latest business results displayed in graphic or descriptive form. The bank teller can inquire and receive an immediate display of a signature or an account balance. The student can request and have displayed course material to which he can respond.

Direct interaction between man and computer will become commonplace. With nearly unlimited storage capacity, greatly increased processing speeds, and direct input and output capability, computing service will be made available to all who desire it on a "dial-up" basis. Today, machines can read printed copy. In the future they will read handwriting. Today, machines can understand and respond to the spoken word to a limited degree. It is not unreasonable to anticipate the possibility of auditory and verbal communication between man and machine in the future.

These new devices and techniques will change many existing concepts and conventions. The printed word as the medium for transmitting information will undoubtedly be replaced by electronic storage and transmittal. There is enough evidence to predict the eventual obsolescence of books. The knowledge of man will be much more efficiently stored, cataloged, and disseminated when done electronically. The library will disappear in its present form. "Book learning" will be obsolete. Students will learn by means of a dialog with the programmed computer which has access to a nearly unlimited supply of information.

Only the future can tell what the future will bring, but it seems certain that it will be exciting.

REVIEW QUESTIONS

12. How is the Certificate in Data Processing earned?

13. What are some implications of miniaturization of computers and computer circuitry?

14. Give some examples of types of memory which require reduced amounts of space.

15. What kind of input and output devices and media can be expected to be a part of information systems of the future?

APPENDIX A
GLOSSARY OF DATA-PROCESSING TERMINOLOGY

access time, (1) the time it takes a computer to locate data or an instruction word in its storage section and transfer it to its arithmetic unit where the required computations are performed. (2) The time it takes to transfer information which has been operated on from the arithmetic unit to the location in storage where the information is to be stored. Synonymous with (read time) and (real time) and related to (write time,) and (time, word, 2).

accounting machine, same as (tabulator).

accumulator, (1) the register and associated equipment in the arithmetic unit of the computer in which arithmetical and logical operations are performed. (2) A unit in a digital computer where numbers are totaled, i.e., accumulated. Often the accumulator stores one operand, and, upon receipt of any second operand, it forms and stores the result of performing the indicated operation on the first and second operands. Related to (adder).

adder, a device which forms, as output, the sum of two, or more numbers presented as inputs. Often no data retention feature is included; i.e., the output signal remains only as long as the input signals are present. Related to (accumulator, 2).

address, (1) an identification, represented by a name, label, or number, for a register or location in storage. Addresses are also a part of an instruction word along with commands, tags, and other symbols. (2) The part of an instruction which specifies an operand for the instruction.

*ADP, A*utomatic *D*ata Processing.

*ALGOL, ALGO*rithmic Language.

algorithmic language, an arithmetic language by which numerical procedures may be precisely presented to a computer in a standard form. The language is intended not only as a means of directly presenting any numerical procedure to any suitable computer for which a compiler exists, but also as a means of communicating numerical procedures among individuals. The language itself is the result of international cooperation to obtain a standardized algorithmic language. The International Algebraic Language is the forerunner of ALGOL. Synonymous with (ALGOL).

alphabetic-numeric, the characters which include letters of the alphabet, numerals, and other symbols such as punctuation or mathematical symbols.

alphameric, a contraction of alphanumeric and alphabetic-numeric.

alphanumeric, a contraction of alphabetic-numeric.

ALU, Arithmetic and Logical Unit, see (arithmetic unit).

analog, the representation of numerical quantities by means of physical variables, e.g., translation, rotation, voltage, or resistance. Contrasted with (digital).

analog computer, see (computer, analog).

analog device, a mechanism which represents numbers by physical quantities, e.g., by lengths, as in a slide rule, or by voltage currents, as in a differential analyzer or a computer of the analog type.

analyst, a person skilled in the definition and development of techniques for the solving of a problem; especially those techniques for solutions on a computer.

application, the system or problem to which a computer is applied. Reference is often made to an application as being either of the computational type, where arithmetic computations predominate, or of the data-processing type, where data-handling operations predominate.

arithmetic unit, the portion of the hardware of a computer in which arithmetic and logical operations are performed. The arithmetic unit generally consists of an accumulator and some special registers for the storage of operands and results, supplemented by shifting and sequencing circuitry for implementing multiplication, division, and other desired operations. Synonymous with ALU.

assemble, (1) to integrate subroutines that are supplied, selected, or generated into the main routine by means of preset parameters, by adapting, or by changing relative and symbolic addresses to absolute form, or by placing them in storage. (2) To operate or perform the functions of an assembler.

assembler, a computer program which operates on symbolic input data to produce machine instructions from that data by carrying out such functions as: translation of symbolic operation codes into computer operating instructions, assigning locations in storage for successive instructions, or computation of absolute addresses from symbolic addresses. An assembler generally translates input symbolic codes into machine instructions item for item and produces as output the same number of instructions or constants which were defined in the input symbolic codes. Synonymous with (assembly routine) and (assembly program) and related to (compiler).

assembly program, same as (assembler).

assembly routine, same as (assembler).

audit trail, a system for tracing items of data from processing step to processing step, particularly from a machine produced report or other machine output back to the original source data.

automatic check, a provision constructed in hardware for verifying the accuracy of information transmitted, manipulated, or stored by any unit or device in a computer. Synonymous with (built-in check), (built-in automatic check) and (hardware check) and related to (program, check, 2).

automatic data processing, data processing performed by a system of electronic or electrical machines so interconnected and interacting as to reduce to a minimum the need for human assistance or intervention. Synonymous with (ADP) and related to (automatic data-processing system).

automatic data-processing equipment, (1) a machine, or group of interconnected machines, consisting of input, storage, computing, control, and output devices, which uses electronic circuitry in the main computing element to perform arithmetic and/or logical operations automatically by means of internally stored or externally controlled programmed instructions. Synonymous with (equipment, electronic data processing). (2) The data-processing equipment which directly supports or services the central computer operation. Clarified by (peripheral equipment).

automatic data-processing system, the term descriptive of an interacting assembly of procedures, processes, methods, personnel, and automatic data-processing equipment to perform a complex series of data-processing operations.

automatic programming, the method or technique by which the computer itself is used to transform or translate programming from a language or form that is easy for a human being to produce into a language that is efficient for the computer to use. Examples of automatic programming are compiling, assembling, and interpretive routines.

automation, (1) the implementation of processes by automatic means. (2) The theory, art, or technique of making a process more automatic. (3) The investigation, design, development, and application of methods of rendering processes automatic, self-moving, or self-controlling.

auxiliary equipment, same as (off-line equipment).
auxiliary storage, see (storage, auxiliary).
base, same as (radix).
base notation, same as (notation, radix)
batch processing, a technique by which items to be processed must be coded and collected into groups prior to processing.

batch total, the sum of certain quantities, pertaining to batches of unit records, used to verify the accuracy of operations on a particular batch of records; e.g., in a payroll calculation, the batches might be departments, and batch totals would be number of employees in the department, total hours worked in the department, total pay for the department. Batches, however, may be arbitrary, such as orders received from 9 a.m. to 11 a.m. on a certain day.

binary, a characteristic, property, or condition in which there are but two possible alternatives; e.g., the binary number system using 2 as its base and using only the digits zero (0) and one (1). Related to (binary-coded decimal).

binary-coded character, one element of a notation system representing alphameric characters such as decimal digits, alphabetic letters, and punctuation marks by a predetermined configuration of consecutive binary digits.

binary-coded decimal, describing a decimal notation in which the individual decimal digits are represented by a pattern of ones and zeros; e.g., in the 8-4-2-1 coded decimal notation, the number 12 is represented as 0001 0010 for 1 and 2, respectively, whereas in pure or straight binary notation it is represented as 1100. Related to (binary).

binary-coded decimal number, a number usually consisting of successive groups of figures, in which each group of four figures is a binary number that represents, but does not necessarily equal arithmetically, a particular figure in an associated decimal number; e.g., if the three rightmost figures of a decimal number are 262, the three rightmost figure groups of the binary-coded decimal number might be 0010, 0110, and 0010.

binary digit, a numeral in the binary scale of notation. This digit may be zero (0), or one (1). It may be equivalent to an "on" or "off" condition, a yes or a no. Often abbreviated to (bit).

binary number, a number, usually consisting of more than one figure, representing a sum, in which the individual quantity represented by each figure has a radix of two. The figures used are 0 and 1.

bit, (1) an abbreviation of binary digit. (2) A single character in a binary number. (3) A single pulse in a group of pulses. (4) A unit of information capacity of a storage device. The capacity in bits is the logarithm to the base two of the number of possible states of the device. Related to (storage capacity).

block diagram, (1) a graphical representation of the hardware in a computer system. The primary purpose of a block diagram is to indicate the paths along which information and/or control flows between the various parts of a computer system. It should not be confused with the term *flow chart.* (2) A coarser and less symbolic representation than a flow chart.

block sort, a sort of one or more of the most significant characters of a key to serve as a means of making workable-sized groups from a large volume of records to be sorted.

boolean algebra, a process of reasoning, or a deductive system of theorems using a symbolic logic and dealing with classes, propositions, or on-off circuit elements. It employs symbols to represent operators such as AND, OR, NOT, EXCEPT, IF . . . THEN, etc., to permit mathematical calculation. Named after George Boole, famous English mathematician (1815–1864).

branch, the selection of one of two or more possible paths in the flow of control, based on some criterion. The instructions which mechanize this concept are sometimes called "branch instructions"; however, the terms *transfer of control* and *jump* are more widely used.

branch instruction, an instruction to a computer that enables the programmer to instruct the computer to choose between alternative subprograms depending upon the conditions determined by the computer during the execution of the program.

B register, (1) same as (index register). (2) A register used as an extension of the accumulator during multiply and divide processes.

buffer, (1) an internal portion of a data-processing system serving as intermediary storage between two storage or data-handling systems with different access times or formats; usually to connect an input or output device with the main or internal high-speed storage. Clarified by (storage, buffer, 4). (2) A logical OR circuit. (3) An isolating component designed to eliminate the reaction of a driven circuit on the circuits driving it; e.g., a buffer amplifier. (4) A diode.

buffer storage, see (storage, buffer).

buffered computer, see (computer, buffered).

bug, a mistake in the design of a routine or a computer, or a malfunction.

byte, (1) a generic term to indicate a measurable portion of consecutive binary digits; e.g., an eight-bit or six-bit byte. (2) A group of binary digits usually operated upon as a unit.

card, eighty (80) column, a punch card with 80 vertical columns representing 80 characters. Each column is divided into two sections, one with character positions labeled zero through nine, and the other labeled eleven (11) and twelve (12). The 11 and 12 positions are also referred to as the X and Y zone punches, respectively. Related to (card, punch) and (card, ninety column).

card field, a set of card columns, either fixed as to number and position or, if variable, then identifiable by position relative to other fields. Corresponding fields on successive cards are normally used to store similar information.

Card, ninety (90) column, a punch card with 90 vertical columns representing 90 characters. The columns are divided in half horizontally, so that the vertical columns in the upper half of the card are numbered 1 through 45 and those in the lower half, 46 through 90. Six punching positions may be used in each column; these are designated, from top to bottom, to represent the digits 0, 1, 3, 5, 7, and 9 by a single punch. The digits 2, 4, 6, and 8 and other characters may be represented by a combination of two or more punches. Related to (card, punch) and (card, eighty column).

card, punch, a heavy stiff paper of constant size and shape, suitable for punching (in a pattern that has meaning) and for being handled mechanically. The punched holes are sensed electrically by wire brushes, mechanically by metal fingers, or photoelectrically by photocells. Related to (card, eighty column) and (card, ninety column).

card punch, a machine which punches cards in designated locations to store data which can be conveyed to other machines or devices by reading or sensing the holes. Synonymous with (card-punch unit).

card reader, (1) a mechanism that senses information punched into cards. (2) An input device consisting of a mechanical punch-card reader and related electronic circuitry which transcribes data from punch cards to working storage or magnetic tape.

card reproducer, see (reproducer, card).

card stacker, a receptacle that accumulates cards after they have passed through a machine.

cathode-ray tube, (1) an electronic vacuum tube containing a screen on which information may be stored by means of a multigrid modulated beam of electrons from the thermionic emitter storage effected by charged or uncharged spots. (2) A storage tube. (3) An oscilloscope tube. (4) A picture tube. Synonymous with (CRT).

cell, (1) the storage for one unit of information, usually one character of one word. (2) A location specified by all or part of the address and possessed of the faculty to store. Specific terms such as column, field, location, and block, are preferable when appropriate.

cell, binary, (1) a cell of one binary digit capacity. (2) A one-bit register or bit position.

central processing unit, same as (main frame, 1).

chad, a small piece of paper tape or punch card removed when punching a hole to represent information.

channel, (1) a path along which information, particularly a series of digits or characters, may flow. (2) One or more parallel tracks treated as a unit. (3) In a circulating storage, a channel is one recirculating path containing a fixed number of words stored serially by word. Synonymous with (band). (4) A path for electrical communication. (5) A band of frequencies used for communication.

character, (1) one symbol of a set of elementary symbols, corresponding to the keys on a typewriter. The symbols usually include the decimal digits 0 through 9, the letters A through Z, punctuation marks, operation symbols, and any other single symbols which a computer may read, store, or write. (2) The electrical, magnetic, or mechanical profile used to represent a character in a computer and its various storage and peripheral devices. A character may be represented by a group of other elementary marks, such as bits or pulses.

character recognition, the technology of using a machine to sense, and encode into a machine language, characters which are written or printed to be read by human beings.

check bit, a binary check digit; often a parity bit. Related to (parity check) and (self-checking number).

check digit, one or more redundant digits carried along with a machine word and used in relation to the other digits in the word as a self-checking, or error-detecting, code to detect malfunctions of equipment in data-transfer operations. Related to (parity check).

circuit, (1) a system of conductors and related electrical elements through which electrical current flows. (2) A communications link between two or more points.

clear, to erase the contents of a storage device by replacing the contents with blanks, or zeros. Contrasted with (hold) and clarified by (erase).

closed loop, see (loop, closed).

closed shop, the operation of a computer facility where programming service to the user is the responsibility of a group of specialists and is effectively the phase of program formulation separated from that of computer implementation. The programmers are not allowed in the computer room to run or oversee the running of their programs. Contrasted with (open shop).

COBOL, Common Business Oriented Language.

code, (1) a system of symbols for meaningful communication. Related to (instruction, 1). (2) A system of symbols for representing data or instructions in a computer or a tabulating machine. (3) To translate the program for the solution of a problem on a given computer into a sequence of machine language or pseudo instructions and addresses acceptable to that computer. Related to (encode). (4) A machine-language program.

code, computer, (1) a system of combinations of binary digits used by a given computer. Synonymous with (code, machine-language). (2) A repertoire of instructions.

code, machine-language, same as (code, computer, 1) and contrasted with (code, symbolic).

code, symbolic, a code which expresses programs in source language, i.e., by referring to storage locations and machine operations by symbolic names and addresses which are independent of their hardware-determined names and addresses. Synonymous with (pseudo code), see (code, 3), and contrasted with (code, machine-language).

coder, a person who prepares instruction sequences from detailed flow charts and other algorithmic procedures prepared by others, as contrasted with a programmer who prepares the procedures and flow charts.

coding, the ordered list in computer code or pseudo code of the successive computer instructions representing successive computer operations for solving a specific problem.

collate, to merge two or more ordered sets of data or cards in order to produce one or more ordered sets which still reflect the original ordering relations. The collation process is the merging of two sequences of cards, each ordered on some mutual key, into a single sequence ordered on the mutual key.

collator, a device used to collate or merge sets or decks of cards or other units into a sequence. A typical example of a card collator has two input feeds, so that two ordered sets may enter into the process, and four output stackers, so that four ordered sets can be generated by the process.Three comparison stations are used to route the cards to one stacker or the other by comparison of criteria specified by plugboard wiring.

common business-oriented language, a specific language by which business data-processing procedures may be precisely described in a standard form. The language is intended not only for presenting any business program directly to any suitable computer for which a compiler exists, but also for communicating such procedures among individuals. Synonymous with (COBOL).

compile, to produce a machine-language routine from a routine written in source language by selecting appropriate subroutines from a subroutine library, as directed by the instructions or other symbols of the original routine, supplying the linkage which combines the subroutines into a workable routine, and translating the subroutines and linkage into machine language. The compiled routine is then ready to be loaded into storage and run; i.e., the compiler does not usually run the routine it produces.

compiler, a computer program more powerful than an assembler. In addition to its translating function, which is generally the same process as that used in an assembler, it is able to replace certain items of input with series of instructions, usually called *subroutines.* Thus, whereas an assembler translates item for item and produces as output the same number of instructions or constants which were put into it, a compiler will do more than this. The program which results from compiling is a translated and expanded version of the original. Synonymous with (compiling routine) and related to (assembler).

compiling routine, same as (compiler).

complement, (1) a quantity expressed to the base n, which is derived from a given quantity by a particular rule; frequently used to represent the negative of the given quantity. (2) A complement on n, obtained by subtracting each digit of the given quantity from $n-1$, adding unity to the least-significant digit, and performing all resultant carries; e.g., the twos complement of binary 11010 is 00110, and the tens complement of decimal 456 is 544. (3) A complement on $n-1$, obtained by subtracting each digit of the given quantity from $n-1$; e.g., the ones complement of binary 11010 is 00101; the nines complement of decimal 456 is 543. Synonymous with (radix minus 1 complement) and (radix complement).

computer, a device capable of accepting information, applying prescribed processes to the information, and supplying the results of these processes. It usually consists of input and output devices, storage, arithmetic and logical units, and a control unit.

computer, analog, a computer which represents variables by physical analogies; thus any computer which solves problems by translating physical conditions such as flow, temperature, pressure, angular positions, or voltage into related mechanical or electrical quantities and uses mechanical or electrical equivalent circuits as an analog for the physical phenomenon being investigated. In general it is a computer which uses an analog for each variable and produces analogs as output. Thus an analog computer measures continuously, whereas a digital computer counts discretely. Related to (data-processing machine).

computer, buffered, a computing system with a storage device which permits input and output data to be stored temporarily in order to match the slow speed of I-O devices with the higher speeds of the computer. Thus, simultaneous input-output-computer operations are possible. A data-transmission trap is essential for effective use of buffering, since it obviates frequent testing for the availability of a data channel.

computer, digital, a computer which processes information represented by combinations of discrete or discontinuous data as compared with an analog computer for continuous data. More specifically, it is a device for performing sequences of arithmetic and logical operations, not only on data, but on its own program. Still more specifically it is a stored-program digital computer capable of performing sequences of internally stored instructions, as opposed to calculators, such as card-programmed calculators, on which the sequence is impressed manually. Related to (data-processing machine).

computer, general-purpose, a computer designed to solve a large variety of problems; e.g., a stored-program computer which may be adapted to any of a very large class of applications.

computer, solid-state, a computer built primarily from solid-state electronic circuit elements.

computer, special-purpose, a computer designed to solve a specific class or narrow range of problems.

computer, stored-program, a computer capable of performing sequences of internally stored instructions and usually capable of modifying those instructions as directed by the instructions.

configuration, a group of machines which are interconnected and are programmed to operate as a system.

console, a portion of the computer which may be used to control the machine manually, correct errors, determine the status of machine circuits, registers, and counters, determine the contents of storage, and manually revise the contents of storage.

control, (1) the part of a digital computer or processor which determines the execution and interpretation of instructions in proper sequence, including the decoding of each instruction and the application of the proper signals to the arithmetic unit and other registers in accordance with the decoded information. (2) Frequently, it is one or more of the components in any mechanism responsible for interpreting and carrying out manually initiated directions. Sometimes it is called *manual control.* (3) In some business applications, a mathematical check. (4) In programming, instructions which determine conditional jumps are often referred to as *control instructions,* and the time sequence of execution of instructions is called the *flow of control.*

control field, a constant location where information for control purposes is placed; e.g., in a set of punch cards, if columns 79 and 80 contain various codes which control whether or not certain operations will be performed on any particular card, then columns 79 and 80 constitute a control field.

control panel, see (panel, control).

control total, a sum of numbers in a specified record field of a batch of records determined repetitiously during the processing operation so that any discrepancy from the control indicates an error. A control total often has some significance in itself but may not, as, e.g., when a control total is determined as the sum of identification numbers of records. Related to (hash total).

control unit, see (control).

conversion, (1) the process of changing information from one form of representation to another, such as, from the language of one type of machine to that of another or from magnetic tape to the printed page. Synonymous with (data conversion). (2) The process of changing from one data-processing method to another or from one type of equipment to another; e.g., conversion from punch-card equipment to magnetic-tape equipment.

conversion, binary to decimal, the process of converting a number written to the base of two to the equivalent number written to the base of ten.

conversion, decimal to binary, the process of converting a number written to the base of ten, or decimal, into the equivalent number written to the base of two, or binary.

convert, (1) to change numerical information from one number base to another. (2) To transfer information from one recorded medium to another.

converter, a device which converts the representation of information or which permits the changing of the method of data processing from one form to another; e.g., a unit which accepts information from punch cards and records the information on magnetic tape, and possibly includes editing facilities.

core storage, same as (storage, magnetic-core).

counter, a device, register, or location in storage for storing numbers or number representations in a manner which permits these numbers to be increased or decreased by the value of another number or to be changed or reset to zero or an arbitrary value.

CPU, Central Processing Unit, same as (main frame, 1).

CRT, Cathode-Ray Tube.

cryogenics, the field of technology which uses devices utilizing properties assumed by metals at absolute zero. At these temperatures large current changes can be obtained by relatively small magnetic field changes.

cybernetics, the field of technology involved in the comparative study of the control and intracommunication of information-handling machines and nervous systems of animals and man in order to understand and improve communication.

data, a general term used to denote any or all facts, numbers, letters, and symbols, or facts that refer to or describe an object, idea, condition, situation, or other factors. It connotes basic elements of information which can be processed or produced by a computer. Sometimes data are considered to be expressible only in numerical form, but information is not so limited. Related to (information).

data, phone, a generic term to describe a family of devices available to facilitate data communication.

data processing, (1) the preparation of source media which contain data or basic elements of information, and the handling of such data according to precise rules of procedure to accomplish such operations as classifying, sorting, calculating, summarizing, and recording. (2) The production of records and reports. Synonymous with (data handling).

data-processing center, a computer installation providing data-processing service for others, sometimes called customers, on a reimbursable or nonreimbursable basis.

data-processing machine, a general name for a machine which can store and process numeric and alphabetic information. Related to (computer, analog), (computer, digital), and (automatic data-processing equipment).

data-processing machine system, an assembly of data-processing machines united by some form of regulated interaction to form an organized whole.

data word, a word which may be primarily regarded as part of the information manipulated by a given program. A data word may be used to modify a program instruction, or to be arithmetically combined with other data words.

debug, (1) to locate and correct any errors in a computer program. (2) To detect and correct malfunctions in the computer itself. Related to (diagnostic routine).

decimal number, a number, usually of more than one figure, representing a sum in which the quantity represented by each figure is dependent on the radix of 10. The figures used are 0, 1, 2, 3, 4, 5, 6, 7, 8, and 9.

decision, the computer operation of determining if a certain relationship exists between words in storage or registers and taking one of alternative courses of action. This is effected by conditional jumps or equivalent techniques. Use of this term has given rise to the misnomer "magic brain"; actually the process consists of making comparisons by use of arithmetic to determine the relationship of two terms (numeric, alphabetic, or a combination of both), e.g., equal and greater than or less than.

decision box, the symbol used in flow charts to indicate a choice, or branching, in the information-processing path.

decrement, (1) the quantity by which a variable is decreased. (2) A specific part of an instruction word in some binary computers; thus a set of digits.

density, character, the number of characters that can be stored per unit of length; e.g., on some makes of magnetic-tape drives, 200 or 556 bits can be stored serially, linearly, and axially to the inch.

diagnostic routine, a routine used to locate a malfunction in a computer or to aid in locating mistakes in a computer program; thus, in general, any routine specifically designed to aid in debugging or trouble shooting. Synonymous with (malfunction routine) and related to (debug, 2).

diagram, (1) a schematic representation of a sequence of subroutines designed to solve a problem. (2) A coarser and less symbolic representation than a flow chart, frequently including descriptions in English words. (3) A schematic or logical arrangement within a component.

digit, a sign or symbol used to convey a specific quantity of information either by itself or with other numbers of its set; e.g., 2, 3, 4, and 5 are digits. The base, or radix, must be specified and each digit's value assigned.

digital, pertaining to the utilization of discrete integral numbers on a given base to represent all the quantities that occur in a problem or a calculation. It is possible to express in digital form all information stored, transferred, or processed by a dual-state condition, e.g., on-off, open-closed, and true-false.

digital computer, see (computer, digital).

diode, a device used to permit current flow in one direction in a circuit and to inhibit current flow in the other. In computers, these are primarily germanium or silicone crystals.

disk, magnetic, a storage device having information recorded on the magnetizable surface of a rotating disk. A magnetic-disk storage system is an array of such devices with associated reading and writing heads which are mounted on movable arms. Related to (storage, disk).

disk storage, see (storage, disk).

display tube, a cathode-ray tube used to display information.

document, (1) a form, voucher, or written evidence of a transaction. (2) To instruct, as by citation of references. (3) To substantiate, as by listing authorities.

documentation, the group of techniques necessary for the orderly presentation, organization, and communication of recorded specialized knowledge in order to maintain a complete record of reasons for changes in variables. Documentation is necessary not so much to give maximum utility as to give an unquestionable historical reference record.

down time, the period during which a computer is malfunctioning, or not operating correctly, due to mechanical or electronic failure, as opposed to available time, idle time, or standby time, during which the computer is functional. Contrasted with (up time).

*EAM, E*lectrical *A*ccounting *M*achines.

edit, to rearrange data or information. Editing may involve the deletion of unwanted data, the selection of pertinent data, the application of format techniques, the insertion of symbols such as page numbers and typewriter characters, the application of standard processes such as zero suppression, and the testing of data for reasonableness and proper range. Editing may sometimes distinguish between input editing (rearrangement of source data) and output editing (preparation of table formats).

*EDP, E*lectronic *D*ata *P*rocessing.

electrical accounting machines, the set of conventional punch-card equipment including sorters, collators, and tabulators. Synonymous with (EAM) and clarified by (tabulating equipment).

electro-mechanical data-processing system, the term used to define a system for data processing utilizing punched-card equipment. Synonymous with (EAM system), (punched-card system), (unit-record system), and (tabulating system).

electronic, pertaining to that branch of science which deals with the motion, emission, and behavior of currents of free electrons, especially in vacuum, gas or photo-tubes, and special conductors or semiconductors. This is contrasted with electric which pertains to the flow of large currents in metal conductors.

electronic data processing, data processing performed largely by electronic equipment. Synonymous with (EDP) and related to (automatic data processing).

electronic data-processing equipment, same as (automatic data-processing equipment, 1).

electronic data-processing machine, same as (automatic data-processing equipment, 1).

electronic data-processing system, the general term used to define a system for data processing by means of machines utilizing electronic circuitry at electronic speed, as opposed to electromechanical equipment.

eleven (11) punch, same as (X punch, 2).

error rate, the total amount of information in error, due to the transmission media, divided by the total amount of information received.

exception principle system, an information system or data-processing system which reports on situations only when actual results differ from planned results. When results occur within a normal range, they are not reported.

execute, to interpret a machine instruction and perform the indicated operation(s) on the operand(s) specified.

executive routine, a routine which controls loading and relocation of routines and in some cases makes use of instructions which are unknown to the general programmer. Effectively, an executive routine is part of the machine itself. Synonymous with (monitor routine), (supervisory routine), and (supervisory program).

external memory, same as (storage, external).

feedback, the part of a closed-loop system which automatically brings back information about the condition under control.

feedback control, a type of system control obtained when a portion of the output signal is operated upon and fed back to the input in order to obtain a desired effect.

ferromagnetic, pertaining to a phenomenon exhibited by certain materials in which the material is polarized in one direction or the other, or reversed in direction, by the application of a positive or negative magnetic field of magnitude greater than a certain amount. The material retains the magnetic polarization unless it is disturbed. The polarization can be sensed by the fact that a change in the field induces an electromotive force, which can cause a current.

field, an assigned area in a record to be marked with information. See (card field).

field, control, see (control field).

file, an organized collection of information directed toward some purpose. The records in a file may or may not be sequenced according to a key contained in each record.

file, detail, a file of information which is relatively transient. This is contrasted with a master file, which contains relatively more permanent information; e.g., in the case of a weekly payroll for hourly employees, the detail file will contain employee number, regular time, overtime, the hours such employee has worked in a given week, and other information changing weekly. The master file will contain the employee's name, number, department, rate of pay, deduction specifications, and other information which regularly stays the same from week to week.

file maintenance, the periodic modification of a file to incorporate changes which occurred during a given period.

film-optical-sensing device, a piece of equipment capable of reading the contents of a film by optical methods; i.e., a system consisting of a light source, lenses, photocells, and a film-moving mechanism. The output of the device is digitized and transferred directly to an electronic computer. An example of such a device is the FOSDIC system developed jointly by the Bureau of Census and the National Bureau of Standards.

fixed-point arithmetic, (1) a method of calculation in which operations take place in an invariant manner and in which the computer does not consider the location of the radix point. This is illustrated by desk calculators or slide rules, on which the operator must keep track of the decimal point. The same is true of many automatic computers, in which the location of the radix point is the programmer's responsibility. Contrasted with (floating-point arithmetic). (2) A type of arithmetic in which the operands and results of all arithmetic operations must be properly scaled to have a magnitude between certain fixed values.

fixed word length, a machine word that always contains the same number of characters or digits.

floating-decimal arithmetic, same as (floating-point arithmetic).

floating-point arithmetic, a method of calculation which automatically accounts for the location of the radix point. This is usually accomplished by handling the number as a signed mantissa times the radix raised to an integral exponent; e.g., the decimal number $+88.3$ might be written as $+.883 \times 10^2$; the binary number $-.0011$, as $-. 11 \times 2^{-2}$. Synonymous with (floating-decimal arithmetic) and contrasted with (fixed-point arithmetic, 1).

flow chart, a graphic representation of the major steps of work in process. The illustrative symbols may represent documents, machines, or actions taken during the process. The area of concentration is on where or who does what, rather than how it is to be done. Synonymous with (process chart) and (flow diagram).

flow diagram, same as (flow chart).

FORTRAN, a programming language designed for problems which can be expressed in algebraic notation, allowing for exponents and up to three subscripts. The FORTRAN compiler is a routine for a given machine which accepts a program written in FORTRAN source language and produces a machine-language routine object program. FORTRAN II added considerably to the power of the original language by giving it the ability to define and use almost unlimited hierarchies of subroutines, all sharing a common storage region if desired. Later improvements have added the ability to use boolean expressions and some

capability for inserting symbolic machine-language sequences within a source program.

FOSDIC, Film-Optical-Sensing Device for Input to Computers, same as (film-optical-sensing device).

game theory, a mathematical process of selecting an optimum strategy in the face of an opponent who has a strategy of his own.

gang punch, to punch identical, or constant, information into all of a group of punch cards.

hard copy, a printed copy of machine output; e.g., printed reports, listings, documents, and summaries.

hardware, the physical equipment or devices forming a computer and peripheral equipment. Contrasted with (software).

hardware check, same as (automatic check).

hash total, a sum of numbers in a specified field of a record or of a batch of records used for checking purposes. No attention is paid to the significance of the total. Examples of such numbers are customer numbers or part numbers. If alphabetic characters have a numerical interpretation to a computer, they also could be added. Related to (control total).

heuristic, pertaining to trial and error methods of obtaining solutions to problems.

heuristic routine, a routine by which the computer attacks a problem, not by a direct algorithmic procedure, but by a trial and error approach frequently involving the act of learning. Synonymous with (heuristic program).

high order, pertaining to the weight or significance assigned to the digits of a number; e.g., in the number 123456, the highest-order digit is 1; the lowest-order digit is 6. One may refer to the three high-order bits of a binary word, as another example. Clarified by (order, 3).

Hollerith, a widely used system of encoding alphanumeric information onto cards, hence the term Hollerith cards is synonymous with punch cards. Such cards were first used in 1890 for the United States census and were named after Herman Hollerith, their originator.

housekeeping operation, a general term for the operation which must be performed for a machine run usually before actual processing begins. Examples of housekeeping operations are: establishing controlling marks, setting up auxiliary storage units, reading in the first record for processing, initializing, set-up verification operations, and file identification.

IDP, Integrated Data Processing.

immediate access, pertaining to the ability to obtain data from, or place data in, a storage device or register directly without serial delay due to other units of data and usually in a relatively short period of time.

index register, a register which contains a quantity which may be used to modify addresses. Synonymous with (B register, 1), and (B box).

indicators, the devices which register conditions, such as high or equal conditions resulting from a comparison of plus or minus conditions that result from a computation. A sequence of operations within a procedure may be varied according to the position of an indicator.

information processing, a less restrictive term than data processing, encompassing the totality of scientific and business operations performed by a computer.

information retrieval, the recovering of desired information or data from a collection of documents or other graphic records.

information-retrieval-system, a system for locating and selecting, on demand, certain documents, or other graphic records, relevant to a given information requirement from a file of such material. Examples of information-retrieval systems are classification, indexing, and machine-searching systems.

information system, the network of all communication methods within an organization. Information may be derived from many sources other than a data-processing unit, such as by telephone, by contact with other people, or by studying an operation.

initialize, (1) to set various counters, switches, and addresses to zero or other starting values, at the beginning of, or at the prescribed points in, a computer routine. (2) Used as an aid to recovery and restart during a long computer run.

in-line processing, same as (on-line).

input, (1) information or data transferred or to be transferred from an external storage medium into the internal storage of the computer. (2) Describing the routines which direct input as defined in (1) or the devices from which such information is available to the computer. (3) The device or collective set of devices necessary for input as defined in (1).

input device, the mechanical unit designed to bring data to be processed into a computer; e.g., a card reader, a tape reader, or a keyboard.

input-output, a general term for the equipment used to communicate with a computer and the data involved in the communication. Synonymous with (I-O).

inquiry, a technique by which the interrogation of the contents of a computer's storage may be initiated at a keyboard.

instruction, (1) a set of characters which defines an operation together with one or more addresses, or no address, and which, as a unit, causes the computer to perform the operation on the indicated quantities. The term instruction is preferable to the terms command and order; command is reserved for a specific portion of the instruction word, i.e., the part which specifies the operation which is to be performed; order is reserved for the ordering of the characters, implying sequence, or the order of the interpolation, or the order of the differential equation. Related to (code, 1). (2) The operation or command to be executed by a computer, together with associated addresses, tags, and indices.

instruction, multiple address, an instruction consisting of an operation code and two or more addresses. Usually specified as a two-address, three-address, or four-address instruction.

integrated data processing, (1) a system that treats as a whole all data-processing requirements to accomplish a sequence of data-processing steps, or a number of related data-processing sequences, and which strives to reduce or eliminate duplicating data entry or processing steps. (2) The processing of data by such a system. Synonymous with (IDP).

interpret, (1) to print on a punch card the information punched in that card. (2) To translate nonmachine language into machine-language instructions.

interpreter, (1) a punch-card machine which will take a punch card with no printing on it, read the information in the punched holes, and print a translation in characters in specified rows and columns on the card. (2) An executive routine which, as the computation progresses, translates a stored program expressed in some machinelike pseudo code into machine code and performs the indicated operations, by means of subroutines, as they are translated. An interpreter is essentially a closed subroutine which operates successively on an indefinitely long sequence of program parameters, the pseudo instructions and operands. It may usually be entered as a closed subroutine and leave by a pseudo-code exit instruction.

interrecord gap, an interval of space or time, deliberately left between recording portions of data or records. Such spacing is used to prevent errors through loss of data or overwriting and permits tape stop-start operations.

I-O, Input-Output.

keyboard entry, (1) an element of information inserted manually, usually via a set of switches or marked punch levers called *keys,* into an automatic data-processing system. (2) A medium as in (1) above for achieving access to or entrance into an automatic data-processing system.

key punch, (1) a special device to record information in cards or tape by punching holes in the cards or tape to represent letters, digits, and special characters. (2) To operate a device for punching holes in cards or tape.

key-verify, to use the punch-card machine known as a verifier, which has a keyboard, to make sure that the information supposed to be punched in a punch card has actually been properly punched. The machine signals when the punched hole and the depressed key disagree.

load-and-go, refers to an automatic coding procedure which not only compiles the program, creating machine language, but also proceeds to execute the created program. Load-and-go procedures are usually part of a monitor.

loading routine, a routine which, once it is itself in storage, is able to bring other information into storage from cards or tape.

loop, (1) a self-contained series of instructions in which the last instruction can modify and repeat itself until a terminal condition is reached. The productive instructions in the loop generally manipulate the operands, while bookkeeping instructions modify the productive instructions and keep count of the number of repetitions. A loop may contain any number of conditions for termination. The equivalent of a loop can be achieved by the technique of straight-line coding, by which the repetition of productive and bookkeeping operations is accomplished by explicitly writing the instructions for each repetition. Synonymous with (cycle, 1). (2) A communications circuit between two private subscribers or between a subscriber and the local switching center.

loop, closed, pertaining to a system with a feedback type of control, so that the output is used to modify the input.

loop, open, pertaining to a control system in which there is no self-correcting action for misses of the desired operational condition, as there is in a closed-loop system.

low-order, pertaining to the weight or significance assigned to the digits of a number; e.g., in the number 123456, the low-order digit is 6. One may refer to the three low-order bits of a binary word, as another example. Clarified by (order, 3).

LPM, Lines Per Minute.

machine language, same as (machine-oriented language).

machine operator, the person who manipulates the computer controls, places information media in the input devices, removes the output, and performs other related functions.

machine-oriented language, (1) a language designed for interpretation and use by a machine without translation. (2) A system for expressing information which is intelligible to a specific machine, e.g., a computer or class of computers. Such a language may include instructions which define and direct machine operations and information to be recorded by, or acted upon, by these machine operations. (3) The set of instructions expressed in the number system basic to a computer, together with symbolic operation codes with absolute addresses, relative addresses, or symbolic addresses. Synonymous with (machine language) and contrasted with (problem-oriented language).

machine-sensible, pertaining to information in a form which can be read by a specific machine.

macroinstruction, (1) an instruction consisting of a sequence of microinstructions which are inserted into the object routine for performing a specific operation. (2) The more powerful instructions which combine several operations in one instruction.

magnetic drum, a cylinder having a surface coating of magnetic material, which stores binary information by the orientation of magnetic dipoles near or on its surface. Since the drum is rotated at a uniform rate, the information stored is available periodically as a given portion of the surface moves past one or more flux-detecting devices called *heads* located near the surface of the drum.

magnetic-ink character recognition, a form of input for an electronic data-processing system using special characters printed with ink which can be magnetized. Magnetic-character readers read and transmit the data electronically to conventional storage devices such as magnetic tape. Used in banking as a principal means of inputing data for processing.

magnetic tape, a tape or ribbon of any material impregnated or coated with magnetic or other material on which information may be placed in the form of magnetically polarized spots.

magnetic-tape unit, the mechanism, normally used with a computer, which handles magnetic tape and usually consists of a tape transport, reading or sensing and writing or recording heads, and associated electrical and electronic equipment. Most units may provide for tape to be wound and stored on reels; however, some units provide for the tape to be stored loosely in closed bins. Clarified by (tape transport) and (paper-tape unit).

main frame, (1) the central processor of the computer system. It contains the main storage, arithmetic unit and special register groups. Synonymous with (CPU) and (central processing unit). (2) All that portion of a computer exclusive of the input, output, peripheral, and, in some instances, storage units.

malfunction, a failure in the operation of the hardware of a computer.

management information system, a communications process in which data are recorded and processed for operational purposes. The problems are isolated for higher-level decision making, and information is fed back to top management to reflect the progress or lack of progress made in achieving major objectives.

mark sensing, a technique for detecting special pencil marks entered in special places on a punch card and automatically translating the marks into punched holes.

master card, a card containing fixed or indicative information for a group of cards. It is usually the first card of that group.

match, a data-processing operation similar to a merge, except that instead of producing a sequence of items made up from the input, sequences are matched against each other on the basis of some key.

matrix, (1) an array of quantities in a prescribed form; in mathematics, usually capable of being subject to a mathematical operation by means of an operator or another matrix according to prescribed rules. (2) An array of coupled circuit elements, e.g., diodes, wires, magnetic cores, and relays, which are capable of performing a specific function such as the conversion from one numerical system to another. The elements are usually arranged in rows and columns. Thus a matrix is a particular type of encoder or decoder. Clarified by (encoder) and (decoder).

medium, the physical substance upon which data are recorded; e.g., magnetic tape, punch cards, and paper.

memory, same as (storage).

memory capacity, same as (storage capacity).

merge, to combine items into one sequenced file from two or more similarly sequenced files without changing the order of the items.

microinstruction, a small single short add, shift, or delete type of command.

MICR, Magnetic Ink Character Recognition.

microsecond, one millionth of a second, 10^{-6} second; abbreviated microsec.

millimicrosecond, same as (nanosecond).

millisecond, one thousandth of a second, 10^{-3} second; abbreviated msec or ms.

mnemonic, pertaining to the assisting of, or intending to assist, human memory. Thus a mnemonic term is usually an abbreviation that is easy to remember, e.g., MPY for multiply and ACC for accumulator.

model, mathematical, the general characterization of a process, object, or concept in terms of mathematics which enables the relatively simple manipulation of variables to be accomplished in order to determine how the process, object, or concept would behave in different situations.

monte carlo method, a trial and error method of repeated calculations to discover the best solution of a problem. Often used when a great number of variables are present with interrelationships so extremely complex as to forestall straightforward analytical handling.

multiple punching, Hollerith cards, the punching of two or more holes in a column of a Hollerith card.

multiplex, the process of transferring data from several storage devices operating at relatively low transfer rates to one storage device operating at a high transfer rate in such a manner that the high-speed device is not obliged to wait for the low-speed devices.

multiplexing, (1) the transmission of a number of different messages simultaneously over a single circuit. (2) Utilizing a single device for several similar purposes or using several devices for the same purpose; e.g., a duplexed communications channel carrying two messages simultaneously.

nanosecond, one thousandth of a millionth of a second, 10^{-9} second. Synonymous with (millimicrosecond).

ninety (90) column card, see (card, ninety (90) column).

nondestructive read, see (read, nondestructive).

notation, base, same as (notation, radix).

notation, radix, (1) an annotation consisting of a decimal number written as a subscript suffix to a number, its decimal value indicating the radix of the number; e.g., 11_2 indicates the number 11 is in the radix of two; 11_8 indicates the number 11 is in the radix of eight. (2) A number written without its radix notation is assumed to be in the radix of 10. Synonymous with (base notation.)

numerical control, descriptive of systems in which digital computers are used for the control of operations, particularly of automatic machines, e.g., drilling or boring machines, the operation control of which is applied at discrete points in the operation or process. Contrasted with (process control) in which control is applied continuously.

object program, see (program, object).

octal, pertaining to eight; usually describing a number system of base, or radix, eight; e.g., in octal notation, octal 214 is 2 times 64, plus 1 times 8, plus 4 times 1, and equals decimal 140. Octal 214 in binary-coded octal is represented as 010, 001, 100; octal 214 as a straight binary number is written 10001100. Note that binary-coded octal and straight binary differ only in the use of commas; in the example shown, the initial zero in the straight binary is dropped. Clarified by (octal number).

octal digit, the symbol 0, 1, 2, 3, 4, 5, 6, or 7 used as a digit in the system of notation which uses 8 as the base, or radix. Clarified by (number systems).

octal number, a number of one or more figures, representing a sum in which the quantity represented by each figure is based on a radix of eight. The figures used are 0, 1, 2, 3, 4, 5, 6, and 7. Clarified by (octal).

off line, descriptive of a system and of the peripheral equipment or devices in a system in which the operation of peripheral equipment is not under the control of the central processing unit. Clarified by (off-line equipment).

off-line equipment, the peripheral equipment or devices not in direct communication with the central processing unit of a computer. Synonymous with (auxiliary equipment).

on line, descriptive of a system and of the peripheral equipment or devices in a system in which the operation of such equipment is under the control of the central processing unit and in which information reflecting current activity is introduced into the data-processing system as soon as it occurs; thus, directly in line with the main flow of transaction processing. Clarified by (on-line equipment); synonymous with (in-line processing) and (on-line processing).

on-line equipment, descriptive of a system and of the peripheral equipment or devices in a system in which the operation of such equipment is under control of the central processing unit and in which information reflecting current activity is introduced into the data-processing system as soon as it occurs; thus, directly in line with the main flow of transaction processing. Synonymous with (in-line processing) and (on-line processing).

on-line processing, same as (on line).

open shop, the operation of a computer facility where computer programming, coding, and operating can be performed by any qualified employee of the organization, not necessarily by the personnel of the computing center itself, and where the programmer may assist in, or oversee the running of his program on the computer. Contrasted with (closed shop).

operand, a quantity entering or arising in an instruction. An operand may be an argument, a result, a parameter, or an indication of the location of the next instruction, as opposed to the operation code or symbol itself. It may even be the address portion of an instruction.

operating system, an integrated collection of service routines for supervising the sequencing of programs by a computer. Operating systems may perform debugging, I-O, accounting, compilation, and storage assignment tasks. Synonymous with (monitor system) and (executive system).

operation, a defined action. The action specified by a single computer instruction or pseudo instruction.

operations research, the use of analytic methods adopted from mathematics for solving operational problems. The objective is to provide management with a more logical basis for making sound predictions and decisions. Among the common scientific techniques used in operations research are the following: linear programming, probability theory, information theory, game theory, monte carlo method, and queuing theory. Synonymous with (OR).

optimize, to rearrange the instructions or data in storage so that a minimum number of time-consuming jumps or transfers are required in the running of a program.

*OR O*perations *R*esearch.

order, (1) a defined successive arrangement of elements or events. This term is losing favor as a synonym for instructions, owing to ambiguity. (2) To sequence or arrange in a series. (3) The weight or significance assigned to a digit position in a number. Clarified by (high-order) and (low-order).

output, (1) the information transferred from the internal storage of a computer to secondary or external storage or to any device outside of the computer. (2) The routines which direct 1. (3) The device or collective set of devices necessary for (1). (4) To transfer from internal storage onto external media.

output device, the part of a machine which translates the electrical impulses representing data processed by the machine into permanent results such as printed forms, punched cards, and magnetic writing on tape.

overpunch, to add holes in a card column that already contains one or more holes. Synonymous with (zone punch) and related to (zone bits).

panel, control, (1) an interconnection device, usually removable, which employs removable wires to control the operation of computing equipment. It is used on punch-card machines to carry out functions which are under the control of the user. On computers it is used primarily to control input and output functions. (2) A device or component of some data-processing machines which permits the expression of instructions in a semifixed computer program by the insertion of pins, plugs, or wires into sockets or hubs in the device in a pattern to represent instructions, and thus make electrical interconnections which may be sensed by the data-processing machine. Synonymous with (plugboard) and related to (pinboard).

paper tape, a strip of paper capable of storing or recording information. Storage may be in the form of punched holes, partially punched holes, carbonization or chemical change of impregnated material, or by imprinting. Some paper tapes, such as punched paper tapes, can be read by the input device of a computer or a transmitting device which sense the pattern of holes that represent coded information.

paper-tape unit, the mechanism which handles punched paper tape and usually consists of a paper-tape transport, sensing and recording or perforating heads and associated electrical and electronic equipment. Clarified by (tape transport) and (magnetic-tape unit).

parallel processing, the operation of a computer so that programs for more than one run are stored simultaneously in its storage and executed concurrently.

parallel running, (1) the running of a newly developed system in a data-processing area in conjunction with the continued operation of the current system. (2) The final step in the debugging of a system, this step follows a system test.

parity bit, a check bit that indicates whether the total number of binary 1 digits in a character or word (excluding the parity bit) is odd or even. If a 1 parity bit indicates an odd number of 1 digits, then a 0 bit indicates an even number of them. If the total number of 1 bits, including the parity bit, is always even, the system is called an even parity system. In an odd parity system, the total number of 1 bits, including the parity bit, is always odd.

parity check, a summation check in which the binary digits in a character or word are added, modulo 2, and the sum checked against a single, previously computed parity digit, i.e., a check which tests whether the number of ones in a word is odd or even. Synonymous with (odd-even check) and related to (redundant check) and to (forbidden-combination check).

PCM, Punch-Card Machine, same as (electrical accounting machine).

peripheral equipment, the auxiliary machines which may be placed under the control of the central computer. Examples of this are card readers, card punches, magnetic tape feeds and high-speed printers. Peripheral equipment may be used on line or off line depending upon computer design, job requirements, and economics. Clarified by (automatic data-processing equipment) and by (off-line equipment).

picosecond, one thousandth of a nanosecond, or 10^{-12} second; abbreviated psec.

plotter, a visual display or board on which a dependent variable is graphed by an automatically controlled pen or pencil as a function of one or more variables.

plugboard, same as (panel, control, 2).

primary storage, see (storage, primary).

printer, high-speed, a printer which operates at a speed more compatible with the speed of computation and data processing so that it may operate on line. At the present time a printer operating at a speed of 250 lines per minute, 100 characters per line, is considered high speed.

printer, line, a device capable of printing one line of characters across a page, i.e., 100 or more characters, simultaneously as continuous paper advances line by line in one direction past type bars or a type cylinder that contains all characters in all positions.

printer, serial, a device capable of printing characters one at a time across a page. Many variations in serial printers exist, e.g., typewriter, stylus or matrix serial printer, and high-speed, multiple-line stylus or matrix serial printer.

problem definition, the art of compiling logic in the form of general flow charts and logic diagrams which clearly explain and present the problem to the programmer in such a way that all requirements involved in the run are presented.

problem-oriented language, (1) a language designed for convenience of program specification in a general problem area rather than for easy conversion to machine instruction code. The components of such a language may bear little resemblance to machine instructions. (2) A machine-independent language with which one needs only to state the problem, not the how of solution. Related to (program generators) and contrasted with (procedure-oriented language).

procedure-oriented language, a machine-independent language which describes how the process of solving the problem is to be carried out; e.g., FORTRAN. Contrasted with (problem-oriented language).

process chart, same as (flow chart).

process control, descriptive of systems in which computers, most frequently analog computers, are used for the automatic regulation of operations or processes. Typical are operations in the production of chemicals during which the operation control is applied continuously and adjustments to regulate the operation are directed by the computer to keep the value of a controlled variable constant. Contrasted with (numerical control).

program, (1) the complete plan for the solution of a problem; more specifically the complete sequence of machine instructions and routines necessary to solve a problem. (2) To plan the procedures for solving a problem. This may involve among other things the analysis of the problem, preparation of a flow diagram, preparing details, testing and developing subroutines, allocation of storage locations, specification of input and output formats, and the incorporation of a computer run into a complete data-processing sytem. Related to (routine).

program check, (1) a system of determining the correct program and machine functioning either by running a sample problem with similar programming and a known answer or by using mathematical or logic checks such as comparing A times B with B times A. (2) A check system built into the program of computers that do not have automatic checking. This check system is normally concerned with programs run on computers which are not self-checking internally. Related to (automatic check).

program, control, a sequence of instructions which prescribe the series of steps to be taken by a system, a computer, or any other device.

program, internally stored, a sequence of instructions stored inside the computer in the same storage facilities as the computer data, as opposed to external storage on punched paper tape and pinboards.

program, object, the program which is the output of an automatic coding system. Often the object program is a machine-language program ready for execution, but it may well be in an intermediate language. Synonymous with (target program) and (object routine) and contrasted with (source program).

punch, (1) to shear a hole by forcing a solid or hollow sharp-edged tool through a material into a die. (2) The hole resulting from (1).

punch, electronic calculating, a card-punch machine which reads a punch card, performs arithmetic and other operations sequentially, and punches the result in a card.

punch card, see (card, punch).

punch-card unit, same as (card punch).

punch tape, a tape, usually paper, upon which data may be stored in the form of punched holes. Hole locations are arranged in columns across the width of the tape. There are usually five to eight positions, or channels, per column with data represented by a binary-coded decimal system. All holes in a column are sensed simultaneously in a manner similar to that for punch cards. Synonymous with (perforated tape).

radix, the quantity of characters for use in each of the digital positions of a numbering system. In the more common numbering systems the characters are some or all of the Arabic numerals as follows:

System Name	Characters	Radix
Binary	(0, 1)	2
Octal	(0, 1, 2, 3, 4, 5, 6, 7)	8
Decimal	(0, 1, 2, 3, 4, 5, 6, 7, 8, 9)	10

Unless otherwise indicated, the radix of any number is assumed to be 10. For positive identification of a radix-10 number, the radix is written as a subscript to the expressed number, e.g., 126_{10}. The radix of any nondecimal numbers is expressed in similar fashion, e.g., 11_2 and 5_8. Synonymous with (base), (base number), and (radix number).

queuing theory, a form of probability theory useful in studying delays or lineups at servicing points.

random access, (1) pertaining to the process of obtaining information from or placing information in storage where the time required for such access is independent of the location of the information most recently obtained or placed in storage. (2) Pertaining to a device in which random access, as defined in definition (1), can be achieved without effective penalty in time.

random-access memory, same as (storage, random-access).

random-access storage, see (storage, random-access).

raw data, data which have not been processed. Such data may or may not be in machine-sensible form.

read, (1) to sense information contained in some source. (2) The sensing of information contained in some source.

read in, to sense information contained in some source and transmit this information to an internal storage.

read, nondestructive, a reading of the information in a register without changing that information.

read out, to sense information contained in some internal storage and transmit this information to a storage external to the computer.

reader, character, a specialized device which can convert data represented in one of the type fonts or scripts read by human beings directly into machine language. Such a reader may operate optically, or, if the characters are printed in magnetic ink, the device may operate magnetically or optically.

reader, high-speed, a reading device capable of being connected to a computer so as to operate on line without seriously holding up the computer. A card reader reading more than 250 cards per minute would be called a high-speed reader. A reader which reads punched paper tape at a rate greater than 50 characters per second could also be called a high-speed reader. Synonymous with (HSR).

reader, magnetic-tape, a device capable of sensing information recorded on a magnetic tape in the form of a series of magnetized spots.

reader, paper-tape, a device capable of sensing information punched on a paper tape in the form of a series of holes.

real time, same as (access time). Clarified by (real-time processing) and (real-time operation).

real-time operation, the use of the computer as an element of a processing system in which the times of occurrence of data transmission are controlled by other portions of the system, or by physical events outside the system, and cannot be modified for convenience in computer programming. Such an operation either proceeds at the same speed as the events being simulated or at a sufficient speed to analyze or control external events happening concurrently.

real-time processing, the processing of information or data in a sufficiently rapid manner that the results of the processing are available in time to influence the process being monitored or controlled. Synonymous with (real-time system).

real-time system, same as (real-time processing).

record mark, a special character used in some computers either to limit the number of characters in a data transfer or to separate blocked or grouped records in tape.

reel, a spool of tape, generally magnetic tape.

register, a hardware device used to store a certain amount of bits or characters. A register is usually constructed of elements such as transistors or tubes and usually contains approximately one word of information. Common programming usage demands that a register have the ability to operate upon information and not merely store information; hardware usage does not make the distinction.

reproducer, card, a device that reproduces a punch card by punching another similar card.

reproducing, to make a duplicate; generally refers to the process of duplicating a punch card or deck of punch cards by means of a reproducing punch.

rewind, to return a film or magnetic tape to its beginning or past location.

rewrite, the process in a storage device of restoring the information in the device to its state prior to reading.

routine, a set of coded instructions arranged in proper sequence to direct the computer to perform a desired operation or sequence of operations. A subdivision of a program consisting of two or more instructions that are functionally related; therefore, a program. Clarified by (subroutine) and related to (program).

row binary, a method of representing binary numbers on a card where successive bits are represented by the presence or absence of punches in successive positions in a row, as opposed to a series of columns. Row binary is especially convenient in 40-bit-word, or less, computers in which the card is frequently used to store 12 binary words on each half of the card.

*SDA, S*ource-*D*ata *A*utomation.

self-checking number, a number with a suffix figure, related to the figure(s) of the number, used to check the number after it has been transferred from one medium or device to another. Related to (check bit), (modulo-*n* check), and (error-detecting code).

sequence, (1) to put a set of symbols into an arbitrarily defined order; i.e., to select A if A is greater than or equal to B, or to select B if A is less than B. (2) An arbitrarily defined order of a set of symbols; i.e., an orderly progression of items of information or of operations in accordance with some rule.

sequence check, a data-processing operation designed to check the sequence of the items in a file assumed to be already in sequence.

serial, (1) the handling of one unit after the other in a single facility, such as to transfer or store in a digit-by-digit time sequence, or to process a sequence of instructions one at a time, sequentially. (2) The time-sequence transmission of, storage of, or logical operation on, the parts of a word with the same facilities for successive parts. Related to (serial operation, 2).

serial access, pertaining to the process of obtaining information from or placing information in storage where the time required for such access is dependent on the necessity for waiting while nondesired storage locations are processed in turn until the desired location is reached.

servomechanism, a device to monitor an operation as it proceeds and to make necessary adjustments to keep the operation under control. A furnace thermostat is an example of a servomechanism.

shift, to move the characters of a unit of information columnwise right or left. For a number, this is equivalent to multiplying or dividing by a power of the base of notation. Related to (arithmetic shift) and (cyclic shift).

simulation, (1) the representation of physical systems and phenomena by computers, models, or other equipment; e.g., an imitative type of data processing in which an automatic computer is used as a model of some entity, as a chemical process. Information enters the computer to represent the factors entering the real process, the computer produces information that represents the results of the process, and the processing done by the computer represents the process itself. (2) In computer programming, the technique of setting up a routine for one computer to make it operate as nearly as possible like some other computer.

simulator, (1) a computer or model which represents a system or phenomenon and which mirrors or maps the effects of various changes in the original, enabling the original to be studied, analyzed, and understood by means of the behavior of the model. (2) A program or routine corresponding to a mathematical model or representing a physical model. (3) A routine which is executed by one computer but which imitates the operations of another computer.

software, the totality of programs and routines used to extend the capabilities of computers, such as compilers, assemblers, narrators, routines, and subroutines. Contrasted with (hardware).

solid state, the electronic components that convey or control electrons within solid materials, e.g., transistors, germanium diodes, and magnetic cores. Thus, vacuum and gas tubes are not included.

sort, to arrange items of information according to rules dependent upon a key or field contained in the items or records; e.g., to digital sort is to sort first the keys on the least-significant digit and to resort on each higher-order digit until the items are sorted on the most-significant digit.

sorter, a machine which puts items of information into a particular order; e.g., it will determine whether A is greater than, equal to, or less than B and sort, or order, accordingly. Synonymous with (sequencer).

source-data automation, the many methods of recording information in coded forms on paper tapes, punched cards, or tags that can be used over and over again to produce many other records without rewriting. Synonymous with (SDA).

source document, a document from which basic data are extracted.

storage, (1) the term preferred to memory. (2) Pertaining to a device in which data can be stored and from which they can be obtained at a later time. The means of storing data may be chemical, electrical, or mechanical. (3) A device consisting of electronic, electrostatic, or electrical hardware or other elements into which data may be entered and from which data may be obtained as desired. (4) The erasable storage in any given computer. Synonymous with (memory).

storage, auxiliary, a storage device in addition to the main storage of a computer, e.g., magnetic tape, disk, or drum. Auxiliary storage usually holds much larger amounts of information than the main storage, and the information is accessible less rapidly. Contrasted with (storage, main).

storage, buffer, (1) a synchronizing element between two different forms of storage, usually between internal and external. (2) An input device in which information is assembled from external or secondary storage and stored ready for transfer to internal storage. (3) An output device into which information is copied from internal storage and held for transfer to secondary or external storage. Computation continues while transfers between buffer storage and secondary or internal storage or vice versa take place. (4) Any device which stores information temporarily during data transfers. Clarified by (buffer).

storage capacity, the number of elementary pieces of data that can be contained in a storage device. Frequently defined in terms of characters in a particular code or words of a fixed size that can be so contained. Synonymous with (memory capacity) and related to (bit, 4).

storage, core, same as (storage, magnetic-core).

storage, disk, the storage of data on the surface of magnetic disks. Related to (disk, magnetic) and (storage, magnetic-disk).

storage dump, a listing of the contents of a storage device or selected parts of it. Synonymous with (memory dump), (core dump), and (memory printout).

storage, external, (1) the storage of data on a device which is not an integral part of a computer, but in a form prescribed for use by the computer. (2) A facility or device, not an integral part of a computer, on which data usable by a computer are stored, such as off-line magnetic-tape units or punch-card devices. Synonymous with (external memory) and contrasted with (storage, internal).

storage, internal, (1) the storage of data on a device which is an integral part of a computer. (2) The storage facilities forming an integral physical part of the computer and directly controlled by the computer. In such facilities all data are automatically accessible to the computer, e.g., magnetic core and magnetic tape on line. Synonymous with (internal memory) and contrasted with (storage, external).

storage, magnetic, a device or devices which utilize the magnetic properties of materials to store information.

storage, magnetic-core, a storage device in which binary data are represented by the direction of magnetization in each unit of an array of magnetic material, usually in the shape of toroidal rings, but also in other forms such as wraps on bobbins. Synonymous with (core storage).

storage, magnetic-disk, a storage device or system consisting of magnetically coated disks, on the surface of which information is stored in the form of magnetic spots arranged in a manner to represent binary data. These data are arranged in circular tracks around the disks and are accessible to reading and writing heads on an arm which can be moved mechanically to the desired disk and then to the desired track on that disk. Data from a given track are read or written sequentially as the disk rotates. Related to (storage, disk).

storage, magnetic-drum, the storage of data on the surface of magnetic drums. Related to (magnetic drum).

storage, magnetic-tape, a storage device in which data are stored in the form of magnetic spots on metal or coated-plastic tape. Binary data are stored as small magnetized spots arranged in column form across the width of the tape. A read-write head is usually associated with each row of magnetized spots so that one column can be read or written at a time as the tape traverses the head.

storage, main, usually the fastest storage device of a computer and the one from which instructions are executed. Contrasted with (storage, auxiliary).

storage, permanent, a method or device used to retain intermediate or final results outside of the machine, usually in the form of punched cards or magnetic tape.

storage, primary, the main internal storage.

storage, program, a portion of the internal storage reserved for the storage of programs, routines, and subroutines. In many systems protection devices are used to prevent inadvertent alteration of the contents of the program storage. Contrasted with (storage, working).

storage, random-access, a storage technique in which the time required to obtain information is independent of the location of the information most recently obtained. This strict definition must be qualified by the observation that we usually mean relatively random. Thus, magnetic drums are of relatively nonrandom access compared to magnetic cores for main storage, but are of relatively random access compared to magnetic tapes for file storage. Synonymous with (random-access memory) and contrasted with (storage, sequential-access).

storage, secondary, the storage facilities not an integral part of the computer, but directly connected to and controlled by the computer; e.g., magnetic drums and magnetic tapes.

storage, sequential access, a storage technique in which the items of information stored become available only in a one after the other sequence, whether or not all the information or only some of it is desired; e.g., magnetic-tape storage. Related to (serial access) and contrasted with (storage, random-access).

storage, working, a portion of the internal storage reserved for the data upon which operations are being performed. Synonymous with (working space) and (temporary storage) and contrasted with (storage, program).

store, (1) to transfer an element of information to a device from which the unaltered information can be obtained at a later time. (2) To retain data in a device from which it can be obtained at a later time.

stored program, a series of instructions in storage to direct the step-by-step operation of the machine. Synonymous with (stored routine).

stored routine, same as (stored program).

subroutine, (1) the set of instructions necessary to direct the computer to carry out a well-defined mathematical or logical operation. (2) A subunit of a routine. A subroutine is often written in relative or symbolic coding even when the routine to which it belongs is not. (3) A portion of a routine that causes a computer to carry out a well-defined mathematical or logical operation. (4) A routine which is arranged so that control may be transferred to it from a master routine and so that, at the conclusion of the subroutine, control reverts to the master routine. Such a subroutine is usually called a *closed subroutine.* (5) A single routine may simultaneously be both a subroutine with respect to another routine and a master routine with respect to a third. Usually control is transferred to a single subroutine from more than one place in the master routine, and the reason for using the subroutine is to avoid having to repeat the same sequence of instructions in different places in the master routine. Clarified by (routine).

summary punch, a card punch operating in conjunction with another machine, commonly a tabulator, to punch into cards data which have been summarized or calculated by the other machine.

symbolic address, a label, alphabetic or alphanumeric, used to specify a storage location in the context of a particular program. Often, programs are first written using symbolic addresses in some convenient code, which are translated into absolute addresses by an assembly program.

symbolic programming, the use of arbitrary symbols to represent addresses in order to facilitate programming.

synchronizer, a storage device used to compensate for a difference in a rate of flow of information or time of occurrence of events when transmitting information from one device to another.

system, an assembly of procedures, processes, methods, routines, or techniques united by some form of regulated interaction to form an organized whole.

system check, a check on the over-all performance of the system, usually not made by built-in computer check circuits; e.g., the use of control totals, hash totals, and record counts.

systems analysis, the examination of an activity, procedure, method, technique, or a business to determine what must be accomplished and how the necessary operations may best be accomplished.

tabulating equipment, the machines and equipment using punch cards. The group of equipment is called tabulating equipment because the main function of installations of punch-card machines for some 20 years before the first automatic digital computer was to produce tabulations of information resulting from sorting, listing, selecting, and totaling data on punch cards. This class of equipment is commonly called *PCM* or *tab equipment.* Similar to (electrical accounting machine), clarified by (tabulator).

tabulator, a machine which reads information from one medium, e.g., cards, paper tape, and magnetic tape, and produces lists, tables, and totals on separate forms or continuous paper. Synonymous with (accounting machine), and clarified by (tabulating equipment).

tape, a strip of material which may be punched, coated, or impregnated with magnetic or optically sensitive substances and used for data input, storage, or output. The data are stored serially in several channels across the tape transversely to the reading or writing motion.

tape drive, same as (tape transport).

tape transport, the mechanism which moves magnetic or paper tape past sensing and recording heads usually associated with data-processing equipment. Synonymous with (tape drive) and (tape feed); related to (tape unit), (magnetic-tape unit), and (paper-tape unit).

transistor, an electronic device utilizing semiconductor properties to control the flow of currents.

twelve (12) punch, same as (Y punch, 2).

unconditional branch, same as (unconditional transfer).

unconditional transfer, an instruction which switches the sequence of control to some specified location. Synonymous with (unconditional branch), (unconditional jump), and (unconditional transfer of control).

underpunch, a punch in one of the lower rows, 1 through 9, of an 80-column, 12-row punch card.

unit, a portion or subassembly of a computer which constitutes the means of accomplishing some inclusive operation or function.

unit record, (1) a separate record that is similar in form and content to other records, e.g., a summary of a particular employee's earnings to date. (2) Sometimes refers to a piece of nontape auxiliary equipment, e.g., card reader, printer, or console typewriter.

update, (1) to put into a master file the changes required by current information or transactions. (2) To modify an instruction so that the address numbers it contains are increased by a stated amount each time the instruction is performed.

utility routine, a standard routine used to assist in the operation of the computer; e.g., a conversion routine, a sorting routine, a print-out routine, or a tracing routine. Synonymous with (utility program).

variable word-length, a machine word may have a variable number of characters. It may be applied either to a single entry whose information content may be changed from time to time, or to a group of functionally similar entries whose corresponding components are of different lengths.

verifier, a device on which a record can be compared or tested for identity character-by-character with a retranscription or copy as it is being prepared.

verify, to check a transcribing operation by a compare operation. It usually applies to transcriptions which can be read mechanically or electrically.

word, an ordered set of characters which occupies one storage location and is treated by the computer circuits as a unit and transferred as such. Ordinarily a word is treated by the control unit as an instruction, and by the arithmetic unit as a quantity. Word lengths may be fixed or variable depending on the particular computer.

word length, the number of characters in a machine word. In a given computer, the number may be constant or variable.

word mark, an indicator to signal the beginning or end of a word.

write, (1) to transfer information, usually from main storage, to an output device. (2) To record data in a register, location, or other storage device or medium.

X Punch, (1) a punch in the X, or 11, row of an 80-column card. (2) A punch in position 11 of a column. The X punch is often used to control or select, or to indicate a negative number as if it were a minus sign. Also called an 11 punch. Synonymous with (eleven (11) punch).

Y punch, (1) a punch in the Y, or 12, row of an 80-column card, i.e., the top row of the card. (2) A punch in position 12 of a column. It is often used for additional control or selection, or to indicate a positive number as if it were a plus sign. Synonymous with (twelve (12) punch).

zero suppression, the elimination of nonsignificant zeros to the left of significant digits, usually before printing.

zone, (1) a portion of internal storage allocated for a particular function or purpose. (2) The three top positions of 12, 11, and 0 on certain punch cards. In these positions, a second punch can be inserted so that, with punches in the remaining positions 1 to 9, alphabetic characters may be represented.

zone punch, same as (overpunch).

APPENDIX B
OCTAL-DECIMAL INTEGER CONVERSION TABLE

OCTAL	0	1	2	3	4	5	6	7
0000	0000	0001	0002	0003	0004	0005	0006	0007
0010	0008	0009	0010	0011	0012	0013	0014	0015
0020	0016	0017	0018	0019	0020	0021	0022	0023
0030	0024	0025	0026	0027	0028	0029	0030	0031
0040	0032	0033	0034	0035	0036	0037	0038	0039
0050	0040	0041	0042	0043	0044	0045	0046	0047
0060	0048	0049	0050	0051	0052	0053	0054	0055
0070	0056	0057	0058	0059	0060	0061	0062	0063
0100	0064	0065	0066	0067	0068	0069	0070	0071
0110	0072	0073	0074	0075	0076	0077	0078	0079
0120	0080	0081	0082	0083	0084	0085	0086	0087
0130	0088	0089	0090	0091	0092	0093	0094	0095
0140	0096	0097	0098	0099	0100	0101	0102	0103
0150	0104	0105	0106	0107	0108	0109	0110	0111
0160	0112	0113	0114	0115	0116	0117	0118	0119
0170	0120	0121	0122	0123	0124	0125	0126	0127
0200	0128	0129	0130	0131	0132	0133	0134	0135
0210	0136	0137	0138	0139	0140	0141	0142	0143
0220	0144	0145	0146	0147	0148	0149	0150	0151
0230	0152	0153	0154	0155	0156	0157	0158	0159
0240	0160	0161	0162	0163	0164	0165	0166	0167
0250	0168	0169	0170	0171	0172	0173	0174	0175
0260	0176	0177	0178	0179	0180	0181	0182	0183
0270	0184	0185	0186	0187	0188	0189	0190	0191
0300	0192	0193	0194	0195	0196	0197	0198	0199
0310	0200	0201	0202	0203	0204	0205	0206	0207
0320	0208	0209	0210	0211	0212	0213	0214	0215
0330	0216	0217	0218	0219	0220	0221	0222	0223
0340	0224	0225	0226	0227	0228	0229	0230	0231
0350	0232	0233	0234	0235	0236	0237	0238	0239
0360	0240	0241	0242	0243	0244	0245	0246	0247
0370	0248	0249	0250	0251	0252	0253	0254	0255

OCTAL	0	1	2	3	4	5	6	7
0400	0256	0257	0258	0259	0260	0261	0262	0263
0410	0264	0265	0266	0267	0268	0269	0270	0271
0420	0272	0273	0274	0275	0276	0277	0278	0279
0430	0280	0281	0282	0283	0284	0285	0286	0287
0440	0288	0289	0290	0291	0292	0293	0294	0295
0450	0296	0297	0298	0299	0300	0301	0302	0303
0460	0304	0305	0306	0307	0308	0309	0310	0311
0470	0312	0313	0314	0315	0316	0317	0318	0319
0500	0320	0321	0322	0323	0324	0325	0326	0327
0510	0328	0329	0330	0331	0332	0333	0334	0335
0520	0336	0337	0338	0339	0340	0341	0342	0343
0530	0344	0345	0346	0347	0348	0349	0350	0351
0540	0352	0353	0354	0355	0356	0357	0358	0359
0550	0360	0361	0362	0363	0364	0365	0366	0367
0560	0368	0369	0370	0371	0372	0373	0374	0375
0570	0376	0377	0378	0379	0380	0381	0382	0383
0600	0384	0385	0386	0387	0388	0389	0390	0391
0610	0392	0393	0394	0395	0396	0397	0398	0399
0620	0400	0401	0402	0403	0404	0405	0406	0407
0630	0408	0409	0410	0411	0412	0413	0414	0415
0640	0416	0417	0418	0419	0420	0421	0422	0423
0650	0424	0425	0426	0427	0428	0429	0430	0431
0660	0432	0433	0434	0435	0436	0437	0438	0439
0670	0440	0441	0442	0443	0444	0445	0446	0447
0700	0448	0449	0450	0451	0452	0453	0454	0455
0710	0456	0457	0458	0459	0460	0461	0462	0463
0720	0464	0465	0466	0467	0468	0469	0470	0471
0730	0472	0473	0474	0475	0476	0477	0478	0479
0740	0480	0481	0482	0483	0484	0485	0486	0487
0750	0488	0489	0490	0491	0492	0493	0494	0495
0760	0496	0497	0498	0499	0500	0501	0502	0503
0770	0504	0505	0506	0507	0508	0509	0510	0511

OCTAL	0	1	2	3	4	5	6	7
1000	0512	0513	0514	0515	0516	0517	0518	0519
1010	0520	0521	0522	0523	0524	0525	0526	0527
1020	0528	0529	0530	0531	0532	0533	0534	0535
1030	0536	0537	0538	0539	0540	0541	0542	0543
1040	0544	0545	0546	0547	0548	0549	0550	0551
1050	0552	0553	0554	0555	0556	0557	0558	0559
1060	0560	0561	0562	0563	0564	0565	0566	0567
1070	0568	0569	0570	0571	0572	0573	0574	0575
1100	0576	0577	0578	0579	0580	0581	0582	0583
1110	0584	0585	0586	0587	0588	0589	0590	0591
1120	0592	0593	0594	0595	0596	0597	0598	0599
1130	0600	0601	0602	0603	0604	0605	0606	0607
1140	0608	0609	0610	0611	0612	0613	0614	0615
1150	0616	0617	0618	0619	0620	0621	0622	0623
1160	0624	0625	0626	0627	0628	0629	0630	0631
1170	0632	0633	0634	0635	0636	0637	0638	0639
1200	0640	0641	0642	0643	0644	0645	0646	0647
1210	0648	0649	0650	0651	0652	0653	0654	0655
1220	0656	0657	0658	0659	0660	0661	0662	0663
1230	0664	0665	0666	0667	0668	0669	0670	0671
1240	0672	0673	0674	0675	0676	0677	0678	0679
1250	0680	0681	0682	0683	0684	0685	0686	0687
1260	0688	0689	0690	0691	0692	0693	0694	0695
1270	0696	0697	0698	0699	0700	0701	0702	0703
1300	0704	0705	0706	0707	0708	0709	0710	0711
1310	0712	0713	0714	0715	0716	0717	0718	0719
1320	0720	0721	0722	0723	0724	0725	0726	0727
1330	0728	0729	0730	0731	0732	0733	0734	0735
1340	0736	0737	0738	0739	0740	0741	0742	0743
1350	0744	0745	0746	0747	0748	0749	0750	0751
1360	0752	0753	0754	0755	0756	0757	0758	0759
1370	0760	0761	0762	0763	0764	0765	0766	0767

OCTAL	0	1	2	3	4	5	6	7
1400	0768	0769	0770	0771	0772	0773	0774	0775
1410	0776	0777	0778	0779	0780	0781	0782	0783
1420	0784	0785	0786	0787	0788	0789	0790	0791
1430	0792	0793	0794	0795	0796	0797	0798	0799
1440	0800	0801	0802	0803	0804	0805	0806	0807
1450	0808	0809	0810	0811	0812	0813	0814	0815
1460	0816	0817	0818	0819	0820	0821	0822	0823
1470	0824	0825	0826	0827	0828	0829	0830	0831
1500	0832	0833	0834	0835	0836	0837	0838	0839
1510	0840	0841	0842	0843	0844	0845	0846	0847
1520	0848	0849	0850	0851	0852	0853	0854	0855
1530	0856	0857	0858	0859	0860	0861	0862	0863
1540	0864	0865	0866	0867	0868	0869	0870	0871
1550	0872	0873	0874	0875	0876	0877	0878	0879
1560	0880	0881	0882	0883	0884	0885	0886	0887
1570	0888	0889	0890	0891	0892	0893	0894	0895
1600	0896	0897	0898	0899	0900	0901	0902	0903
1610	0904	0905	0906	0907	0908	0909	0910	0911
1620	0912	0913	0914	0915	0916	0917	0918	0919
1630	0920	0921	0922	0923	0924	0925	0926	0927
1640	0928	0929	0930	0931	0932	0933	0934	0935
1650	0936	0937	0938	0939	0940	0941	0942	0943
1660	0944	0945	0946	0947	0948	0949	0950	0951
1670	0952	0953	0954	0955	0956	0957	0958	0959
1700	0960	0961	0962	0963	0964	0965	0966	0967
1710	0968	0969	0970	0971	0972	0973	0974	0975
1720	0976	0977	0978	0979	0980	0981	0982	0983
1730	0984	0985	0986	0987	0988	0989	0990	0991
1740	0992	0993	0994	0995	0996	0997	0998	0999
1750	1000	1001	1002	1003	1004	1005	1006	1007
1760	1008	1009	1010	1011	1012	1013	1014	1015
1770	1016	1017	1018	1019	1020	1021	1022	1023

OCTAL	0	1	2	3	4	5	6	7
2000	1024	1025	1026	1027	1028	1029	1030	1031
2010	1032	1033	1034	1035	1036	1037	1038	1039
2020	1040	1041	1042	1043	1044	1045	1046	1047
2030	1048	1049	1050	1051	1052	1053	1054	1055
2040	1056	1057	1058	1059	1060	1061	1062	1063
2050	1064	1065	1066	1067	1068	1069	1070	1071
2060	1072	1073	1074	1075	1076	1077	1078	1079
2070	1080	1081	1082	1083	1084	1085	1086	1087
2100	1088	1089	1090	1091	1092	1093	1094	1095
2110	1096	1097	1098	1099	1100	1101	1102	1103
2120	1104	1105	1106	1107	1108	1109	1110	1111
2130	1112	1113	1114	1115	1116	1117	1118	1119
2140	1120	1121	1122	1123	1124	1125	1126	1127
2150	1128	1129	1130	1131	1132	1133	1134	1135
2160	1136	1137	1138	1139	1140	1141	1142	1143
2170	1144	1145	1146	1147	1148	1149	1150	1151
2200	1152	1153	1154	1155	1156	1157	1158	1159
2210	1160	1161	1162	1163	1164	1165	1166	1167
2220	1168	1169	1170	1171	1172	1173	1174	1175
2230	1176	1177	1178	1179	1180	1181	1182	1183
2240	1184	1185	1186	1187	1188	1189	1190	1191
2250	1192	1193	1194	1195	1196	1197	1198	1199
2260	1200	1201	1202	1203	1204	1205	1206	1207
2270	1208	1209	1210	1211	1212	1213	1214	1215
2300	1216	1217	1218	1219	1220	1221	1222	1223
2310	1224	1225	1226	1227	1228	1229	1230	1231
2320	1232	1233	1234	1235	1236	1237	1238	1239
2330	1240	1241	1242	1243	1244	1245	1246	1247
2340	1248	1249	1250	1251	1252	1253	1254	1255
2350	1256	1257	1258	1259	1260	1261	1262	1263
2360	1264	1265	1266	1267	1268	1269	1270	1271
2370	1272	1273	1274	1275	1276	1277	1278	1279

OCTAL	0	1	2	3	4	5	6	7
2400	1280	1281	1282	1283	1284	1285	1286	1287
2410	1288	1289	1290	1291	1292	1293	1294	1295
2420	1296	1297	1298	1299	1300	1301	1302	1303
2430	1304	1305	1306	1307	1308	1309	1310	1311
2440	1312	1313	1314	1315	1316	1317	1318	1319
2450	1320	1321	1322	1323	1324	1325	1326	1327
2460	1328	1329	1330	1331	1332	1333	1334	1335
2470	1336	1337	1338	1339	1340	1341	1342	1343
2500	1344	1345	1346	1347	1348	1349	1350	1351
2510	1352	1353	1354	1355	1356	1357	1358	1359
2520	1360	1361	1362	1363	1364	1365	1366	1367
2530	1368	1369	1370	1371	1372	1373	1374	1375
2540	1376	1377	1378	1379	1380	1381	1382	1383
2550	1384	1385	1386	1387	1388	1389	1390	1391
2560	1392	1393	1394	1395	1396	1397	1398	1399
2570	1400	1401	1402	1403	1404	1405	1406	1407
2600	1408	1409	1410	1411	1412	1413	1414	1415
2610	1416	1417	1418	1419	1420	1421	1422	1423
2620	1424	1425	1426	1427	1428	1429	1430	1431
2630	1432	1433	1434	1435	1436	1437	1438	1439
2640	1440	1441	1442	1443	1444	1445	1446	1447
2650	1448	1449	1450	1451	1452	1453	1454	1455
2660	1456	1457	1458	1459	1460	1461	1462	1463
2670	1464	1465	1466	1467	1468	1469	1470	1471
2700	1472	1473	1474	1475	1476	1477	1478	1479
2710	1480	1481	1482	1483	1484	1485	1486	1487
2720	1488	1489	1490	1491	1492	1493	1494	1495
2730	1496	1497	1498	1499	1500	1501	1502	1503
2740	1504	1505	1506	1507	1508	1509	1510	1511
2750	1512	1513	1514	1515	1516	1517	1518	1519
2760	1520	1521	1522	1523	1524	1525	1526	1527
2770	1528	1529	1530	1531	1532	1533	1534	1535

OCTAL	0	1	2	3	4	5	6	7
3000	1536	1537	1538	1539	1540	1541	1542	1543
3010	1544	1545	1546	1547	1548	1549	1550	1551
3020	1552	1553	1554	1555	1556	1557	1558	1559
3030	1560	1561	1562	1563	1564	1565	1566	1567
3040	1568	1569	1570	1571	1572	1573	1574	1575
3050	1576	1577	1578	1579	1580	1581	1582	1583
3060	1584	1585	1586	1587	1588	1589	1590	1591
3070	1592	1593	1594	1595	1596	1597	1598	1599
3100	1600	1601	1602	1603	1604	1605	1606	1607
3110	1608	1609	1610	1611	1612	1613	1614	1615
3120	1616	1617	1618	1619	1620	1621	1622	1623
3130	1624	1625	1626	1627	1628	1629	1630	1631
3140	1632	1633	1634	1635	1636	1637	1638	1639
3150	1640	1641	1642	1643	1644	1645	1646	1647
3160	1648	1649	1650	1651	1652	1653	1654	1655
3170	1656	1657	1658	1659	1660	1661	1662	1663
3200	1664	1665	1666	1667	1668	1669	1670	1671
3210	1672	1673	1674	1675	1676	1677	1678	1679
3220	1680	1681	1682	1683	1684	1685	1686	1687
3230	1688	1689	1690	1691	1692	1693	1694	1695
3240	1696	1697	1698	1699	1700	1701	1702	1703
3250	1704	1705	1706	1707	1708	1709	1710	1711
3260	1712	1713	1714	1715	1716	1717	1718	1719
3270	1720	1721	1722	1723	1724	1725	1726	1727
3300	1728	1729	1730	1731	1732	1733	1734	1735
3310	1736	1737	1738	1739	1740	1741	1742	1743
3320	1744	1745	1746	1747	1748	1749	1750	1751
3330	1752	1753	1754	1755	1756	1757	1758	1759
3340	1760	1761	1762	1763	1764	1765	1766	1767
3350	1768	1769	1770	1771	1772	1773	1774	1775
3360	1776	1777	1778	1779	1780	1781	1782	1783
3370	1784	1785	1786	1787	1788	1789	1790	1791

OCTAL	0	1	2	3	4	5	6	7
3400	1792	1793	1794	1795	1796	1797	1798	1799
3410	1800	1801	1802	1803	1804	1805	1806	1807
3420	1808	1809	1810	1811	1812	1813	1814	1815
3430	1816	1817	1818	1819	1820	1821	1822	1823
3440	1824	1825	1826	1827	1828	1829	1830	1831
3450	1832	1833	1834	1835	1836	1837	1838	1839
3460	1840	1841	1842	1843	1844	1845	1846	1847
3470	1848	1849	1850	1851	1852	1853	1854	1855
3500	1856	1857	1858	1859	1860	1861	1862	1863
3510	1864	1865	1866	1867	1868	1869	1870	1871
3520	1872	1873	1874	1875	1876	1877	1878	1879
3530	1880	1881	1882	1883	1884	1885	1886	1887
3540	1888	1889	1890	1891	1892	1893	1894	1895
3550	1896	1897	1898	1899	1900	1901	1902	1903
3560	1904	1905	1906	1907	1908	1909	1910	1911
3570	1912	1913	1914	1915	1916	1917	1918	1919
3600	1920	1921	1922	1923	1924	1925	1926	1927
3610	1928	1929	1930	1931	1932	1933	1934	1935
3620	1936	1937	1938	1939	1940	1941	1942	1943
3630	1944	1945	1946	1947	1948	1949	1950	1951
3640	1952	1953	1954	1955	1956	1957	1958	1959
3650	1960	1961	1962	1963	1964	1965	1966	1967
3660	1968	1969	1970	1971	1972	1973	1974	1975
3670	1976	1977	1978	1979	1980	1981	1982	1983
3700	1984	1985	1986	1987	1988	1989	1990	1991
3710	1992	1993	1994	1995	1996	1997	1998	1999
3720	2000	2001	2002	2003	2004	2005	2006	2007
3730	2008	2009	2010	2011	2012	2013	2014	2015
3740	2016	2017	2018	2019	2020	2021	2022	2023
3750	2024	2025	2026	2027	2028	2029	2030	2031
3760	2032	2033	2034	2035	2036	2037	2038	2039
3770	2040	2041	2042	2043	2044	2045	2046	2047

OCTAL	0	1	2	3	4	5	6	7
4000	2048	2049	2050	2051	2052	2053	2054	2055
4010	2056	2057	2058	2059	2060	2061	2062	2063
4020	2064	2065	2066	2067	2068	2069	2070	2071
4030	2072	2073	2074	2075	2076	2077	2078	2079
4040	2080	2081	2082	2083	2084	2085	2086	2087
4050	2088	2089	2090	2091	2092	2093	2094	2095
4060	2096	2097	2098	2099	2100	2101	2102	2103
4070	2104	2105	2106	2107	2108	2109	2110	2111
4100	2112	2113	2114	2115	2116	2117	2118	2119
4110	2120	2121	2122	2123	2124	2125	2126	2127
4120	2128	2129	2130	2131	2132	2133	2134	2135
4130	2136	2137	2138	2139	2140	2141	2142	2143
4140	2144	2145	2146	2147	2148	2149	2150	2151
4150	2152	2153	2154	2155	2156	2157	2158	2159
4160	2160	2161	2162	2163	2164	2165	2166	2167
4170	2168	2169	2170	2171	2172	2173	2174	2175
4200	2176	2177	2178	2179	2180	2181	2182	2183
4210	2184	2185	2186	2187	2188	2189	2190	2191
4220	2192	2193	2194	2195	2196	2197	2198	2199
4230	2200	2201	2202	2203	2204	2205	2206	2207
4240	2208	2209	2210	2211	2212	2213	2214	2215
4250	2216	2217	2218	2219	2220	2221	2222	2223
4260	2224	2225	2226	2227	2228	2229	2230	2231
4270	2232	2233	2234	2235	2236	2237	2238	2239
4300	2240	2241	2242	2243	2244	2245	2246	2247
4310	2248	2249	2250	2251	2252	2253	2254	2255
4320	2256	2257	2258	2259	2260	2261	2262	2263
4330	2264	2265	2266	2267	2268	2269	2270	2271
4340	2272	2273	2274	2275	2276	2277	2278	2279
4350	2280	2281	2282	2283	2284	2285	2286	2287
4360	2288	2289	2290	2291	2292	2293	2294	2295
4370	2296	2297	2298	2299	2300	2301	2302	2303

OCTAL	0	1	2	3	4	5	6	7
4400	2304	2305	2306	2307	2308	2309	2310	2311
4410	2312	2313	2314	2315	2316	2317	2318	2319
4420	2320	2321	2322	2323	2324	2325	2326	2327
4430	2328	2329	2330	2331	2332	2333	2334	2335
4440	2336	2337	2338	2339	2340	2341	2342	2343
4450	2344	2345	2346	2347	2348	2349	2350	2351
4460	2352	2353	2354	2355	2356	2357	2358	2359
4470	2360	2361	2362	2363	2364	2365	2366	2367
4500	2368	2369	2370	2371	2372	2373	2374	2375
4510	2376	2377	2378	2379	2380	2381	2382	2383
4520	2384	2385	2386	2387	2388	2389	2390	2391
4530	2392	2393	2394	2395	2396	2397	2398	2399
4540	2400	2401	2402	2403	2404	2405	2406	2407
4550	2408	2409	2410	2411	2412	2413	2414	2415
4560	2416	2417	2418	2419	2420	2421	2422	2423
4570	2424	2425	2426	2427	2428	2429	2430	2431
4600	2432	2433	2434	2435	2436	2437	2438	2439
4610	2440	2441	2442	2443	2444	2445	2446	2447
4620	2448	2449	2450	2451	2452	2453	2454	2455
4630	2456	2457	2458	2459	2460	2461	2462	2463
4640	2464	2465	2466	2467	2468	2469	2470	2471
4650	2472	2473	2474	2475	2476	2477	2478	2479
4660	2480	2481	2482	2483	2484	2485	2486	2487
4670	2488	2489	2490	2491	2492	2493	2494	2495
4700	2496	2497	2498	2499	2500	2501	2502	2503
4710	2504	2505	2506	2507	2508	2509	2510	2511
4720	2512	2513	2514	2515	2516	2517	2518	2519
4730	2520	2521	2522	2523	2524	2525	2526	2527
4740	2528	2529	2530	2531	2532	2533	2534	2535
4750	2536	2537	2538	2539	2540	2541	2542	2543
4760	2544	2545	2546	2547	2548	2549	2550	2551
4770	2552	2553	2554	2555	2556	2557	2558	2559

OCTAL	0	1	2	3	4	5	6	7
5000	2560	2561	2562	2563	2564	2565	2566	2567
5010	2568	2569	2570	2571	2572	2573	2574	2575
5020	2576	2577	2578	2579	2580	2581	2582	2583
5030	2584	2585	2586	2587	2588	2589	2590	2591
5040	2592	2593	2594	2595	2596	2597	2598	2599
5050	2600	2601	2602	2603	2604	2605	2606	2607
5060	2608	2609	2610	2611	2612	2613	2614	2615
5070	2616	2617	2618	2619	2620	2621	2622	2623
5100	2624	2625	2626	2627	2628	2629	2630	2631
5110	2632	2633	2634	2635	2636	2637	2638	2639
5120	2640	2641	2642	2643	2644	2645	2646	2647
5130	2648	2649	2650	2651	2652	2653	2654	2655
5140	2656	2657	2658	2659	2660	2661	2662	2663
5150	2664	2665	2666	2667	2668	2669	2670	2671
5160	2672	2673	2674	2675	2676	2677	2678	2679
5170	2680	2681	2682	2683	2684	2685	2686	2687
5200	2688	2689	2690	2691	2692	2693	2694	2695
5210	2696	2697	2698	2699	2700	2701	2702	2703
5220	2704	2705	2706	2707	2708	2709	2710	2711
5230	2712	2713	2714	2715	2716	2717	2718	2719
5240	2720	2721	2722	2723	2724	2725	2726	2727
5250	2728	2729	2730	2731	2732	2733	2734	2735
5260	2736	2737	2738	2739	2740	2741	2742	2743
5270	2744	2745	2746	2747	2748	2749	2750	2751
5300	2752	2753	2754	2755	2756	2757	2758	2759
5310	2760	2761	2762	2763	2764	2765	2766	2767
5320	2768	2769	2770	2771	2772	2773	2774	2775
5330	2776	2777	2778	2779	2780	2781	2782	2783
5340	2784	2785	2786	2787	2788	2789	2790	2791
5350	2792	2793	2794	2795	2796	2797	2798	2799
5360	2800	2801	2802	2803	2804	2805	2806	2807
5370	2808	2809	2810	2811	2812	2813	2814	2815

OCTAL	0	1	2	3	4	5	6	7
5400	2816	2817	2818	2819	2820	2821	2822	2823
5410	2824	2825	2826	2827	2828	2829	2830	2831
5420	2832	2833	2834	2835	2836	2837	2838	2839
5430	2840	2841	2842	2843	2844	2845	2846	2847
5440	2848	2849	2850	2851	2852	2853	2854	2855
5450	2856	2857	2858	2859	2860	2861	2862	2863
5460	2864	2865	2866	2867	2868	2869	2870	2871
5470	2872	2873	2874	2875	2876	2877	2878	2879
5500	2880	2881	2882	2883	2884	2885	2886	2887
5510	2888	2889	2890	2891	2892	2893	2894	2895
5520	2896	2897	2898	2899	2900	2901	2902	2903
5530	2904	2905	2906	2907	2908	2909	2910	2911
5540	2912	2913	2914	2915	2916	2917	2918	2919
5550	2920	2921	2922	2923	2924	2925	2926	2927
5560	2928	2929	2930	2931	2932	2933	2934	2935
5570	2936	2937	2938	2939	2940	2941	2942	2943
5600	2944	2945	2946	2947	2948	2949	2950	2951
5610	2952	2953	2954	2955	2956	2957	2958	2959
5620	2960	2961	2962	2963	2964	2965	2966	2967
5630	2968	2969	2970	2971	2972	2973	2974	2975
5640	2976	2977	2978	2979	2980	2981	2982	2983
5650	2984	2985	2986	2987	2988	2989	2990	2991
5660	2992	2993	2994	2995	2996	2997	2998	2999
5670	3000	3001	3002	3003	3004	3005	3006	3007
5700	3008	3009	3010	3011	3012	3013	3014	3015
5710	3016	3017	3018	3019	3020	3021	3022	3023
5720	3024	3025	3026	3027	3028	3029	3030	3031
5730	3032	3033	3034	3035	3036	3037	3038	3039
5740	3040	3041	3042	3043	3044	3045	3046	3047
5750	3048	3049	3050	3051	3052	3053	3054	3055
5760	3056	3057	3058	3059	3060	3061	3062	3063
5770	3064	3065	3066	3067	3068	3069	3070	3071

OCTAL	0	1	2	3	4	5	6	7
6000	3072	3073	3074	3075	3076	3077	3078	3079
6010	3080	3081	3082	3083	3084	3085	3086	3087
6020	3088	3089	3090	3091	3092	3093	3094	3095
6030	3096	3097	3098	3099	3100	3101	3102	3103
6040	3104	3105	3106	3107	3108	3109	3110	3111
6050	3112	3113	3114	3115	3116	3117	3118	3119
6060	3120	3121	3122	3123	3124	3125	3126	3127
6070	3128	3129	3130	3131	3132	3133	3134	3135
6100	3136	3137	3138	3139	3140	3141	3142	3143
6110	3144	3145	3146	3147	3148	3149	3150	3151
6120	3152	3153	3154	3155	3156	3157	3158	3159
6130	3160	3161	3162	3163	3164	3165	3166	3167
6140	3168	3169	3170	3171	3172	3173	3174	3175
6150	3176	3177	3178	3179	3180	3181	3182	3183
6160	3184	3185	3186	3187	3188	3189	3190	3191
6170	3192	3193	3194	3195	3196	3197	3198	3199
6200	3200	3201	3202	3203	3204	3205	3206	3207
6210	3208	3209	3210	3211	3212	3213	3214	3215
6220	3216	3217	3218	3219	3220	3221	3222	3223
6230	3224	3225	3226	3227	3228	3229	3230	3231
6240	3232	3233	3234	3235	3236	3237	3238	3239
6250	3240	3241	3242	3243	3244	3245	3246	3247
6260	3248	3249	3250	3251	3252	3253	3254	3255
6270	3256	3257	3258	3259	3260	3261	3262	3263
6300	3264	3265	3266	3267	3268	3269	3270	3271
6310	3272	3273	3274	3275	3276	3277	3278	3279
6320	3280	3281	3282	3283	3284	3285	3286	3287
6330	3288	3289	3290	3291	3292	3293	3294	3295
6340	3296	3297	3298	3299	3300	3301	3302	3303
6350	3304	3305	3306	3307	3308	3309	3310	3311
6360	3312	3313	3314	3315	3316	3317	3318	3319
6370	3320	3321	3322	3323	3324	3325	3326	3327

OCTAL	0	1	2	3	4	5	6	7
6400	3328	3329	3330	3331	3332	3333	3334	3335
6410	3336	3337	3338	3339	3340	3341	3342	3343
6420	3344	3345	3346	3347	3348	3349	3350	3351
6430	3352	3353	3354	3355	3356	3357	3358	3359
6440	3360	3361	3362	3363	3364	3365	3366	3367
6450	3368	3369	3370	3371	3372	3373	3374	3375
6460	3376	3377	3378	3379	3380	3381	3382	3383
6470	3384	3385	3386	3387	3388	3389	3390	3391
6500	3392	3393	3394	3395	3396	3397	3398	3399
6510	3400	3401	3402	3403	3404	3405	3406	3407
6520	3408	3409	3410	3411	3412	3413	3414	3415
6530	3416	3417	3418	3419	3420	3421	3422	3423
6540	3424	3425	3426	3427	3428	3429	3430	3431
6550	3432	3433	3434	3435	3436	3437	3438	3439
6560	3440	3441	3442	3443	3444	3445	3446	3447
6570	3448	3449	3450	3451	3452	3453	3454	3455
6600	3456	3457	3458	3459	3460	3461	3462	3463
6610	3464	3465	3466	3467	3468	3469	3470	3471
6620	3472	3473	3474	3475	3476	3477	3478	3479
6630	3480	3481	3482	3483	3484	3485	3486	3487
6640	3488	3489	3490	3491	3492	3493	3494	3495
6650	3496	3497	3498	3499	3500	3501	3502	3503
6660	3504	3505	3506	3507	3508	3509	3510	3511
6670	3512	3513	3514	3515	3516	3517	3518	3519
6700	3520	3521	3522	3523	3524	3525	3526	3527
6710	3528	3529	3530	3531	3532	3533	3534	3535
6720	3536	3537	3538	3539	3540	3541	3542	3543
6730	3544	3545	3546	3547	3548	3549	3550	3551
6740	3552	3553	3554	3555	3556	3557	3558	3559
6750	3560	3561	3562	3563	3564	3565	3566	3567
6760	3568	3569	3570	3571	3572	3573	3574	3575
6770	3576	3577	3578	3579	3580	3581	3582	3583

OCTAL	0	1	2	3	4	5	6	7
7000	3584	3585	3586	3587	3588	3589	3590	3591
7010	3592	3593	3594	3595	3596	3597	3598	3599
7020	3600	3601	3602	3603	3604	3605	3606	3607
7030	3608	3609	3610	3611	3612	3613	3614	3615
7040	3616	3617	3618	3619	3620	3621	3622	3623
7050	3624	3625	3626	3627	3628	3629	3630	3631
7060	3632	3633	3634	3635	3636	3637	3638	3639
7070	3640	3641	3642	3643	3644	3645	3646	3647
7100	3648	3649	3650	3651	3652	3653	3654	3655
7110	3656	3657	3658	3659	3660	3661	3662	3663
7120	3664	3665	3666	3667	3668	3669	3670	3671
7130	3672	3673	3674	3675	3676	3677	3678	3679
7140	3680	3681	3682	3683	3684	3685	3686	3687
7150	3688	3689	3690	3691	3692	3693	3694	3695
7160	3696	3697	3698	3699	3700	3701	3702	3703
7170	3704	3705	3706	3707	3708	3709	3710	3711
7200	3712	3713	3714	3715	3716	3717	3718	3719
7210	3720	3721	3722	3723	3724	3725	3726	3727
7220	3728	3729	3730	3731	3732	3733	3734	3735
7230	3736	3737	3738	3739	3740	3741	3742	3743
7240	3744	3745	3746	3747	3748	3749	3750	3751
7250	3752	3753	3754	3755	3756	3757	3758	3759
7260	3760	3761	3762	3763	3764	3765	3766	3767
7270	3768	3769	3770	3771	3772	3773	3774	3775
7300	3776	3777	3778	3779	3780	3781	3782	3783
7310	3784	3785	3786	3787	3788	3789	3790	3791
7320	3792	3793	3794	3795	3796	3797	3798	3799
7330	3800	3801	3802	3803	3804	3805	3806	3807
7340	3808	3809	3810	3811	3812	3813	3814	3815
7350	3816	3817	3818	3819	3820	3821	3822	3823
7360	3824	3825	3826	3827	3828	3829	3830	3831
7370	3832	3833	3834	3835	3836	3837	3838	3839

OCTAL	0	1	2	3	4	5	6	7
7400	3840	3841	3842	3843	3844	3845	3846	3847
7410	3848	3849	3850	3851	3852	3853	3854	3855
7420	3856	3857	3858	3859	3860	3861	3862	3863
7430	3864	3865	3866	3867	3868	3869	3870	3871
7440	3872	3873	3874	3875	3876	3877	3878	3879
7450	3880	3881	3882	3883	3884	3885	3886	3887
7460	3888	3889	3890	3891	3892	3893	3894	3895
7470	3896	3897	3898	3899	3900	3901	3902	3903
7500	3904	3905	3906	3907	3908	3909	3910	3911
7510	3912	3913	3914	3915	3916	3917	3918	3919
7520	3920	3921	3922	3923	3924	3925	3926	3927
7530	3928	3929	3930	3931	3932	3933	3934	3935
7540	3936	3937	3938	3939	3940	3941	3942	3943
7550	3944	3945	3946	3947	3948	3949	3950	3951
7560	3952	3953	3954	3955	3956	3957	3958	3959
7570	3960	3961	3962	3963	3964	3965	3966	3967
7600	3968	3969	3970	3971	3972	3973	3974	3975
7610	3976	3977	3978	3979	3980	3981	3982	3983
7620	3984	3985	3986	3987	3988	3989	3990	3991
7630	3992	3993	3994	3995	3996	3997	3998	3999
7640	4000	4001	4002	4003	4004	4005	4006	4007
7650	4008	4009	4010	4011	4012	4013	4014	4015
7660	4016	4017	4018	4019	4020	4021	4022	4023
7670	4024	4025	4026	4027	4028	4029	4030	4031
7700	4032	4033	4034	4035	4036	4037	4038	4039
7710	4040	4041	4042	4043	4044	4045	4046	4047
7720	4048	4049	4050	4051	4052	4053	4054	4055
7730	4056	4057	4058	4059	4060	4061	4062	4063
7740	4064	4065	4066	4067	4068	4069	4070	4071
7750	4072	4073	4074	4075	4076	4077	4078	4079
7760	4080	4081	4082	4083	4084	4085	4086	4087
7770	4088	4089	4090	4091	4092	4093	4094	4095

Octal	Decimal
10000	4096
20000	8192
30000	12288
40000	16384
50000	20480
60000	24576
70000	28672

APPENDIX C
BIBLIOGRAPHY OF RELATED REFERENCE
AMTERIALS

Arnold, Robert R., Harold C. Hill, and Aylmer V. Nichols, *Introduction to Data Processing*. New York: John Wiley and Sons, Inc., 1966.

Awad, Elias M., *Business Data Processing*. Englewood Cliffs, N. J.: Prentice-Hall, Inc., 1965.

Bergamini, David, and the Editors of Life, *Mathematics*. New York: Time Incorporated, 1963.

Brown, R. Gene, and Kenneth S. Johnston, *Paciolo on Accounting*. New York: McGraw-Hill Book Company, 1963.

Burck, Gilbert, and the Editors of Fortune, *The Computer Age*. New York: Harper and Row, Publishers, 1965.

Cashman, Thomas J., *Review Manual for Certificate in Data Processing*. Anaheim, Calif.: Anaheim Publishing Co., 1964.

Chapin, Ned, *An Introduction to Automatic Computers*. Princeton, N. J.: D. Van Nostrand Co., Inc., 1963.

Computers and Thought, eds., Edward A. Feigenbaum and Julian Feldman. New York: McGraw-Hill Book Company, 1963.

Cutler, Donald, *Introduction to Computer Programming*. Englewood Cliffs, N. J.: Prentice-Hall, Inc., 1964.

Davis, Gordon B., *An Introduction to Electronic Computers*. New York: McGraw-Hill Book Company, 1965.

Desmonde, William H., *Computers and Their Uses*. Englewood Cliffs, N. J.: Prentice-Hall, Inc., 1964.

Elliott, C. Orville, and Robert S. Wasley, *Business Information Processing Systems*. Homewood, Illinois: Richard D. Irwin, Inc., 1965.

271

Favrett, Andrew G., *Introduction to Digital Computer Applications*. New York: Reinhold Publishing Corp., 1965.

Gibson, E. Dana, *International Data Processing*. Elmhurst, Illinois: The Business Press, 1965.

Gregory, Robert H., and Richard L. Van Horn, *Business Data Processing and Programming*. Belmont, Calif.: Wadsworth Publishing Co., Inc., 1963.

Grossman, Alvin, and Robert L. Howe, *Data Processing for Educators*. Chicago: Educational Methods, Inc., 1965.

Haga, Enoch, *Understanding Automation*. Elmhurst, Illinois: The Business Press, 1965.

Hearle, Edward F. R., and Raymond J. Mason, *A Data Processing System for State and Local Governments*. Englewood Cliffs, N. J.: Prentice-Hall, Inc., 1963.

Inman, Kenneth L., *Fundamentals of Electronic Data Processing*. Englewood Cliffs, N. J.: Prentice-Hall, Inc., 1965.

Laurie, Edward J., *Computers and How They Work*. Cincinnati, Ohio: South-Western Publishing Co., 1963.

Martin, E. Wainwright, Jr., *Electronic Data Processing, An Introduction*. Homewood, Illinois: Richard D. Irwin, Inc., 1961.

McGill, Donald A. C., *Punched Cards: Data Processing for Profit Improvement*. New York: McGraw-Hill Book Company, 1962.

McMillan, Claude, and Richard F. Gonzales, *Systems Analysis, A Computer Approach to Decision Models*. Homewood, Illinois: Richard D. Irwin, Inc., 1965.

Moder Joseph J., and Cecil R. Phillips, *Project Management With CPM and PERT*. New York: Reinhold Publishing Corp., 1964.

Nelson, Oscar S., and Richard S. Woods, *Accounting Systems and Data Processing*. Cincinnati, Ohio: South-Western Publishing Co., 1961.

O'Neal, Leeland R., *Electronic Data Processing Systems: A Self-Instructional Programmed Manual*. Englewood Cliffs, N. J.: Prentice-Hall, Inc., 1964.

Postley, John A., *Computers and People*. New York: McGraw-Hill Book Co., Inc., 1960.

Ralston, Anthony, *A First Course in Numerical Analysis*. New York: McGraw-Hill Book Company, 1965.

Randall, Clarence B., Sally W. Weimer, and Maynard S. Greenfield, *Systems and Procedures for Automated Accounting*. Cincinnati, Ohio: South-Western Publishing Co., 1962.

Saxon, James A., *Programming the IBM 7090: A Self-Instructional Programmed Manual*. Englewood Cliffs, N. J.: Prentice-Hall, Inc., 1963.

Saxon, James A., *COBOL: A Self-Instructional Programmed Manual*. Englewood Cliffs, N. J.: Prentice-Hall, Inc., 1963.

Saxon, James A., *Programming the RCA 301: A Self-Instructional Programmed Manual*. Englewood Cliffs, N. J.: Prentice-Hall, Inc., 1965.

Saxon, James A., and Richard W. Senseman, *Programming and Wiring the UNIVAC 1004 Card Processor: A Self-Instructional Programmed Manual*. Englewood Cliffs, N. J.: Prentice-Hall, Inc., 1964.

Saxon, James A., and William S. Plette, *Programming the IBM 1401: A Self-Instructional Programmed Manual*. Englewood Cliffs, N. J.: Prentice-Hall, Inc., 1962.

Schmidt, Richard N., and William E. Meyers, *Electronic Business Data Processing*. New York: Holt, Rinehart and Winston, Inc., 1963.

Schmidt, Richard N., and William E. Meyers, *Introduction to Computer Science and Data Processing*. New York: Holt, Rinehart and Winston, Inc., 1965.

Schultz, Louise, *Digital Processing: A System Orientation*. Englewood Cliffs, N. J.: Prentice-Hall, Inc., 1963.

Sprowls, R. Clay, *Computers, A Programming Problem Approach*. New York: Harper and Row, Publishers, 1966.

Schweyer, Herbert E., *Analytical Models for Managerial and Engineering Economics*. New York: Reinhold Publishing Corp., 1964.

Shils, Edward B., *Automation and Industrial Relations*. New York: Holt, Rinehart and Winston, 1963.

Swallow, Kenneth P., and Wilson T. Price. *Elements of Computer Programming*. New York: Holt, Rinehart and Winston, 1965.

Taube, Mortimer, *Computers and Common Sense*. New York: McGraw-Hill Book Company, 1961.

Van Ness, Robert G., *Principles of Punched Card Data Processing,* Rev. ed., Elmhurst, Illinois: The Business Press, 1962, 1964.

Weinstein, Seymour M., and Armand Keim, *Fundamentals of Digital Computers*. New York: Holt, Rinehart and Winston, Inc., 1965.

INDEX

275